Writing, Thinking, and the Brain

How Neuroscience Can Improve Writing Instruction

Tracey Tokuhama-Espinosa, Jovi R. S. Nazareno, and Christopher Rappleye

AF794823

TEACHERS COLLEGE PRESS
TEACHERS COLLEGE | COLUMBIA UNIVERSITY
NEW YORK AND LONDON

Published by Teachers College Press,® 1234 Amsterdam Avenue, New York, NY 10027

Library of Congress Cataloging-in-Publication Data is available at loc.gov

ISBN 978-0-8077-8634-5 (paper)
ISBN 978-0-8077-86352X (hardcover)
ISBN 978-0-8077-8271-2 (ebook)

Printed on acid-free paper
Manufactured in the United States of America

Contents

Scan this QR code to view select downloadable tables and figures, as well as online appendixes and the full list of references:

List of Figures and Tables

Acknowledgments

This project emerged from the reflections of a small writing group made up of people devoted to making their thinking visible in a variety of genres. We thank everyone who put kindling onto this fire by openly sharing successes and stumbles in their own writing and thinking processes. We give a special nod to Marie Kaye, who helped shape the original structure of the ThinkWrite model and whose experience as a teacher, editor, and ghostwriter catalyzed a wealth of reflection and revision. We also wish to thank the many writers and educators who came before us, who gifted us the value of a writing group and of our own and collective thoughts.

The research, writing, beta-testing, and reformulation of the ThinkWrite model evolved slowly but surely over several years, on several continents, and with dozens of students. We lived many waves of literacy movements, including the science of reading, and saw our work nurtured by better and more refined studies related to the neuroscience of writing. We are grateful for the professional and peer feedback from critical friends and colleagues.

We appreciate Allison Scott and the encouragement and time spent on helping shape this book into its final form, and her predecessor, Jean Word, for seeing the potential in this idea years ago. We also thank John Bylander for the detailed copyediting and wordsmithing.

Finally, we are all so thankful for our silent partners and loved ones for giving up their time so that the three of us could create together. Tracey is especially grateful to her husband and children for their constant celebration of these shared accomplishments, and to her mother and best editor, who never fails to inspire. Jovi wishes to express her love and gratitude to her ʻohana for all their unwavering encouragement, with a special thank-you to her mom and grandma for being her first teachers, to her oldest brother for being her first editor, and to her husband and son for their constant inspiration. Chris would like to express his thanks to those at MICDS including Jay Rainey, Sally Maxwell, Scott Small, Lynn Mittler—and to Elizabeth Helfant in particular—for their support. He is grateful to be a part of such a thoughtfully engaged department, and for his students for their continuing inspiration. He would like to thank Tracey and Jovi for including him in this incredible conversation. And, for their patient support and enthusiasm, he is forever grateful to and for Anne, Emma, Francis, and Henry, who bring everything meaningful to life.

Introduction

We have been lucky enough to have some wonderful teachers in our lives. This book is both dedicated to, and meant for, all of them.

WHO SHOULD READ THIS BOOK

This book is for people like Miss Harris, who intuitively nurtured our love for storytelling and turned it into writing. She cleverly gave us nursery school kids a piece of newsprint, and we were invited to draw a picture of anything we wanted on that sprawling 14 × 11–inch terrain. It could be from real life or from our imagination; all she wanted was a drawing. After we finished the drawing, she asked us to tell her about it. She would ask about every line and squiggle. She asked us to elaborate. She made us go into details. She listened. She cared about what we were thinking, not just what we had drawn. After we shared what the picture meant, she chose a single sentence from our narrative. She confirmed the sentence with us. If we agreed, she wrote the sentence underneath our picture. She then rewrote the same sentence in dotted lines instead of complete letters, so the outline of the letters was clear. Then it was our turn. We traced over each letter. When we finished, she applauded! Then she asked us to rewrite the entire sentence ourselves. When we finished, she told us that we had written a story about our picture. She asked us to "read" it again. It was an amazing feeling for our 4-year-old selves.

This book is also meant for teachers like Ms. Houston, who had a large 4th-grade class but did everything to treat us like individuals. She smiled at each of us as we came into class in the morning, she commented on our lunch choice, and she listened attentively in circle time. She was instructed to use SRA (Science Research Associates) reading kits to entertain some of us in the reading corner while she tutored others one-on-one on the main carpet during reading time. We would race to do card after card of exercises in the SRA boxes, hoping to finish each colored segment and be the first in class to do so. The card prompts involved choosing one word that was better than the other choices (they did not ask us to choose our own word), or to read short passages and then note the main ideas from their list of preselected ideas. They were boring, uncreative, and uninspiring. But we felt a sense of accomplishment as we finished all 20 cards in each segment, and at least one child got to work one-on-one with Ms. Houston.

We were also lucky to have teachers like Ms. Clayton in 10th-grade. Ms. Clayton was young, overly ambitious, and blindly believed in our abilities to become writers. She drilled core ideas that have become pillars of metacognition into our heads. One of the most memorable was to ask at the end of each paragraph, "So what?" This helped us reassess just how related (or not) our writing was to the assignment. Were we going on tangents, or just following stream-of-consciousness, or did we get lost on the way to the punch line of our idea? She was subtle but consistent. She didn't coddle us, she shaped us. She was tough and memorable.

This book is also for people like Mrs. White, who taught AP English at a large public high school. She would have us read out *The Adventures of Huckleberry Finn* in loud animated voices and then challenge us on what in our own lives was faintly related to what Huck was experiencing. She wove the current civil rights issues into classic literature, reminding us that there were reoccurring themes in life and in fiction. Then she would make us read our own essays out loud to the group and hear how others interpreted ideas differently, and listen to what they thought about what we had put on paper. She also praised how some students could brilliantly explain ideas in class debate and then asked, "now why can't you just write like you speak?" to call attention to the leap from speaking to writing.

We also benefited from teachers who would not have called themselves writing teachers. This book is for people like Professor Cheever, who taught history at a major university, who once commented to one of us that every single proper name, from Shakespeare to Beethoven, was misspelled in one of our first university papers, but also said that the bigger idea "had merit." He realized that the lack of spelling abilities did not mean poor logic; he separated thinking ability from spelling and the writing that resulted.

This is for the writing teachers who shaped us but did not know at the time what they were doing to our brains. It is for teachers who probed the thinking behind the writing, like Miss Harris; for those who did not have enough time to be as personalized as they wanted to, like Ms. Houston; for teachers out to shape how learners self-assess, like Ms. Clayton; or those who challenged us to find meaning beyond our own realities, like Mrs. White; or those who knew all learners "have merit," like Professor Cheever. This book is for our best teachers, and it is for the worst. It is for teachers in their strongest moments and in their weakest. It is for the great teachers made poorer by the system and for poor teachers made better by the system. It is for teachers who know about good writing intuitively and those who have learned it through study and practice. We hope all teachers, novices and experts, technically accurate or with lack of refined skills, intuitively attuned and professionally acute, can learn from the information in this book because it is about how we *approach* writing, not just a to-do list of steps.

HOW TO READ THIS BOOK

Looking at writing with the brain in mind changes the things we value in classrooms. ThinkWrite can be used with any literacy curriculum. ThinkWrite depends on reorganizing the process of instruction, not on changing the content. It does not depend on district or even schoolwide adoption; a single teacher can begin applying it today, right now.

In Chapter 1, we show how ThinkWrite fits into the larger history of literacy development and note the inspirations that have come from earlier research. By listening to literacy experts and university composition instructors; special needs, bilingual, and early childhood development researchers; and professional writers as well as writing teachers on the front lines in schools today, we came across patterns of concerns that we sought to address through ThinkWrite. We also consider technology and how it has reframed the vital thinking behind writing. We are concerned, as are many teachers, that something is being lost when students lean too heavily on AI for writing support, but we are also enthusiastic that many aspects of learning can be more personalized, thanks to edtech tools. One of the main messages of the book is that the writing process improves thinking, which means skipping steps in this writing process can mean gaps in the development of critical cognitive skills development. We also summarize five powerful lessons learned from the past and show the natural evolution of literacy instruction over the past 170 years leading up to ThinkWrite.

In Chapter 2, we introduce the 15 stages of thinking from the ThinkWrite model. We introduce a new concept to the learning sciences, *holonic thinking*, or thinking through *holons*, to show the reader that everything in the world can be described as a part of something else, and it can also be broken down into smaller parts. Holonic thinking allows us to focus on writing at the smallest of scales (like punctuation marks) and then pull back to the macroscopic view of teaching and learning in context (like the ways students influence each other in a classroom or how culture changes the educational experience). This approach permits us to better think of ideal literacy instruction within students' contexts and cultures. Teaching the exact same unit or lesson varies in its results because the people (students and teachers) and contexts (neighborhoods, communities, and cultures) are different. Valuing this saves frustration and celebrates new kinds of classroom opportunities. Holons also exist at the level of the brain, not just in language and in classrooms. We use holonic thinking to explain how the brain *neuro*constructively builds up literacy. The brain, human language, and classroom instruction are all huge ideas, and when discussed together can seem overwhelming. By using holons to explain the brain, social contexts, and language, we hope the connections between them become clearer and that those links make the bridge between thinking and writing more visible.

Finally, we explore the idea that "diagnosis is half the cure" when problems arise in writing instruction, as well as how breaking problems down into their smallest parts—holonic thinking—can lead to more accurate interventions. Rather than saying a student has a "language" problem, which could mean thousands of different issues, ThinkWrite uses holonic thinking and neuroscience to more accurately pinpoint what problems a student likely has to help select the most appropriate activities.

In Chapters 3, 4, and 5, we explain why using all 15 stages of thinking at different times in the writing process is beneficial to the final writing project. Rather than a single linear process of thinking, ThinkWrite leverages the brain's natural tendency to jump from one kind of thinking to another. This is called *toggling*. It is common for a teacher to want students to "be on task" or to "stay focused" to get through a lesson successfully. A closer look at neural activity confirms that most of the time, the brain is not just doing one thing in a focused way but is more likely to be jumping from one idea to another. This is why some play-based approaches to learning that let the child take the lead in directing the lesson are so successful. Co-construction of the learning experience is a great way to leverage the brain's naturally rotating levels of attention!

To explain how *toggling* benefits the writing process, we will talk about how the brain requires high levels of energy (*cognitive load*) to learn new things and how toggling saves energy for the most important aspects of learning in Chapter 6. One key aspect of the ThinkWrite approach is to raise metacognitive awareness of, and control over, this toggling process, so writers can learn to sustain their efforts in one stage when needed and shift strategically to another stage with greater self-knowledge and purpose. Key benefits of toggling are that the writer never experiences writer's block and that the dozens of activities available for each of the 15 stages of thinking offer student choice and autonomy in their learning.

Chapter 7 is the most practical chapter of the book and shares tools to coach writers and make the thinking behind writing visible. Here we look at how to evaluate, assess, and offer feedback to writers using new ThinkWrite tools, such as the PPPP (product, process, progress, potential) and spider rubrics, to help students learn to self-assess and monitor their progress as writers. One of our favorite aspects of ThinkWrite evaluation tools is that they can and should be used by students and teachers alike, thus helping learners become more autonomous in their learning and self-evaluation.

To structure the tools, interventions, and activities into a recognizable framework, in Chapter 8 we use Universal Design for Learning (UDL) principles. UDL is based on the architectural concept that "some people can do stairs, but everyone can do ramps; so let's use ramps." To do this, we break writing and thinking down to their smallest parts, combine that with teacher knowledge of the range of learners, and use a variety of ThinkWrite tools. The ThinkWrite approach within the UDL framework is complementary to all other curricular structures and can be used in any school for students pre-K through university. This is because ThinkWrite is an approach to teaching, not a replacement of curriculum.

Finally, in Chapter 9, we remind readers of some key Mind, Brain, and Education (MBE) science principles guiding the structure of ThinkWrite, and then move from the theoretical foundations to its practical applications. We then address teachers who may love the idea of ThinkWrite, but have some "yes, but" hesitations due to perceived barriers to implementation. We share our own journeys and challenges when we first started using ThinkWrite to explain some roadblocks to implementation and how they were conquered.

This book is meant for teachers who want to not only read about the theoretical underpinning of a new model for teaching writing, but who want to live the writing experience. A key element of the ThinkWrite model is honoring differentiation for literacy instruction, and this book structure tries to reflect that flexibility. As with the ThinkWrite model itself, readers have the choice of where to start their journey in this book. Just as the ThinkWrite model is drawn as a circle (see Figure 1.1) and can be started at any stage, readers are encouraged to jump between chapters in the book as needed. We think many policymakers will benefit from the lessons from the experts in Chapter 1 and the detailed literature review in Appendix A as well as the complete Reference list found in the online supplemental materials, but teachers might want to begin with the model itself in Chapter 3 or want a clearer understanding of the value of toggling between neural networks in the brain and start with Chapter 6. Those teachers who love the brain may find it fun to start with Chapter 2. Others might want to see how the ThinkWrite structure fits into their current literacy program and will begin with Chapter 8. Many will want to apply new tools for evaluating writing and begin with Chapter 7, and teachers of all levels will want to read Chapter 9, which practically addresses the challenges and opportunities of using ThinkWrite in their own classrooms. All approaches work; you can start your journey where you feel most comfortable or interested. As stand-alone sections, the design of the ThinkWrite model invites flexibility to approach the book in reading blocks that fit each reader's needs. You can also continue your journey at ***ThinkWriteMBE.com***.

Now, we invite you to dive into the content. You can continue to the wisdom from earlier researchers and the rationale for ThinkWrite, or jump into a chapter of your choice.

Scan this QR code to view select downloadable tables and figures, as well as online appendixes and the full list of references:

CHAPTER 1

A Story of Learning to Write

One of the big ideas of this book is to explain why writing is one of, if not *the,* most complex task in the human brain. Sports require physical coordination to accurately place body parts in sync to catch a high fly ball. Reciting a poem requires memory of the meaning of words to place the right emphasis. Debate requires attention, perspective taking, and cognitive empathy to determine what the other person might be thinking. Digital literacy requires executive functions to prioritize cognitive logic. Science and math require a hierarchical notion of concepts to resolve problems. Writing requires all those things simultaneously.

We began writing together in an online group to motivate our own projects. One person was authoring the great American novel, another was writing technical manuals, and the other was working on peer-reviewed articles. As a loosely organized online writing group, we tried to follow basic guidelines of quick introductions and 1-minute summaries of writing goals for the hour, then intense silence as we wrote, followed by a debriefing. As time went on, the debriefings became longer as we found ourselves examining our writing processes. It seemed just as common to find ourselves apologetically saying we had not advanced as we had hoped because we were caught in a "rabbit hole of research," or spent a lot of time "reflecting," or trying "to understand" what was really being asked of us, or got caught "mind wandering" and linking loose ideas. It was not until several months into this process that collectively we came to realize that the rabbit holes, the reflections, the understanding, and the mind wandering were all part of the writing itself. When we began to share this insight with friends, colleagues, and anyone who cared about writing, the news was met first with surprise, then relief, and then with something that can only be described as vengeance-like conviction ("I *knew* it!"), followed by celebration. After developing a full-scale model of what we called the "stages" of the thinking behind the writing we were experiencing (Figure 1.1), we realized that this theory of teaching writing had merit, not only in our own personal writing processes, but it seemed that everyone exposed to it was relieved to know that their own writing processes, often "slowed" by too much thinking, were actually "correct" and could even be considered efficient.

Figure 1.1. The ThinkWrite Model

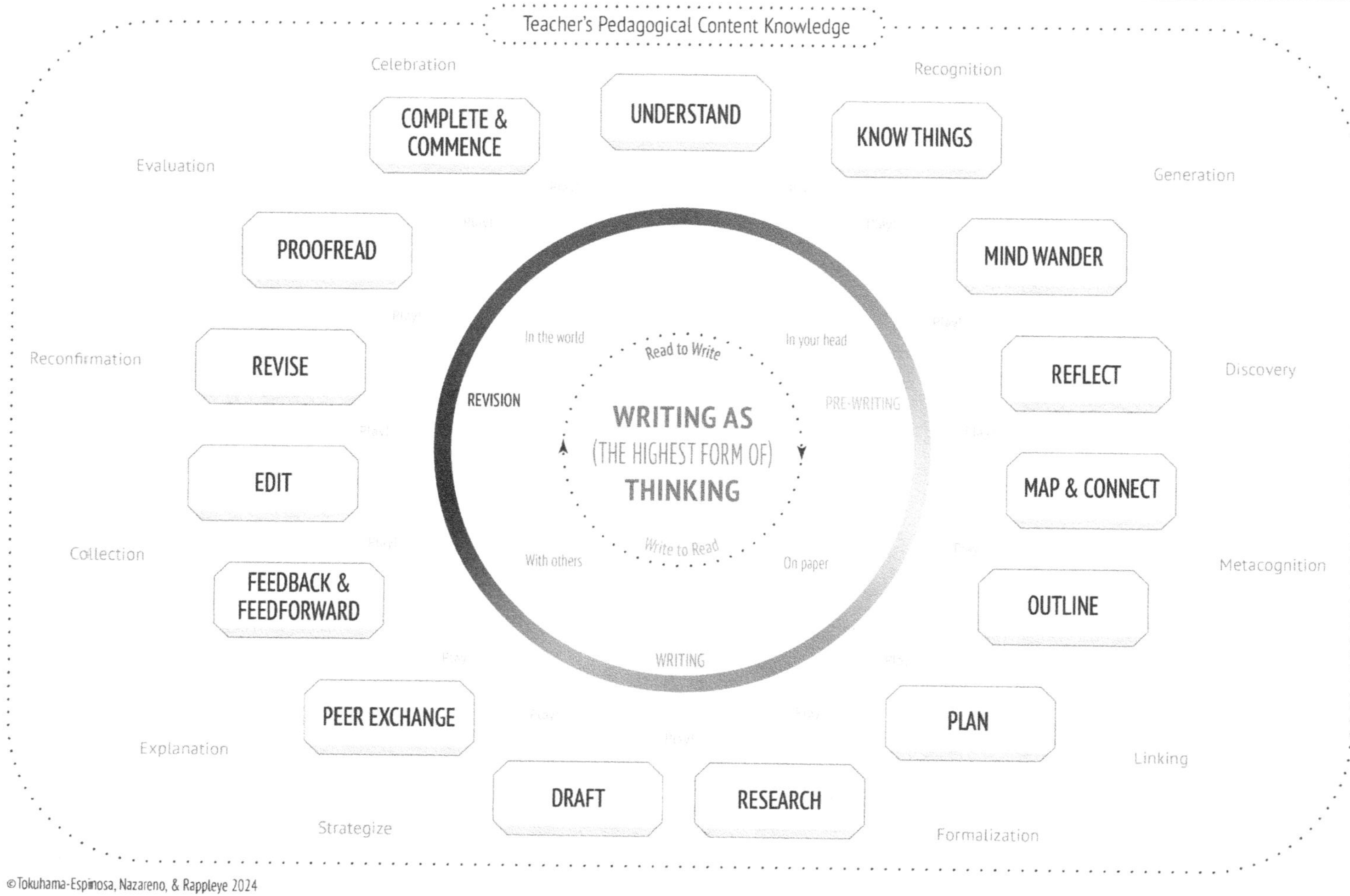

Source: Authors. All rights reserved.

THINK TO WRITE, WRITE TO THINK

Learning about the neural networks that underpin the thinking behind the writing brought our writing group some wonderful *"aha!"* moments, not the least of which was great self-compassion for our processes. These experiences helped us appreciate that there are so many ways writing can go wrong, yet all can be "fixed" easily if we diagnose the root causes of the problems correctly. Many of these problems were grounded in the quality of the thinking behind the writing, not the technical aspects of writing itself. We found that the correct diagnosis of where thinking was going awry was made easier by using the *ThinkWrite* model. As we experimented with our own students, we realized how ThinkWrite has the power to change their self-perceptions as writers, giving them more autonomy to choose the thinking paths they need to reach their writing goals and find more success with greater rewards. We watched growth mindsets emerge and student confidence rise. These students became better writers by becoming better thinkers, which in turn improved their writing, which continued to benefit their thinking, and so on, in a never-ending spiral upward. Better writers, better thinkers. Better thinkers, better writers.

Intelligence and Language

Language has suffered a "chicken or the egg" existence with intelligence for a long time. Are we smart because words give us the power to think, or do we have language because we are smart? The human brain has an innate language sense that permits us to speak, which is what sets us apart from other mammals (Chomsky, 1967; Dehaene, 2009; Pinker, 2003). In Greenspan and Shanker's (2009) book *The First Idea: How Symbols, Language, and Intelligence Evolved From Our Primate Ancestors to Modern Humans,* they explain how the longer larynx in our throats gave humans the ability to use a far greater number of sounds than other apes, and in doing so, sophisticated language emerged. Because our primitive ancestors had this greater range, they could label a larger number of objects in a nuanced way, and these new subtleties led to the possibility of more complex thoughts. In 1921, the German philosopher Ludwig Wittgenstein said that "the limits of my language mean the limits of my world," suggesting that language shapes perception and thought (Wittgenstein, 1921). Oscar Wilde called language "the parent, and not the child, of thought" (Wilde, 1891, p. 14) for this reason as well as from his own personal experience. As vocabulary grows, so does the ability to share a range of thoughts. Recent studies have similarly tied a more subtle and detailed vocabulary for emotions with greater self-awareness and self-regulation, which also turns out to be important for academic success as well as being an important life skill (e.g., Gallingane & Han, 2015). This explains why modern education has always tied "smarts" to having strong language skills.

Whether or not all people think in words all the time is still being debated, but this does not mean language is not used for all thinking, though this might sound counterintuitive. Some people report that they do not think using words (or have an inner voice; see Hurlburt & Akhter, 2008), but most do (Perrone-Bertolotti et al., 2014). And all existing tools to measure intelligence incorporate language and, ironically enough, even tests that are "nonverbal" rely on language. Why? Because non-verbal tests of intelligence rely on *mental schema* of related objects that are categorized with conceptual labels, and labels are language driven (Davis et al., 2020; Gilboa & Marlatte, 2017; Tse et al., 2007; R. Sternberg, personal communication, August 13, 2022). Thinking through language is well documented in studies that show that even the *in*ability to speak words does not mean you do not think with words. People who have suffered strokes and can't express themselves by speaking still show brain scans tracing multiple language pathways in the brain (Halai et al., 2017).

All IQ tests, such as the Stanford-Binet, Woodcock-Johnson, and Wechsler scales, and assessment tools commonly used in schools, such as Power School, Pearsons, and all U.S. state exams, use language skills as proxies for intelligence (Costa & Faria, 2018). Robert Sternberg, one of the greatest theorists and researchers on intelligence, coalesced various definitions and determined that *intelligence* is

> the capacity to learn from experience, using metacognitive processes to enhance learning, and the ability to adapt to the surrounding environment; it may require different adaptations within different social and cultural contexts (Niu & Brass, 2011; Saklofske et al., 2015; Sternberg, 2004). (Sternberg, 2018, p. 145)

Experience, metacognitive processes, learning, and adaptation to changing cultural contexts are all mediated by language. All modern theories of intelligence, including Gardner's theory of multiple intelligences (1983) and Sternberg's triarchic theory of intelligence (1997), consider language as a mediator of intelligence since language is the most prominent cultural artifact (Sternberg, 2018). Evidence from philosophy (e.g., Vashkevych et al., 2021), psychology (e.g., Lupyan & Clark, 2015; Moore, 1968), education (e.g., Sandel, 1998), evolutionary psychobiology (e.g., Pinker, 2010; Premack, 1976), linguistics (e.g., Oller, 1981), cognitive science (e.g., Ünal & Papafragou, 2020), and now neuroscience (e.g., Zhang et al., 2022) shows the link between language and intelligence. Thinking and writing have a special relationship in the brain, in part due to writing's circular role in both capturing and shaping thinking.

Speaking contributes to elaborated thought (Ünal & Papafragou, 2020; Vygotsky, 1934), as cognition and language advance hand in hand (Dancygier, 2017; Nippold, 2016; Pinker, 2003). This can be stimulated by strong classroom structures (Zwiers & Crawford, 2011), especially if experienced in a range of contexts (Shaules, 2019). The evolution of thinking and language and their influence on one another are further enhanced and result in leaps in human development due to written language (Greenspan & Shanker, 2009). Speaking and writing abilities are different, though complementary, neural pathways in the brain. While humans easily learn to speak as a part of socialization, they must explicitly learn to read and write (Dehaene, 2009). The expectation that reading and writing are "common knowledge" for all members of society is a relatively recent phenomenon. Out of the 300,000 years of human existence on earth, people have only spoken for the past 50,000 years, known how to write for the past 5,000 years, and only for 170 years has it been expected that everyone in society should do so (Figure 1.2).

Figure 1.2. The History of Human Language from Speaking to Writing

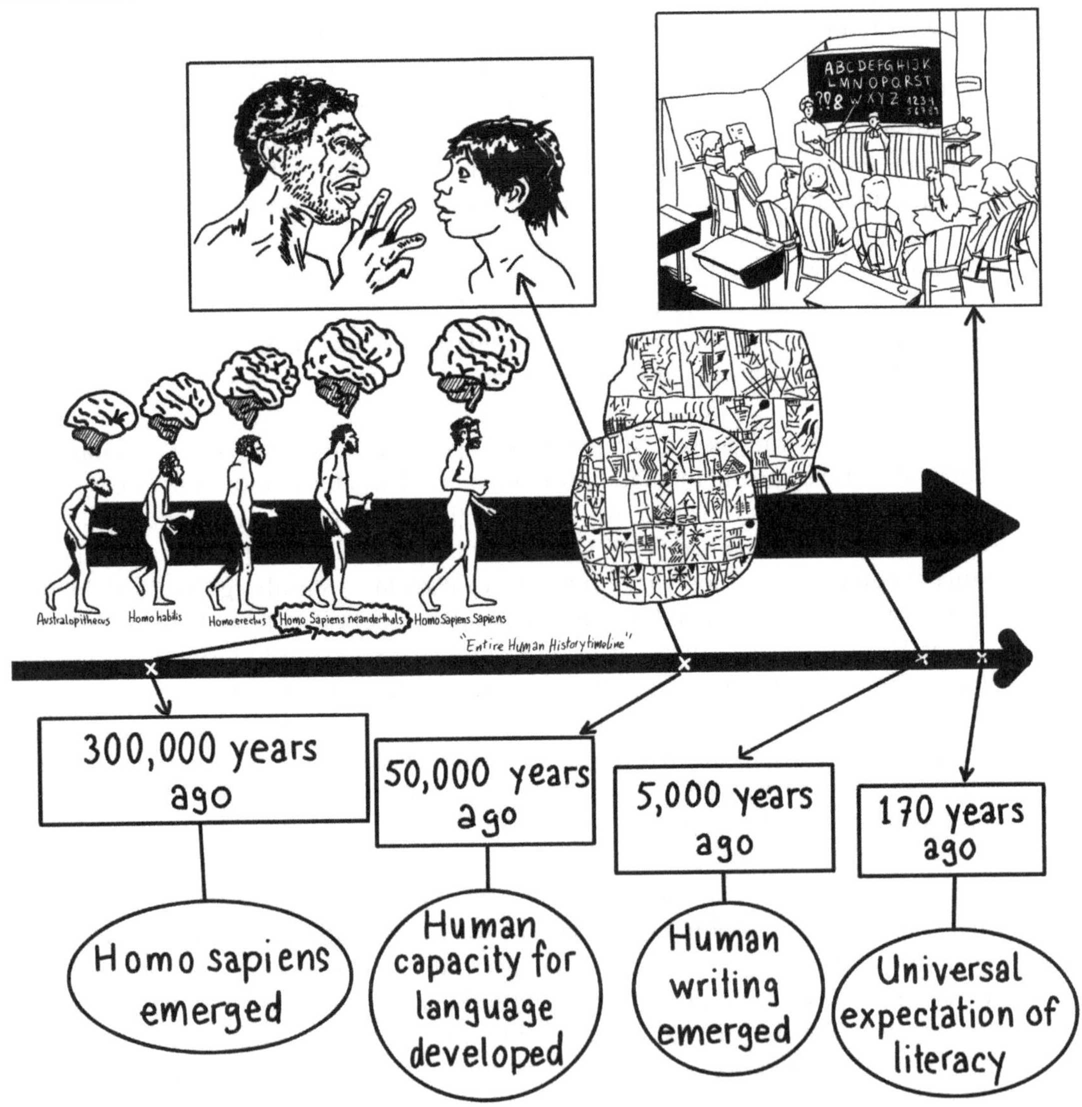

Learning how to do something and to do it well requires practice and refinement, both over an individual's lifespan as well as over the span of human history, resulting in epigenetic changes based on a combination of nature and nurture over time, and humans have not been literate long enough to avoid problems. According to Donna Coch, reading neuroscientist at Dartmouth College, "humans have been reading and writing for only about 5,000 years; on an evolutionary scale, that is very little time for the development of a neural region specialized for the cultural invention of reading" (Coch, 2016, p. 191), which also plays a role in writing. Formal writing instruction recruits neural networks originally developed for other purposes, which cues the activation of the genes necessary for us to wire these diverse networks together to reach the expressive potential that writing affords us. The brain adapts to what it does most; the "newness" of writing in human history might explain the prevalence of language difficulties as the precision of neural network refinement is still under way (Dehaene, 2009). Just as it takes a child around 5 to 7 years to rehearse enough of the key neural networks to learn to write spontaneously (Cummins, 2013), the human species needs several generations before advanced cognitive skills, like writing, become habituated to the extent that they are retrieved effortlessly. By integrating the learning sciences into writing instruction, ThinkWrite approaches the writing process with increased granularity, and by naming the thinking stages involved in writing in recognizable terms aims to advance that process.

To better understand how the brain learns to write, a good starting point is understanding how it learns to read (Rosenblatt, 2019). Many of the neural networks required for writing draw on those developed for reading, and both reading and writing recruit neural networks originally evolved for other purposes (Dehaene, 2009; Wolf & Stoodley, 2008). While "literacy" means both reading and writing, most of what is known about literacy in the brain is limited to reading.

Reading vs. Writing

Applying what we know about literacy and the brain has been complicated by several factors.

First, reading and writing are often not taught as complementary processes in school but rather as separate events with separate purposes despite evidence that using them together as a system benefits the learner (e.g., Nan, 2018); learning to read helps writing, and writing helps reading. The modalities of language, like speaking, listening, reading, and writing, are not always presented as parts of the whole of language experience. We see this in distinct activities in several language standards (e.g., Cox et al., 2018) that separate out vocabulary from grammar, or sentence phrasing from storytelling, which all play roles in good writing but are often taught separately. Rather than teach language elements as integrated pieces and allow students to show and share their own emerging skills using all the elements together, we often limit "correct" answers to a small number of options on multiple-choice tests, some measuring knowledge of grammar, others for vocabulary, and yet others for assessing the quality of a strong essay. The categorization of these elements into separate standards can discourage awareness of the underlying connection between them.

In many classrooms, particularly in advanced grades, it is common for there to be an instructional shift between reading in one genre and writing in another. For example, we often ask students to read a poem (one genre) and then write an analytical essay about the poem (another genre). This can be a missed opportunity for strengthening student awareness of the formal elements of the read genre, especially those that might not otherwise be the subject or focus of an assigned formal literary analysis, as important as formal analysis is. For example, reading a story could be followed by asking children to write their own stories, but this does not happen as frequently as one would expect in our schools. Before writing outlines for their own stories or essays, students could be asked to backward engineer the outline of a well-known story to identify the essential elements (introductions, supporting examples, conclusions, etc.) on their own. Not doing so is a missed opportunity to use the complementary skills of reading and writing in a natural way. Similarly, the absence of models of developmentally appropriate analytical writing can lead to missed or partial understandings. We will talk more about this in Chapter 2 as we think about a more holistic approach to language development in education.

Second, time is often the enemy of sufficient rehearsal for writing skills: reading dominates the time dedicated to literacy in many classrooms, and writing receives only a fraction of instruction time in schools. In a recent study on 4th-grade boys and literacy instruction, it was found that most of the focus on literacy is on reading, not writing. Of the reading topics and relative time exposure that were focused on, Everett and Moten (2022) cite six topics (disciplinary exposure, concept of reading, ability to decode multisyllabic vocabulary words, reading fluency, reading comprehension, and capacity to read across multiple genres) and just two writing topics (ability to write texts that nurture intellectual and personal development, and capacity to write across multiple genres), which were the main focus of instruction. Other studies around the world show similar patterns and quantify this in terms of student time, not just quantity of topics. In Norway, for example, only 19% of 1st-graders were asked to write during the fall semester. When queried about this, teachers responded that students were asked to write less as they needed to prioritize reading (Håland et al., 2019).

Reading also takes precedence over writing in language skill building. For example, vocabulary is a key component of language; the more vocabulary one has, the better and more accurately people can express themselves. Vocabulary instruction in 2nd- and 3rd-grade classrooms seems to be mainly tied to pre-reading activities (learning the words that might come up in a text that will be read in the future), rather than to a learner's search for the right word as they write a sentence (Sparapani et al., 2018). This discrepancy in time and quality instruction between reading and writing has existed for decades. In *The Reader, the Scribe, the Thinker: A Critical Look at the History of American Reading and Writing Instruction* (1987) by E. Jennifer Monagban and E. Wendy Saul, they traced the imbalance of reading to writing instruction back to the 1960s, suggesting that reading has been given priority over writing for at least the past 60 years.

Some teachers prioritize reading over writing because of a belief in a hierarchy of skills. That is, they think that reading must be taught before writing. This is actually not true. While writing is a more complex process in the brain than reading (using more brain networks simultaneously than reading, as we will see in Chapter 2), children can learn to read by writing. For example, the highly successful Montessori instructional process favors allowing children to generate ideas and then express them through writing; in this way, they learn to read by seeing their own writing (Richardson, 1997). A child might ask the teacher, "how do you spell my name?" and in learning to write, she then learns to read. From a teacher's perspective, it may seem natural to divide reading and writing in our schools, but from the brain's perspective, this does not make a lot of sense. (There are similar examples about how we teach math, dividing up skill sets like addition and multiplication, when the brain might do better seeing those presented together.) The neat curricular divisions of skill sets taught in schools are not necessarily the most natural way for the brain to learn (Tokuhama-Espinosa, 2019).

Another reason that reading is given more time in school than writing is that it is often relatively easier to teach and grade. While learning to read is a huge mental process, writing is even harder and requires about twice as many steps to teach. Whatever the reason, despite being a cornerstone of strong academic outcomes and lifelong learning, writing is often given relatively less direct instructional time.

A final reason that writing is not given as much instructional time as other subjects may have to do with the challenge of guiding such an individualized and subjective process. Writing simultaneously represents and directs the interior neural development of the individual writer. The forms of writing—those patterns that make up "voice," the selection of genre, the unique connections, and so on—are not just the form into which some previously formed thinking is "poured." Form in writing in this sense develops out of individual experience, capacities, and choices. Our thinking processes shape our writing, and the experience of writing and the choices we make shape our thinking and our future capacity for both thinking and writing. Culturally we also value writing as an expression of individual identity, from one's handwriting to the unique voice that concerns the maneuvers, patterns of diction, and rhythms of syntax that characterize one individual's writing (and thinking) versus another's. Although math and coding and the sciences, particularly at the most advanced levels, can certainly be expressive pursuits, we more readily recognize writing as aligned to the arts in its capacity to preserve and externalize one's individual identity in an enduring form and in a social space. Writing instruction is not only about teaching young learners to conform to conventions—though such teaching of forms is important—it also involves recognizing our responsibility for nurturing the individual writer's unique contributions to the larger conversation. Writing may be functional, as in a shopping list, email solicitation, or communication of directions to a gathering, but it can also be performative, as in a love poem, a statement of philosophy in a job application, or the creation of a novel, or persuasive as in an argumentative essay, or a combination of all of these. Due to the highly varied aims of writing, the challenges of guiding the development of individual voices, and the demands of the complex thinking involved, writing instruction often restricts itself to teaching the mastery of a few forms and at a technical level. Such restrictions are simultaneously a driver of and driven by limited instructional time for writing.

Processes vs. Products

In an age when some say generative AI can be trained to write just like humans (even using our own voice!), thoughtful teachers and society as a whole should pause to ask *why* we should care just as much, or more, about the *process* of writing than the final *product*. ThinkWrite values the way thinking improves writing and writing improves thinking. If the end product—an ad for detergent, a college essay, a shopping list, or memo—can be generated by AI, why shouldn't we allow this to be? Because quality writing is linked to quality thinking. There is a disciplined precision to writing, a form of thinking that is useful for the individual and for society. Writing's effect on an individual's thinking and underlying neural development is beneficial to cognition more broadly, not just for literacy. Reaching our human potential means leveraging our ability to think, and that ability, in turn, is inextricably linked to the *process* of learning to write. Generative AI can, and perhaps should, take over tasks in which the only goal is a product, but we teach writing in schools with the goal of educating, not just producing. Strong literacy programs have always valued not only the product but also the process, progress, and potential of the writing and writer (more about this in Chapter 7). One of the major implications of the ThinkWrite model is that writing is not just a set of skills to be mastered in the narrow sense of merely acquiring abstract competencies, but that these competencies are best gained in the pursuit of the self-directed experience of mastery, necessary for meeting our needs for both autonomy and belonging (see Niemiec & Ryan, 2009), to be a part of a larger community, and to make our thinking clear in that context. Humans should learn to write well not just because their academic success depends on it, but rather because society's future depends on good thinkers whose ideas can best be remembered if documented in writing. Technology's infringement on the thinking process is a concern, but it also has the potential to benefit and even elevate thinking if used appropriately (more about this in Chapter 9).

Thanks to advancements in the learning sciences, including those in education and neuroscience, we now have new tools to approach both our understanding of how the brain learns to write and what teachers can do to take advantage of this information to teach better. The neuroscience of writing is a recent phenomenon because both neuroscience and writing are relatively new on the stage of human knowledge, both emerging just a few centuries ago. One of the insights we hope to share in this book is the way we can make this invisible thinking more visible using research. ThinkWrite was catalyzed by our reflections about writing but was born of a natural evolution of thinking about writing instruction in school contexts over the past century. To offer a firm foundation on which to build this new evidence-based approach to writing, we dove into the research to learn from experts.

There is a significant body of research on writing that we engaged with in order to develop ThinkWrite, from understanding how Greeks and Romans focused on phonics, to early literacy in the United States as far back as 1635, to the role of whole-word approaches in the 19th and 20th centuries, to the reading wars that marked the latter half of the 20th century, to the more recent debate between balanced reading and the emerging discourse on the science of reading (Figure 1.3).

We sought wisdom from four major contributors to the discussion on writing best practices (Figure 1.4). First and foremost was wisdom from teachers of writing and composition, including assessment and evaluation, the role of student agency, online writing, teacher-to-teacher advice, and personal experiences of writing instruction. Second, we leveraged information from professional writers ranging from technical manuals to inspirational and motivational guides. Third, and often overlooked in mainstream writing programs, was wisdom from language experts, including research from ESL, EAL, bilingualism, multiliteracy, special education, and learning difficulties. Finally, we sought wisdom from cognitive development researchers, including developmental literacy, research on the reading brain, and the few studies done on the neuroscience of writing.

While it is outside the scope of the present book to detail our expansive review of the literature, we have included an online supplement (Appendix A) for those who wish to do a deep dive on how the history of reading and writing influenced the development of ThinkWrite, including helpful bibliographies for further reading. In this section, we provide a synthesis of the five key lessons we learned from our research that have shaped the ThinkWrite model.

LESSONS LEARNED

The literature review and wisdom from the experts led to five important ideas about literacy instruction.

Figure 1.3. Formal Early Literacy in the United States

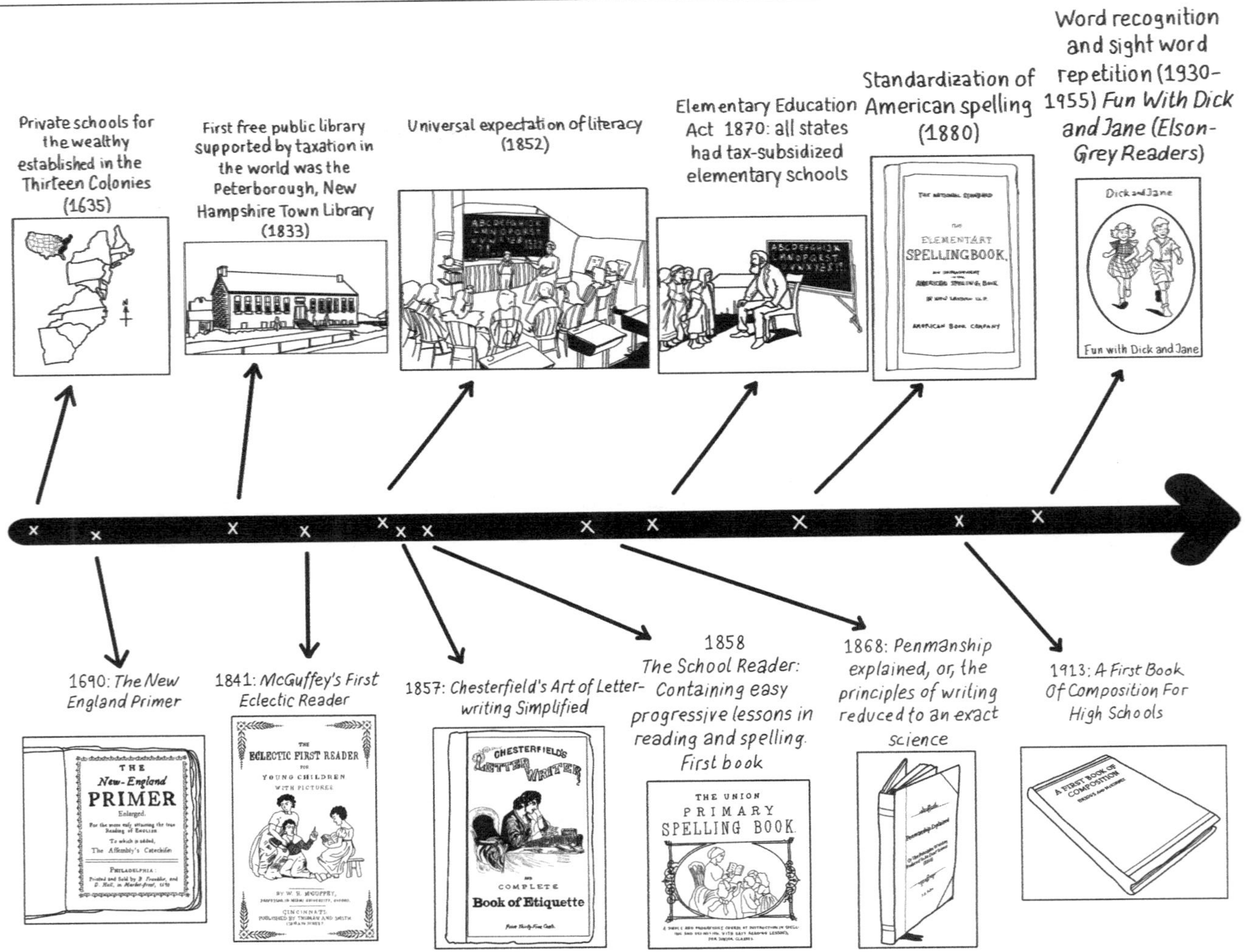

Figure 1.4. Wisdom From the Experts

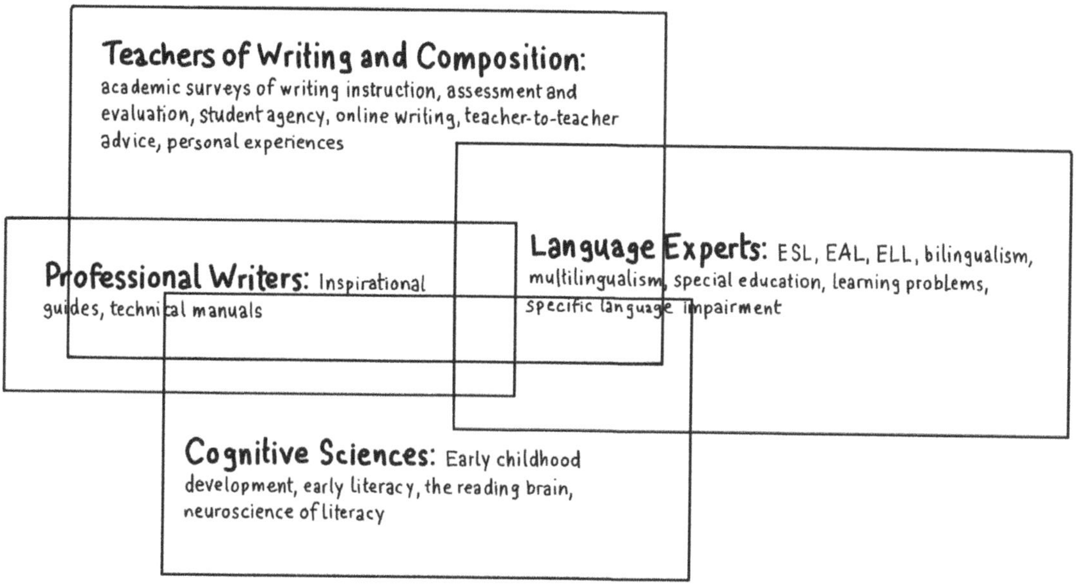

Lesson 1. To Write Well, the Invisible Thinking Behind Good Writing Needs Acknowledgment

Writing is both visible and invisible. Currently, school systems around the world have a bias toward the visible; we judge people as being "good" or "bad" writers based on the written products they produce, like outlines, drafts, or revisions. However, as counterintuitive as it might seem, most of the writing process is *invisible* as evidenced from the literature from neuroscience and literacy (Ellis & Bloch, 2021). Education's tools, such as rubrics and standardized test scores, measure the physical essay but not the quality of the thinking that went into it.

In her 1982 essay "The Winds of Change: Thomas Kuhn and the Revolution in the Teaching of Writing," Maxine Hairston observed that even while the writing *process* had come to be the conventional approach to writing, most writing *instruction* and *feedback* lagged behind, reflecting a focus on the written *product*. (This, despite the fact that Murray's influential book *A Writer Teaches Writing* [1968] had already triggered a look into the processes of writing 14 years before her own work.) Sadly, today most feedback and rubrics continue to focus on the written product rather than the thinking process; most rubrics related to thinking are separate from writing (Joseph et al., 2020). Students' products continue to be valued more than their processes (thinking) or their progress as individuals.

A focus on the product and the ignoring of the process can lead to a downward spiral in learning. Because the effort that goes into writing is not often rewarded, students can get discouraged by teacher feedback that privileges lingering errors in the final product, and because the grade is prized over the thinking, students consider themselves "failures" as writers. Because the thinking is not rewarded, students may stop putting effort and energy into the thinking that underpins the writing process, making some even resort to generative AI like ChatGPT, which skips the unrewarded thinking and simply generates a good product (Bai et al., 2023). If teachers reward only the product and not the thinking behind the writing, we anticipate more and more students will turn to ChatGPT because the effort and energy needed to *think* will not be recognized nor prized in grading.

Lesson 2. To Write Well, We Need to Attend to the Social Context of Writing

Writing is a social activity (Boscolo & Gelati, 2019; Graham & Harris, 2019; Ives et al., 2022; Williams, 2022) and must be learned within the context and culture of the learner for it to be authentic (Bruyère & Pendergrass, 2020; He, 2020; Winstead & Alterio, 2021). However, writing is often treated as an individual skill, despite the fact that people are deeply influenced by each other as they think through expectations, read and interpret each other's ideas and feelings, and learn from each other's perspectives (e.g., Hsin & Snow, 2017; Seih et al., 2011). Part of the socialization of writing is related to feedback.

If treated to positive, constructive, personalized feedback, many students learn to thrive off of it, and even seek it out (Henderson et al., 2019a, 2019b). Too much of the writing experience takes place as a unidirectional structure, however, of teacher-to-student instruction, despite evidence of the numerous benefits of peer exchanges to develop and grow ideas (e.g., Bürgermeister et al., 2021). Exchanging ideas with peers gives students the opportunity to hear what others think, which broadens perspectives. As an added benefit, peer exchange also teaches social conventions about how to communicate, which in turn supports writing (e.g., Yu & Liu, 2021). Peer feedback is a stepping stone to writing for authentic audiences (Behizadeh, 2019), an opportunity in turn that taps into important emotional centers in the writer and helps motivate self-confidence (Sari et al., 2022).

Related to the variety of social contexts are the different realities of language use among home, neighborhood, and school (Hornberger & Link, 2012). The linguistic diversity of children in the United States is unequaled around the world and poses some tricky problems. Children who communicate well at home but differently from the school language can suffer academically (Hagemann, 2001). Many students speak in the neighborhood slang, which is not accepted in their schools, and they are punished or marginalized for having been brought up with different languages rather than celebrated for their bilingualism (Bohney, 2016). Several authors from the 1970s to the present have spoken about culturally relevant pedagogies (e.g., Hammond, 2014; Thompson & Mixon, 1996) that leverage communication tools like hip hop pedagogy (Buffington & Day, 2018; Ladson-Billings, 1995) to allow students to show they understand concepts, and can express them in multimodal approaches. Others in bilingual education have shown how clearly demarcating the space for different "Englishes" could benefit students who use something other than "standard" English at home (Hammond, 2014), such as kids in Hawaii who speak Pidgin (also known as Hawaii Creole English) at home but can learn to use English in school (Khan & Akter, 2021).

Lesson 3. To Write Well, Students Should Learn to Write in Multiple Genres

Literacy programs in U.S. classrooms have evolved in the past 50 years. The Library Association's Recommended Reading List has expanded and now includes a greater variety of authors than ever before in its history (American Library Association, 2023). The number of genres has also expanded to include *mangas*, graphic novels, along with the traditional short stories and chapter books. While the science of how to teach reading has exploded (e.g., Christenson, 2023; Duke & Cartwright, 2021; Hiebert, 2023; Petscher et al., 2020; Shanahan, 2020), the science of how we write has not kept pace in part because of the sheer number of writing genres in which learning can occur. In a recent critique of the current, limited system, John Warner's *Why They Can't Write: Killing the Five-Paragraph Essay and Other Necessities* (2018) points out that there are many policies about writing that have failed our students, most notably the dependence on teaching the five-paragraph argumentative essay at the cost of more varied forms of expression.

We found there are more than 200 different genres of writing (Figure 1.5). The Common Core State Standards (CCSS) "cover" a few dozen (Carmichael et al., 2010). Writing poetry is a different talent from writing a short story, *and a different way of thinking* as expressed by different neural correlates (e.g., Jacobs & Willems, 2018). Writing a short story is different from a research paper; writing a newspaper article is different from journaling; writing a comedy is different from an obituary; writing a sitcom is different from writing a play; writing a romantic novel is different from a historical novel; and texting is different from the typical five-paragraph argumentative essay taught in most high school classrooms. All genres of writing stimulate distinct forms of thinking, but not all genres are celebrated in school (see Haim & Ravid, 2022, for an example). Students can often be good at one kind of writing but not so good at others. When the genre they are not so good at is the one that is graded, they label themselves "poor" writers, and their motivation to grow as a writer is stunted (Torres et al., 2020). There is no "hierarchy" of writing genres, although formal writing is prized over the informal, and schools often prioritize evidence from standardized tests over imagination (Willson & Falcon, 2018).

Figure 1.5. Genres of Writing

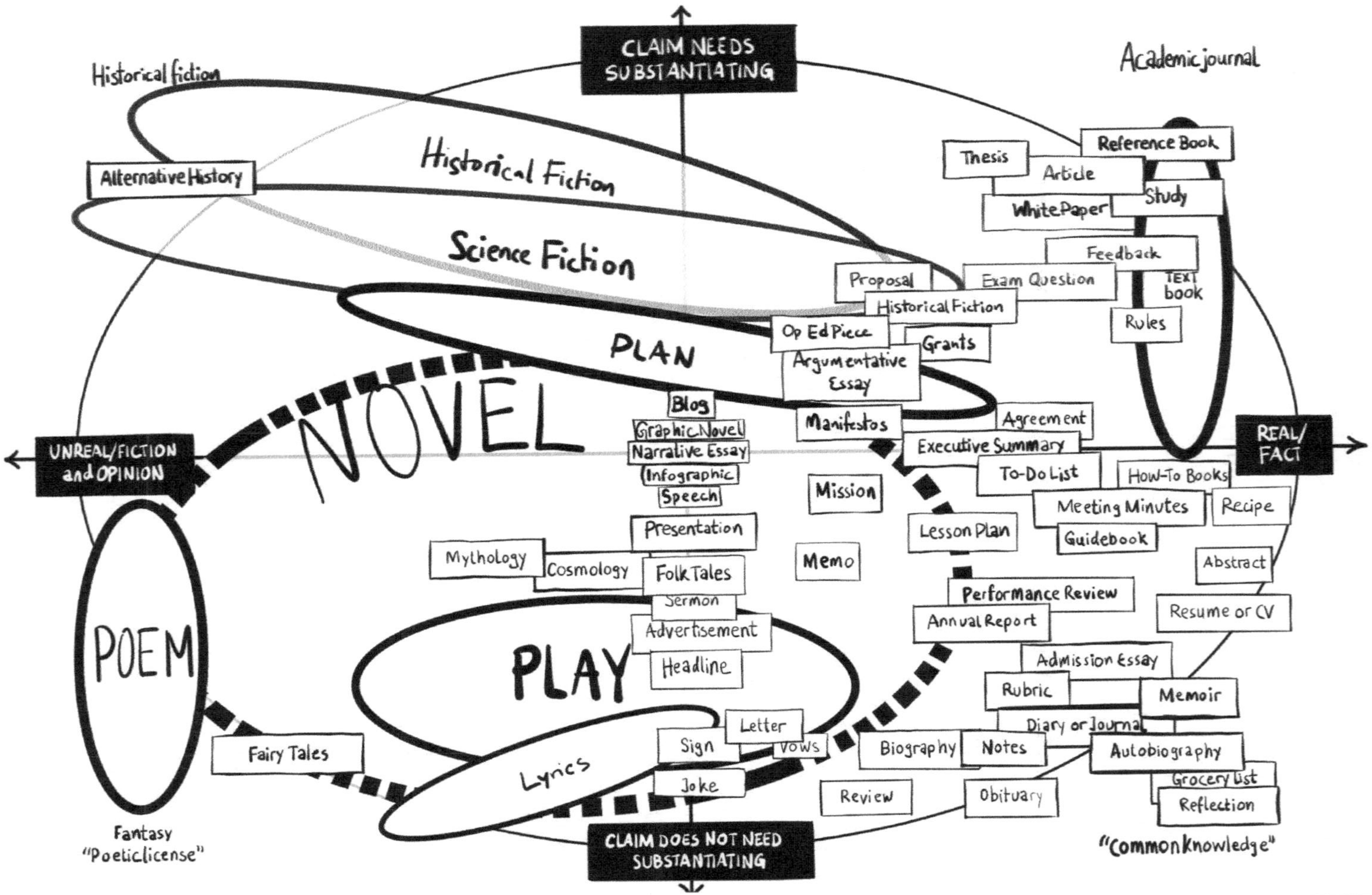

We also know people write not just for academic success but also for artistic expression, historical documentation, or simply as one of many ways to communicate with others (Dunlap, 2009; Messner, 2023). Of the 200+ genres, some are more school related than others, like the essay, and others are more "free," like free-verse poetry or texting. There are also genres of writing like instructional manuals and list making, which differ from the ability to write a good eulogy or a dedication in a book. Writing can involve personal feelings and perspective-taking, like in a memoir or autobiography, or it can be "distant" and evidence based, such as in a research paper or lab report. Some genres can employ other genres within them (e.g., a novel can contain a grocery list or poem or essay), and some creative writing can combine the expectations of one genre in the context of another (e.g., a novel in the form of a sequence of dialogues). People can write abbreviated texts, structured emails, or reflective sonnets. People also write in these different genres using tools like pencils and paper or digital tools like computers. Most teachers intuitively know the difference in the thinking stages used to write a message to a parent, a good exam question, and well-thought-out feedback comments, but many have not yet had the chance to see all these different genres in a single umbrella framework before (Figure 1.5) or consider their production using a range of tools from pencils to AI.

Despite the existence of these many genres of writing (Devitt, 2004), most school programs are structured around just a handful (Fang, 2021). A few decades ago, these categories were collectively called "EDNA": Exposition, Description, Narration and Argumentation, which described the four types of essays to be learned in school (Brand, 1998). The limited number of genres seems to go against the recommendations of excellent writing instructors like Jim Burke (2003) and Steven Graham (et al., 2019) who have long argued that becoming a good writer means learning to write in multiple genres. Currently, book after book on teaching writing generally limits their formats to just a few genres (e.g., Gear, 2020) of writing based on the Common Core Standards (2010) (a) narrative, (b) expository (informative/expository), and (c) persuasive (opinion/argument). Heightened awareness of genres gives writers insight including a greater consciousness of rules as conventions and how these shape the expectations of our readers and meaning-making, and with which writers can playfully and meaningfully engage. The more genres one is exposed to, the broader the range of thinking skills that are developed (Smith, 1994).

While there are no hierarchies in genres of writing, there are different levels of thinking that are involved in each. Jotting down a grocery list is writing, but it takes less mental effort than composing the lyrics to a song or writing a skit. The mental effort is the *cognitive load*, or energy, needed by the brain to take up and consider information as we work and learn (Klepsch & Seufert, 2020; Xu et al., 2021). To celebrate learning, teachers need to celebrate thinking; to celebrate thinking, they need to leverage the most important tool they have: writing in all its genres (Atkins et al., 2021; Bruce, 2020).

Lesson 4. To Write Well, People Need to Read Broadly

In a related concept, reading widely is an opportunity to build a writer's schema of different genres (Driscoll et al., 2020; Tardy et al., 2020). This helps construct a writer's sense of the world's complexity and internalize the possibilities of what it means to be a writer in different contexts. Representative works from multiple cultural backgrounds can help bridge the perceived gap between school English and the marginalized versions of "Englishes" of students' neighborhoods. Writing in a different genre can be a way to find one's true voice, and that in turn can be a driver to further mastery (Xu, 2023).

Reading to write and writing to read are complementary processes. The literature reviewed echoes many teachers' intuitions, as well as evidence from Graham, MacArthur, and Herbert's work in 2019: When students write about what they have read, their comprehension of texts improves and their writing improves (Jaramillo et al., 2023; Vandermeulen, 2023; Walther & Biggs-Tucker, 2023). Win-win! Wide and extensive reading acquaints the brain with perspectives and others' internal thinking processes that are otherwise inaccessible (Eekhof et al., 2021; Firman et al., 2022). What's more, when reading is done in a broad range of genres, the brain is exposed to syntactical norms and possibilities in a range that far exceeds that which it gets from direct grammatical instruction (Barnes et al., 2021; Freeman et al., 2016). Additionally, and paradoxically, we find our voice through the voices of others. We do this by registering our own affective and cognitive response to another's writing and recalling those possibilities if rehearsed enough when later engaged in our own writing tasks (Gibbs, 2015; Pasupathi & Oldroyd, 2015). A related but different point is that when teachers ask students to take notes in their own words based on things they have read, they are improving both reading and writing skills (Vandermeulen et al., 2023). Taking notes should not be an option, nor should it be left to chance (Wilson et al., 2023); note-taking skills should be taught explicitly in school as this enhances thinking, reading, and writing.

Lesson 5. To Write Well, People Need Time: All Teachers Should be Writing Teachers

In 1968, Benjamin Bloom identified time as the main problem with student achievement. In his article he suggested that over 90% of the students in any given classroom would be able to master the content of whatever was taught if they had enough time to do so. Bloom questioned the use of time boundaries to determine aptitude in school, or worse yet, to judge intelligence (1968). Why is writing "good" only when you can answer an essay question within a certain amount of time? (Mairano et al., 2022). Many professional writers would certainly tell you that they have missed more than one deadline in the name of a better end product! Time is one of the factors that can contribute to understanding; some people need more time than others at different stages of their learning. Timed exams are important when lives are at stake, for example, so learning how to revive a drowning victim with CPR *should* be a time-bound skill. But should writing a poem be based on whether you can do so within the allotted 20 minutes? Most poets would argue otherwise (Ryan & Daffern, 2020). Copying writing from an example does not take much time, but generating new ideas, searching your mind for the right word, looking up examples, seeing optional formats, experimenting, getting feedback, revising . . . all take time.

Time also factors into teaching writing as signaled by Stephen Graham, who pointed out that the key to good writing instruction was the amount of time it was given in the curriculum (Graham et al., 2019). He noted:

> At the most basic level, effective writing instruction depends on time (NCOW, 2003). Teachers who devote more time to writing instruction apply multiple methods more often to promote writing growth (e.g., Gilbert & Graham, 2010; Hsiang et al., 2018). In effect, quality writing instruction cannot occur if sufficient time is not available. (p. 277)

Graham says that the burden of time is on both teachers and policymakers. At the teacher level, *all teachers* need to assume the role of writing teachers and make space for writing activities in class (Russell, 2020; Wolpert-Gawron, 2014); it should not just be considered a topic to be taught in English class, but rather a modality woven into all subjects (Bell-Nolan, 2015). At the level of policymakers, school systems should not account for teaching hours based on the subject but rather on the skills, of which writing is one, which would democratize the sense of responsibility that all teachers should have around writing (Kinneavy, 2020). Graham (2019) noted that teachers around the world reported spending far less than the recommended 1 hour per day on writing skills, mostly because not all teachers feel this is in their job mandate. Few teachers aside from the language arts instructor even feel the obligation to correct writing errors (Williamson, 2022). Given the importance of time in learning to write, and matching this with toggling (Chapter 6), it is worth asking ourselves if a *better use of time*, not just the amount of time, would make a difference in writing outcomes.

It is clear that writing does not get enough time in the school curriculum to yield satisfactory results (Bazerman & Russell, 2020). The consequence is an average literacy level just above middle school for the U.S. population (Department of Education, 2019), which is both shocking and sobering. To resolve this problem and give more time to writing we only have two options: We either extend the school day to have more time for writing (Bazerman & Russel, 1994), which does not seem likely, or we convince all teachers they should support writing in their individual classes. When all teachers are "writing teachers" this also has additional benefits, such as insights into student thinking and improved teacher understanding of student needs (Bean & Melzer, 2021). If all teachers were asked to support writing, the amount of time-on-task would increase to an acceptable level, and writing levels would increase across subjects as would comprehension of content.

In the early 2000s, the International Baccalaureate (IB) Programme, one of the most intense and well-researched curricula in the world (Jaafar et al., 2021), proclaimed that all teachers are writing teachers. Several had whispered this for centuries (e.g., Emig, 2020; Freisinger, 1980; Graves, 2008), and many presumed this was already baked into the K–12 curriculum by the time Charles Bazerman and David R. Russell compiled *Landmark Essays on Writing Across the Curriculum* in 1994, but this message had not been articulated to such a wide range of teachers around the world in such a definitive way before. Indeed, few policies around writing have ever been mandated, and this one had decades of research behind it. School success is tied to literacy success; as the brain adapts to what it does most, more writing across the curriculum would improve thinking as well as success in school. This took a while to sink in.

Many IB teachers who taught math or computer science had to mentally digest this before accepting the logic behind the policy. Those in art pushed back as they felt the purpose of their subject was precisely to free up students from feeling bound to written words. Those in physical education and health, history, civics, and philosophy all saw the link between documentation and learning but were not completely convinced either. Watching our own children go through this process and the ways that creative teachers began incorporating math journals into school, for example, was instructive. One of our children's IB math teachers asked the kids to just "write anything" they wanted in the journal, including their frustrations with math itself. To his surprise, this led to incredible insights that helped break through many mental blocks about math and made visible the interiorized social and emotional context within which students' learning struggles play out. Comments like "I just get so frustrated when I don't know what to do with the parenthesis" helped the teacher identify roadblocks to learning and design better instructional interventions. Other comments, like "math makes me feel stupid," gave teachers a reminder to praise smart guesses, even when they were incorrect. "I don't get why little numbers [square roots] don't work the same way as big number [integers]" helped the teacher see the world of numbers through the 7th-grader's eyes and to take the time to say that while "3" might look the same in addition as in algebra, a "3" used as a cube functioned differently. The insights that all the teachers began to have improved their ability to respond to individual needs by making the students' thinking more visible (Ritchhart et al., 2011) and therefore gave them actionable steps to intervene. Furthermore, it gave the students the opportunity to use words in new ways and applied them to subjects in which they had not developed enough vocabulary to permit conversations to take place. Making the invisible visible and appreciating the many ways of knowing that humans are capable of showed teachers, students, and parents that education was complex but also manageable, logical, and creative. These math journals showed that writing can be an important tool for metacognitive awareness (Kesebir & Oksuz, 2022) by exposing emotional and cognitive challenges. Additionally, student writing improved, meaning thinking improved.

Those who supported the idea that all teachers are writing teachers from the start probably realized three things. First, they realized that by strengthening writing, they would be improving cognitive abilities needed in all subject areas (Çavdar & Doe, 2012). Second, they also realized that every subject taught in school depends on the written word (Dockrell et al., 2011). Students who were incapable of interpreting written instructions, descriptions, or visuals were at a disadvantage in the modern world (Met, 2008). Third, they also realized that while anyone can claim to be a genius inside their own heads, the only way to know this for sure is to share one's ideas with others in a common language (spoken and written), and the only way to preserve those good ideas over time is through writing, as it is the only "tangible documentation of thought" (Mahootian, 2012, p. 192). Thinking together or along with others is heavily dependent on language (Mercer, 2002). Without writing, people have a hard time sharing ideas and documenting them.

There are a handful of conclusions that can be drawn from this expert advice. First, tailoring writing assignments to individual needs personalizes the experience, which motivates students (e.g., Camacho et al., 2021; Wright et al., 2020). Second, positive learning environments foster responsible intellectual risk-taking (e.g., Cleghorn, 2023; MacKinnon & Archer-Kuhn, 2023). Third, writing is a process that produces products, but only the product, not the process, is typically graded in school. To make the thinking process more visible for coaching, students and teachers alike need to learn vocabulary that permits these conversations. Furthermore, the literature suggests that the definition of a "good" writer has been made narrow by the limited number of writing genres taught in school. We would like to celebrate the many ways people can be good writers in all genres. Some people are good at lab reports and poor at poetry, and others are great storytellers but terrible at research papers; knowledge of different genres plays a role in becoming a good writer (Viriya & Wasanasomsithi, 2017). Research shows that 4th- and 5th-grade kids can teach each other to be good writers (grammar, syntax, vocabulary, spelling) but are unaware of different genres of writing (Wilson & Wen, 2022), and this lack of knowledge of different writing genres remains a problem even postsecondary (Peter & Singaravelu, 2021). This means few people even know how many different ways (genres) there are to be great writers. The current curricula prize the five-paragraph argumentative essay over most other forms (Warner, 2018), leaving many students feeling their work is inadequate when they might actually excel in different genres. Approaching a broader range of genres can help connect the subject to a student's growing sense of being a writer, leveraging motivating emotions while engaging with the material and shaping the writing.

WHY THINKWRITE? WHY NOW?

Because humans' past experiences and cultural habits are so powerful, they create ingrained ideas that are hard to change; if you have done something one way for a while, it makes it hard to get your brain to link to new ways of doing things. As teachers we often fall back on familiar patterns in writing instruction, though they may not be fully supported by research. This is a common process in the brain called *heuristics*. It is easier and takes less energy to use the shortcuts of prior knowledge than to try and learn something new and more contextually appropriate. Even when faced with evidence, we often find it more comfortable to use what we are familiar with than spend the energy to adopt a new perspective (Khalidi, 2023).

The wisdom from writing experts motivates us to offer the following advice. We would like to challenge you to move out of your comfort zone of prior knowledge and be open to new information generated in the learning sciences as we introduce new concepts in the rest of this book. We also encourage you to take notes as you read, share your findings with others, get feedback on your evolving thinking, and give yourself time to explore. Your personal comfort with this change in thinking about writing instruction will be the foundation on which we can move forward toward literacy instruction founded on a new neuroscience of writing.

The Evidence and the Urgency

While there are many excellent programs to help students learn to write, some of which integrate the exciting new information being generated by the learning sciences, we were motivated to search for a new model in ThinkWrite for many reasons. Consider the macro-level arguments for a new writing approach (Figure 1.6).

Writing is the highest form of thinking (Tokuhama-Espinosa, 2021). Thinking and writing are mutually beneficial: Deep thinking facilitates coherent writing (Bean & Melzer, 2021; Halpern, 2013), while learning to write well improves your thinking (Bean & Melzer, 2021; Nickerson et al., 2014), partially because writing improves reading (Graham & Hebert, 2010), and knowledge intake through reading is fundamental to learning. Academic success hinges on writing (College Board, 2003), as shown in studies all around the world (e.g., Kuiken & Vedder, 2021), with "normal" as well as neurodivergent brains (e.g., Molitor et al., 2016). A good job depends on being successful in a range of literacies, including from writing skills to digital literacy (Day, 2023). Democratic societies depend on literate individuals (Cope & Kalantzis, 2014; Kellner & Share, 2007; Khan, 2020; Polizzi, 2020). As the National Commission on Writing in America's Schools and Colleges proclaimed, "Writing today is not a frill for the few, but an essential skill

Figure 1.6. Writing Is the Highest Form of Thinking

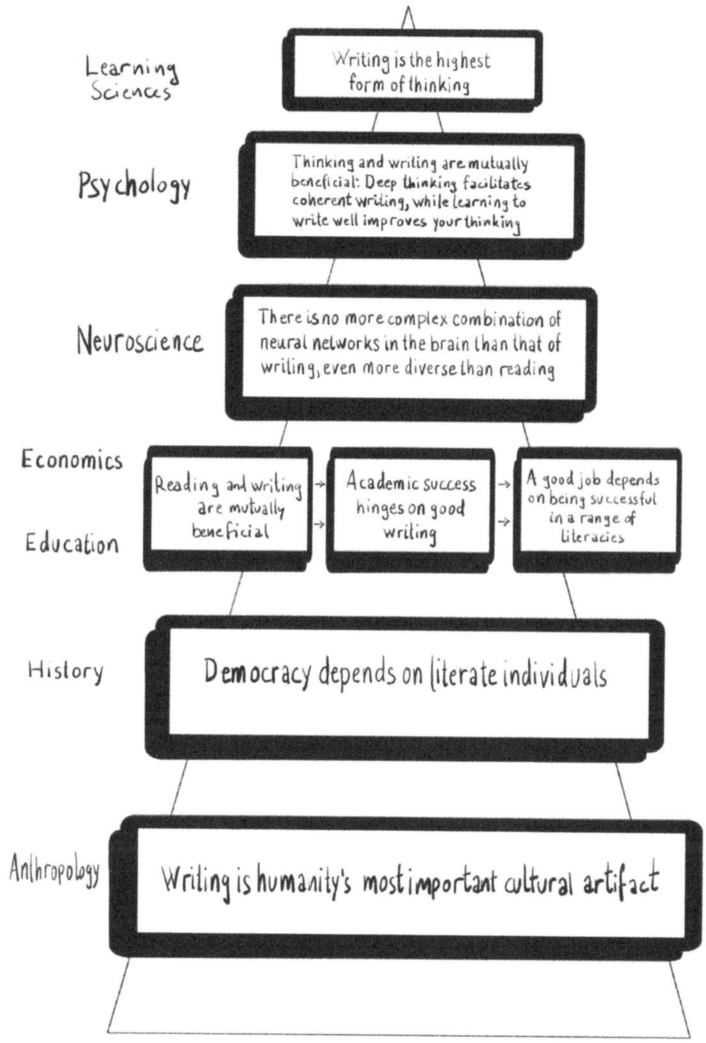

Artwork by Gabriel Espinosa Tokuhama for Tracey Tokuhama-Espinosa.

for the many," (College Board, 2003, p. ii). They go on to link individual and national potential to writing:

> America will never realize its potential as an engine of opportunity and economic growth until a writing revolution puts language and communication in their proper place in the classroom. Writing is how students connect the dots in their knowledge. (College Board, 2003, p. 3)

All of the above statements suggest that writing is humanity's most important cultural artifact. They take on even more importance for us as educators when we realize that the following statements are *also* true:

- While humans speak intuitively, they cannot learn to read or write without instruction. Writing must be learned explicitly, not just implicitly (Dehaene, 2009).
- Learning to read and write have only been considered required school subjects for the past five generations, and we have yet to perfect the best way to teach (Murphy & Thaiss, 2020).
- In 2018, most Americans read at a 7th- to 8th-grade level and wrote with even less ability (U.S. Department of Education, 2019).
- Nearly two-thirds of high school graduates read and write below grade level (Blank, 2023).
- The inability to read and write well are risk factors for criminal activity and incarceration. Three out of five people in prison cannot read, and 85% of youth offenders struggle to read (Duwe & Henry-Nickie, 2021).
- Writing, despite being the highest form of thinking and involved in all academic subjects, is far less researched than other academic areas such as reading, art, physical education, or STEM content (College Board, 2003).
- More than a third of 2nd-grade students believe they are "not good writers" (Seban & Tavşanlı, 2015), and this self-perception worsens into middle school, where it levels out, and remains low through high school (Pajares et al., 2007).
- According to the National Center for Educational Statistics, 21% of adults in the United States (about 43 million) are illiterate or functionally illiterate. Worldwide, the United Nations estimates that more than 260 million children were out of school in 2017, and 773 million adults—two-thirds of whom are women—remained illiterate in 2018 (AI for Good, 2022).
- Illiteracy is correlated with poverty; 43% of adults with the lowest literacy levels live in poverty (Rae, 2020). Levels of adult literacy are correlated with levels of political participation and efficacy, as well as trust in government (Ugur-Cinar et al., 2020).
- Low levels of literacy may be costing the U.S. economy $2.2 trillion a year (Nietzel, 2020).

Many adults, even those working in schools, continue to feel self-conscious and insecure about their writing long after their formal education has ended. Formal teacher education programs vary widely in their preparation of teachers to instruct students in writing. Graham reports that while some education programs prepare teachers well, surveys show "this is not typically the case" (Graham, 2019, p. 293), and many teachers do not feel well prepared to teach writing. He suggests this is due to the lack of sufficient direct instruction in best practices and its theoretical foundations, and a lack of opportunities to practice them. In this, the formal teaching of educators echoes the challenges to writing instruction more generally (Graham, 2019). Graham also points to a perceived lack of institutional support for writing instruction due to a lack of recognition of writing's importance and its role in learning within the context of an overfull curriculum. Given this situation, teachers often fall back on what worked well for them as individuals in the classroom, shaped as we all are by our own past experience. But that may not be what meets the needs of our students. And while teachers may feel the need to differentiate writing instruction, they may not feel they have the expertise, resources, or time to do so (Al-Shaboul et al., 2021).

The struggle to improve literacy has been ongoing ever since the inception of formal education (Tierney & Pearson, 2021). Typical, standardized intelligence tests use language, literacy, and math as proxies for "smart" (Gardner, 2011) but do so in a limited way (Chen & Gardner, 2018; Sternberg, 2020). These "literacy" tests generally are limited to measuring reading skills, which are easier and less costly to evaluate than writing skills, despite the knowledge that writing involves even more complex thinking than reading and would be a better measure of general intelligence (Parkin et al., 2020). Knowing how to write not only serves as a protective factor for health (Zajacova & Lawrence, 2018) and wealth (Ungureanu & Tomita, 2021), but it is also correlated with political stability (Ali et al., 2021) and having a sense of trust in your community (e.g., Barrera-Osorio et al., 2020; Goldin, 1999). Writing well and critical thinking are inseparable (Halpern, 2013).

Despite the many excellent writing programs in existence, there do not seem to be as many good writers in the world as would be expected. The problem? Perhaps we have not been playing with a full deck, or, at the least, we have not been privy to all the "rules" of the writing game. Most literacy programs are based solely on educational studies and are not yet nurtured by other learning sciences. Learning how humans learn to write requires more than just understanding curriculum milestones; it means unifying distinct levels or units of analysis from the learning sciences that range from cultural comparisons, to psychological well-being in classrooms, to a child's brain and biology.

While international comparative policies, national goals, institutional mission statements, and department objectives can all be aligned, a child's life still might not be in sync with requirements. To teach to each child's strengths within their cultural contexts and to adjust for their personal risk and protective factors, teachers are reminded to take advantage of a more microscopic contributor: neural networks. ThinkWrite uses research from all the learning sciences (instructional design, neuropsychology, AI, cultural anthropology, educational psychology, cognitive neuroscience, social linguistics, and others) and suggests writing instruction begin where the student is, not where the textbooks say they should be. Using the brain's hierarchy of the writing trajectory, we believe people can become great writers.

ThinkWrite Is Complementary to Any Curriculum

We close with the reminder that while ThinkWrite can be implemented as a programmatic approach to writing instruction and lesson planning, it can also serve as a complementary process, which can be used with any writing curriculum. It is our hope that by explaining the neural underpinnings of writing, teachers will modify their approach to developing the thinking behind the writing as well as extend their empathy to struggling writers. We hope that the labels we apply to the invisible thinking will offer missing vocabulary needed to facilitate better conversations about the emergent writing process. We are in debt to earlier scholars who highlighted the needs of current writing students (Appendix A) and hope we have added to the conversation about the best ways to teach writing.

To physically decipher what is happening in the brain when we write, we now turn to Chapter 2.

CHAPTER 2

The Neuroscience of Writing

In this chapter, we look at how the brain manages the thinking behind the writing using learning trajectories. To explain this, we will introduce what we hope becomes a favorite word: *holons*. We will start with how language, the brain, and thinking are related and then explain the networks related to learning more generally. Following this, in Chapters 3, 4, and 5, we will look at each of the 15 stages of the ThinkWrite model, broken down into prewriting, writing, and revision.

LEARNING TRAJECTORIES AND THEIR NEURAL NETWORKS

Writing requires many different types of thinking sustained by different sets of neural networks in the brain. These networks are stimulated by different kinds of in- and out-of-school activities. The key to teaching writing with the brain in mind is to appreciate that the brain has multiple systems and ways to order the thinking stages behind the writing process. Understanding and labeling these systems gives us tools to talk about them and eventually manage them. It's exciting to think that the brain is the most complex thing in the universe, and teachers get to change it every day in their classrooms!

We now know that the neural networks involved in writing are numerous and each is part of the larger whole of writing. For example, recognizing letters (Polk et al., 2002) uses a different neural pathway from understanding their corresponding sounds (Takashima et al., 2014), or word meaning (Lin et al., 2024), which is in turn different from the pathways that relate to the motor coordination needed to use a pencil to write that letter (Planton et al., 2013). Added to these elements of writing (letters, sounds, meaning, holding a pencil) are other elements, like a student's motivational state and their prior knowledge of the content being written about, which are also supported by dozens of other neural pathways. To explain the complexity of the brain and learning, we want to introduce this idea of *holons*.

HOLONS: PARTS AND WHOLE

Hopefully by the end of this chapter, *holon* will be one of your favorite words, as it has become one of ours. A holon is defined as something that is at once a part of something else but also a whole unto itself.

For example, take a leaf. A leaf is part of a tree, but it is a whole unto itself. The leaf can also be broken down into its smaller parts, but each of those parts can also be broken down even further. A leaf's vein, for example, can also be broken down into the xylem and phloem, and so on. In the opposite direction, the leaf is part of a tree, but the tree can also be a part of a forest (Figure 2.1).

In another example, the word *love* can be a part of a sentence ("I love you") but also has a meaning unto itself. The *mother* can be a part of a family or community, but she is also her own self. A *hand* is a part of the body, but it is also an entity in and of itself. Parts and whole are easily understood by even very young children, but the process of thinking through holons is far less common. Thinking through holons means habituating a three-step thought process: First, remembering that everything is always a part as well as a whole; second, considering that the parts themselves can always be reduced further into even smaller subparts; third, challenging ourselves to constantly imagine how everything is part of a bigger whole. The goal of this chapter is to ensure that literacy instruction always incorporates a habituated look at the ways content can be made smaller, and how it also fits as a part into other structures and systems.

Everything in the natural world is a holon: You, me, the leaf, the word, and everything else we can name can be broken down into smaller parts and viewed in the context of larger wholes. The book in your hands is a holon as it can be broken down into chapters, and those chapters into core concepts, and the concepts into paragraphs, and the paragraphs into sentences and the sentences into words, and so on. But the book can also be a part of a larger whole of your personal library or your professional development. Thinking through holons is beneficial as it reminds us as teachers to break down concepts and big ideas into smaller parts for easier instruction, *but we must also remember to bring all of those pieces back together again*. For example, by asking students to write a complete story bringing together everything they know about characters, using the right vocabulary, structuring the outline in such a way as to reach the climax at the right time, including a moral, and so on.

Holons are useful in thinking about language and writing, and about how the brain works. They are also useful to explain teachers, students, and their relationships, which we'll look at in Chapter 9.

The Holons of the Brain

The brain can be broken down into smaller parts, but it is also a part of your body, and your body is part of your family, and your family is a part of society, and so on.

Figure 2.1. Holon: Leaf

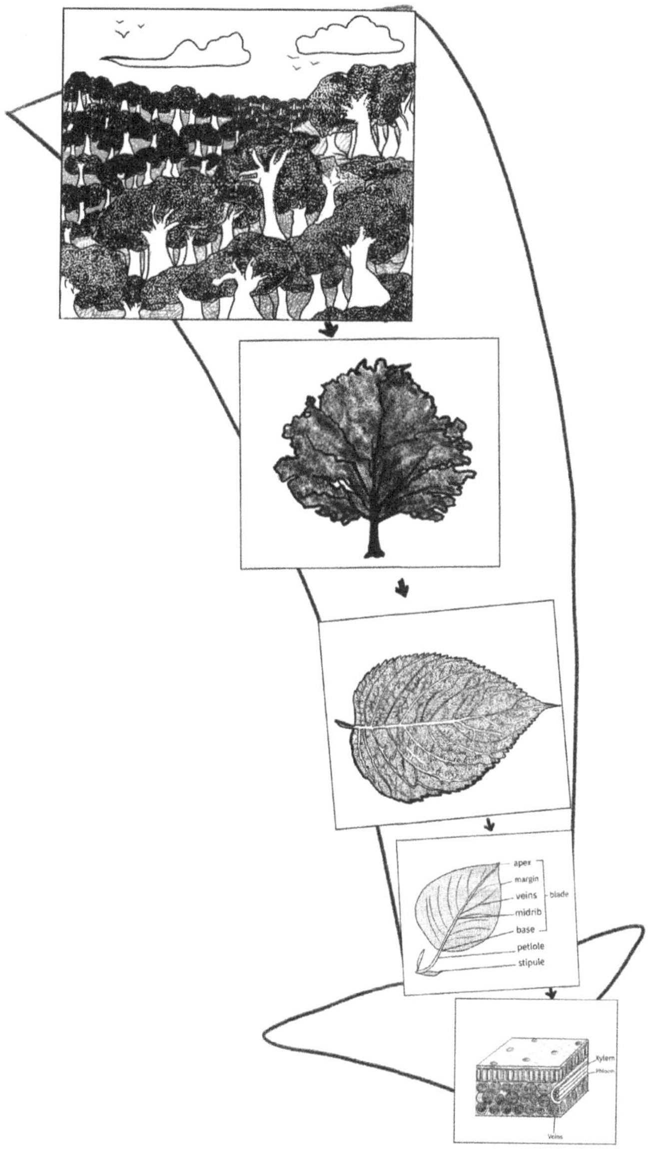

Artwork by Gabriel Espinosa Tokuhama for Tracey Tokuhama-Espinosa.

The brain can be broken down into hemispheres, and the hemispheres can be broken down into lobes; the lobes can be broken down into networks which are subserved by pathways, which in turn are made up of synapses, which can be broken down into neurotransmitters, which can be broken down into electrical and chemical elements, and so on (Figure 2.2). In the opposite direction, the brain

Figure 2.2. Holons in the Brain (Smaller Parts)

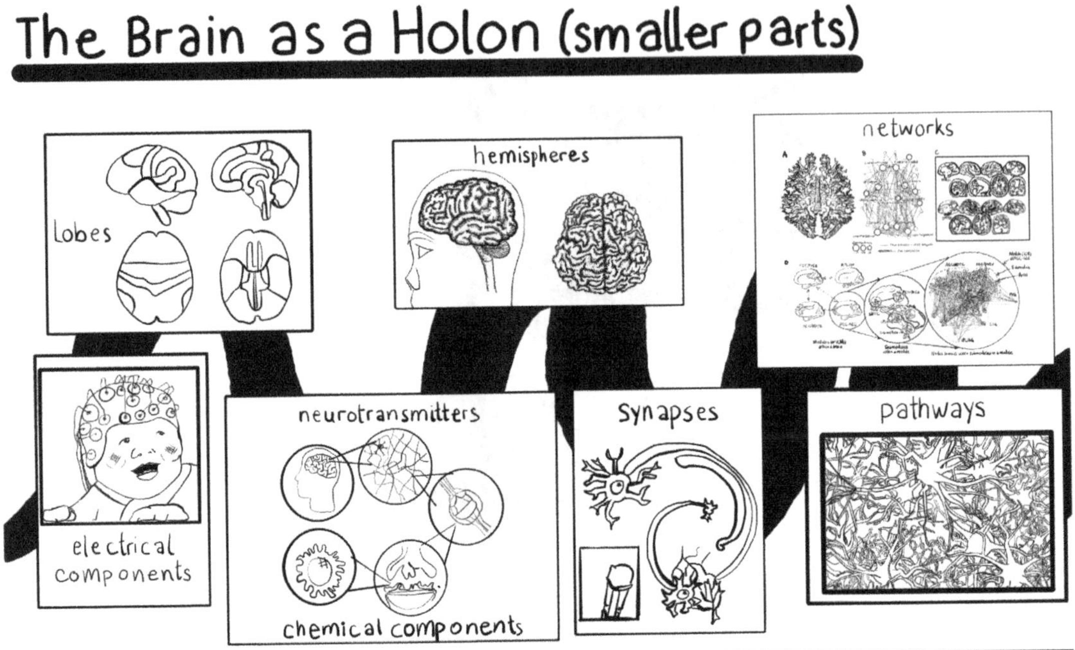

is a holon that is part of an individual's body, but that body is a kid in a classroom, and that classroom is an element in society, and that society is part of a city, and the city is part of the state, and so on (Figure 2.3).

Teachers don't need to memorize brain parts, but they do need to acknowledge that learning to write involves different networks and can be stimulated in different stages of thinking. They also need to know that roadblocks to learning can sometimes be caused by problems with memory systems, other times attention problems, and yet other times by social–emotional contexts, or by learning the sub-elements of language itself. The key idea for teachers is that each sub-element is managed by distinct networks in the brain, requiring different kinds of interventions. A good diagnosis is half the cure.

The Holons of Language

Language can be broken down into listening, speaking, reading, and writing, which can be further broken down into smaller and smaller units. Similarly, language can be seen as one subject out of many in a school curriculum. Breaking down literacy into its smallest parts is a key way to ensure students have the foundations for good writing. The logical construction of skills from the smallest units, like letters in the kindergarten years, up through complex

Figure 2.3. Holons in the Brain (Larger Parts): The Dynamic Teaching–Learning Process

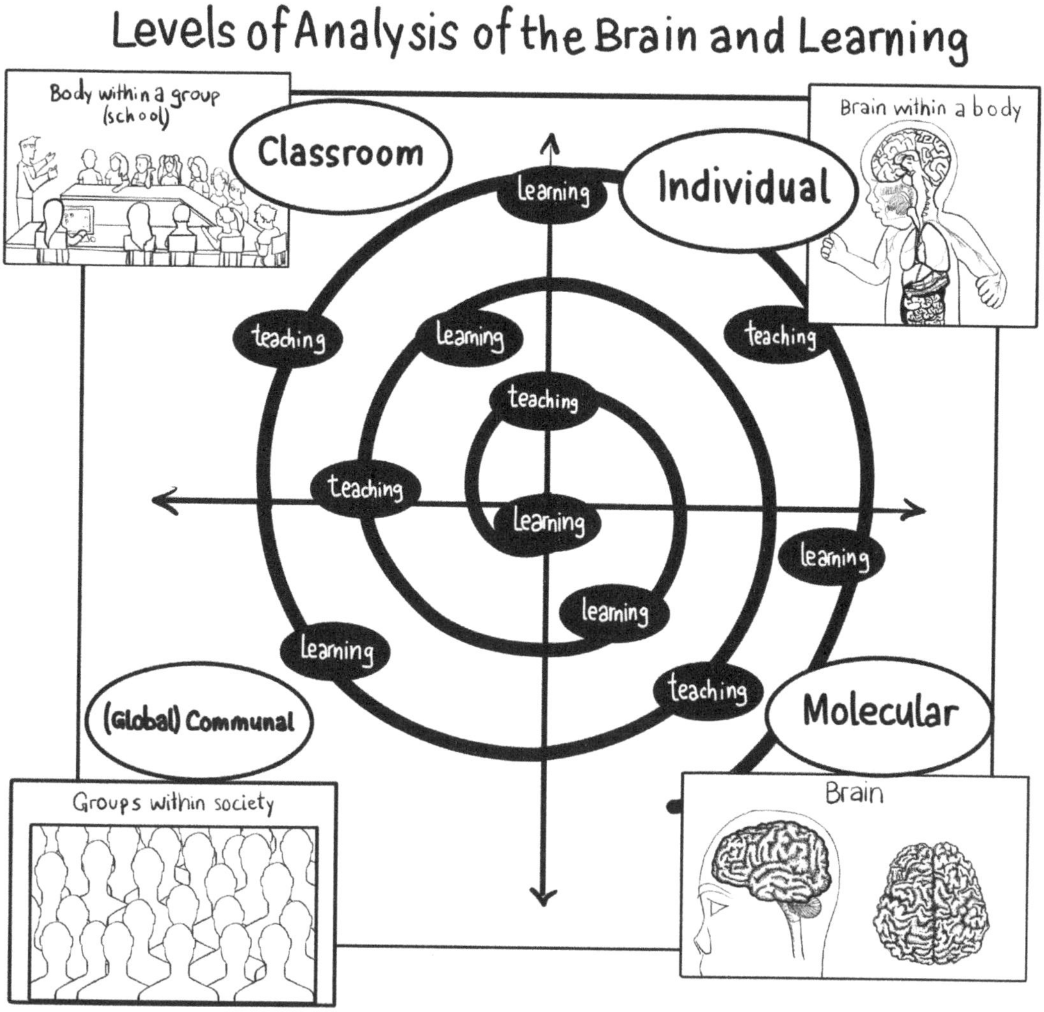

ideas, like writing whole essays in high school, follows an intuitive design. Mastery of orthographic control in the elementary years, for example, helps free up the brain's attention for other types of thinking and higher-order skills later on.

On the other hand, to suggest an overly hierarchical alignment of holons can be misleading. Young children can construct and share meaningful stories through dictation (Veraksa et al., 2020) even before gaining full orthographic control (Gimenez et al., 2014). Surprisingly, some students who struggle with some "basic" holons of writing may still have great facility with other holons of writing "higher" up in our conceptual understanding of the writing process. F. Scott Fitzgerald was a notoriously poor speller (Boland, 2013), for example, though few would doubt his contribution to the world of letters. ThinkWrite tells us that (1) a hierarchy of learning concepts exists in a trajectory and that (2) there is a large range of human variability that determines how and when individuals reach each milestone, much of which is due to individual experience. By naming the sub-elements in writing that may be missing or causing roadblocks to optimal performance in writing, we can intervene more effectively. Holons are useful to understand in writing because each one correlates to distinct neural pathways in the brain.

Writing consists of hundreds of holons that range from phonemes to syllables (one neural pathway [Omura et al., 2004]); letters to words (a different neural pathway [Jung, 2020]); words to sentences (yet another neural pathway [Fairhall, 2024]); or sentences to paragraphs (a distinct neural pathway [Trompenaars et al., 2017]) (Figure 2.4). Successful language instruction occurs when these smaller pieces are all brought back into the larger whole once the separate parts have been taught. Holons can also be thought of as parts of speech, literary devices, vocabulary, and so on. Breaking down writing into its smallest parts is what we do naturally as we organize content in school for literacy.

One can teach through holons by starting at the most macro level of communication or the most micro level of a single sound; the key is to disaggregate each part into its smallest and largest parts. Being able to name the letter "b" is important, but the use of the letter "b" in a sentence relies on not only the letter "b" but also on rules for spelling, the ways that combinations of letters change sounds (how "b" sounds in the word "bubble" compared to the sound in the word "thumb," for example), and a host of other language rules. While knowing the parts is vital, parts alone do not construct the whole without purposeful connections. This is the difference between knowing a lot of body parts in isolation (hand, heart, hair) versus knowing how the body as a whole functions, or how a single moment in history can teach us a lesson about people or important characters, but history as a whole can help explain human nature. Each piece of language contributes to communication, and the ability to read and write requires hundreds of different pathways, most of which occur without our conscious perception.

Holons are also extremely useful in getting to the heart of language problems because they more precisely label the language problems and target them with more precise interventions. It turns out that writing involves hundreds of neural pathways, which we have classified into 16 neural networks (Tokuhama-Espinosa & Borja, 2023), which can then be grouped into four categories: sensory, context, general cognitive networks, and domain-specific networks (Figure 2.5), which we explain next.

Figure 2.4. Holons and Hierarchies in Language and Communication

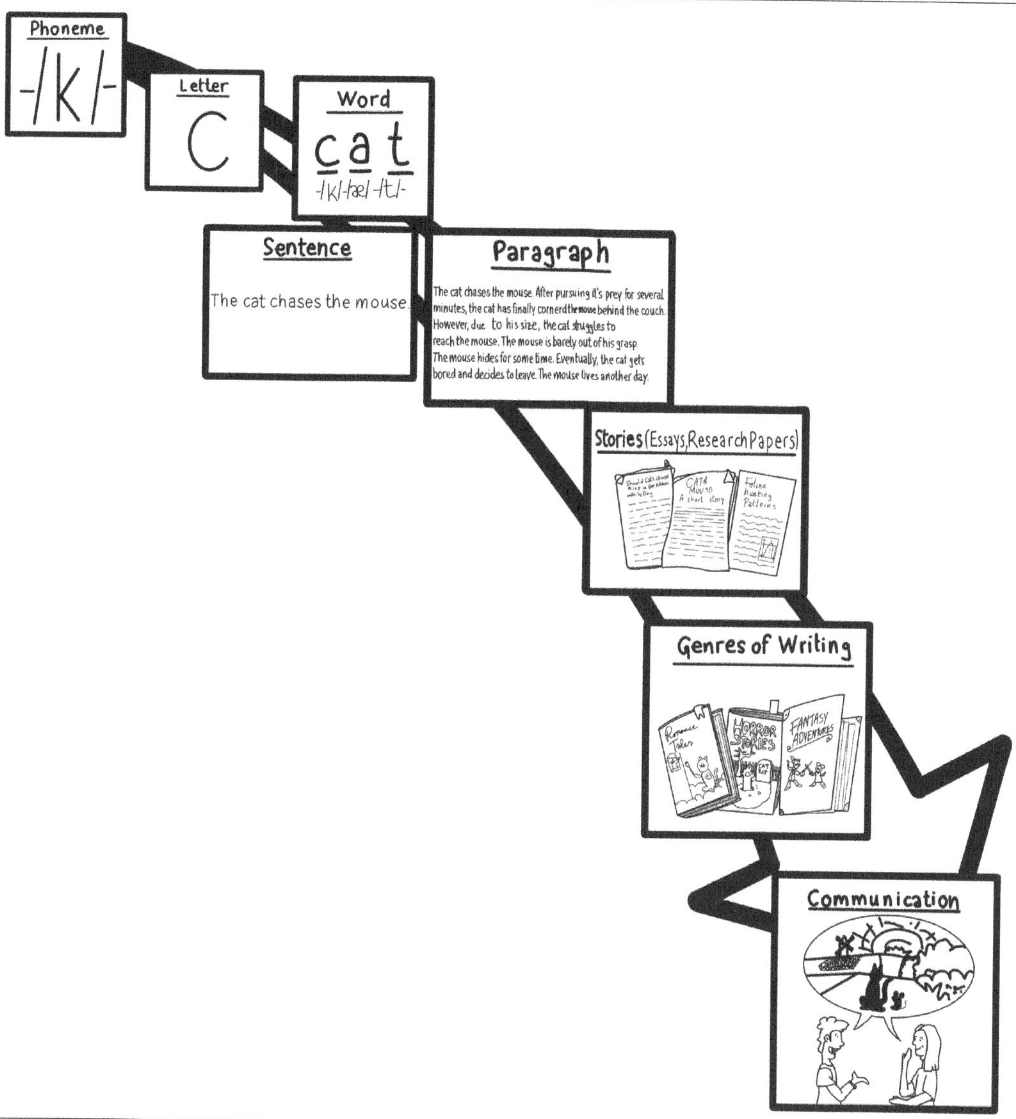

FOUR CATEGORIES OF NEURAL NETWORKS FOR LANGUAGE

All learning is filtered through the senses, as Aristotle pointed out over 2,000 years ago. Once the senses perceive the world and the context of learning itself, then the brain uses general cognitive abilities to understand, analyze, and use the new information. The specific domain areas of learning—language, math, science, art,

Figure 2.5. Four Categories of Neural Networks

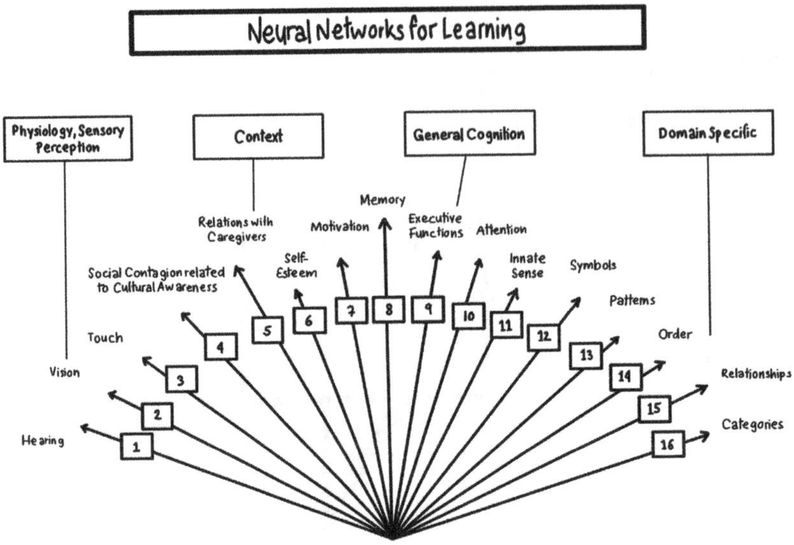

and so on—also bring their own networks to the learning process. Human learning follows a pattern of sensory perception, memory checks, attention, and decisions about how to use the brain's limited energy (Sepp et al., 2019). Learning is also relatively unique for each person as no two people have the same lived experiences (Simpson, 2023), which means, thanks to the brain's plastic response to experience—the development of stronger or weaker neural connections in response to patterns of stimulus—each brain is also unique. The typical patterns of learning combine with the unique individual to contribute to the neural pathways for writing. Each of these networks is made up of smaller elements, called pathways. The four categories of networks are explained briefly below.

Sensory Networks

Sensory networks relate to how the brain perceives the world around it. Writing involves just three, not five, of the senses: seeing, hearing and touch, or graphomotor processes (writing does not depend on taste or smell at all, except in metaphorical thinking). The sensory perception networks in turn branch off into multiple pathways (Figure 2.6). Teachers can use knowledge of the sensory networks to scale up interventions in classrooms as many learning problems involve poor eyesight, hearing, and/or graphomotor control. This can look like a child who has a problem with language, but the problem "disappears" once the child is given glasses, a hearing aid, or exercise to improve handwriting.

Vision involves seeing colors, brightness, and contrast. But it also is related to visual crowding and how the brain perceives saliency (what jumps off the page) (Łuniewska et al., 2022). Most interestingly, the visual networks perceive letters differently than other objects in the "letterbox" network (Dehaene, 2013). The way writing is presented on the page, the typefaces used, or colors chosen all influence the ability to read and eventually to write.

Hearing involves pitch and tempo (Grabowski, 2022) and being able to determine sarcasm and the correct rhythm of a conversation (Farrall, 2012). Fascinatingly, hearing relates to hand gestures and the memory of poems, songs, and speeches (e.g., Cook, 2018). Auditory processing, another pathway in hearing in the brain, is how your brain hears what it is reading or composes the right string of words to make a sentence eloquent or cumbersome (Burke, 2015). Believe it or not, the brain actually hears human language sounds in different neural pathways from nonspeech sounds (Belin, 2018). Something like a fire engine siren is perceived by the ear in the same way as a voice but is processed in the brain differently because language is special. Human speech sounds even occupy more brain real estate: "the speech area is significantly larger as compared with others" (Shklovsky et al., 2019, p. 577).

The more a child is read to, the clearer the voices in their head when reading on their own. Once the brain perceives another person talking, it also has to classify the sounds it perceives. There are subclassifications of language sounds. For example, some sounds are very close like "b" and "p," which are harder for the brain to distinguish compared to very distant sounds, like "k" and "l" sounds (Coch, 2021). The brain becomes more accurate in categorizing these language sounds through exposure. The more rehearsal, the easier it is for the brain to distinguish similar sounds. The sounds of some words have somatic and emotional resonance beyond that suggested by the meaning of the word alone, suggesting some cross-domain "wiring" of the sounds of language to the brain's emotion systems, a fact to which skillful writers are especially attuned. This means reading, rhythming, singing, and other word games that employ language sounds benefit writing.

Finally, from an auditory perspective, depending on the language, certain patterns are "normal" to the brain and others are not. For example, "th" in English is common, but "th" in Spanish is not (Whitley, 2002). This is important for writing teachers to know because when the brain is reading and writing, it is also *listening* to what it sees on paper (Emmorey & Lee, 2021)! Fluent writers actually "hear" what they are reading. Again, this means that the greater rehearsal and familiarity the brain has with words and word patterns, the easier it will be to write.

Touch and graphomotor networks include visuomotor coordination to string letters together in a way that is legible (Unell et al., 2021). As your fingertips are some of the most sensitive parts of your body, writing with a pen or pencil offers your brain feedback about the shape of letters in a way that keyboarding cannot

(Frangou, 2016), meaning writing by hand increases neural pathways for memory (Smoker et al., 2009). It is now known that handwriting on paper reinforces memory more than writing on tablets or keyboarding on a computer (Ihara et al., 2021).

"Haptic" or touch memory is also used to increase the number of ways your brain can retrieve knowledge of written material. In Montessori education, kids trace letters in the sand (or draw letters on each other's backs) to increase the neural pathways for letter recognition (Mooney et al., 2018). In some cultures, skillful calligraphy itself is prized and cultivated for its expressive capacities (Labuschagne, 2017). Like sound, the shape of language, something graphic designers are very well aware of—whether in font style or the style of handwriting—can convey its own energy and both capture and generate emotional resonance. While some who struggle with orthographic control may benefit greatly from keyboarding, in general teachers who leverage all sensory network inputs during writing instruction help students connect more memory pathways, leading to better learning.

Contextual and Social Networks

In addition to sensory networks, contextual networks also play a role in learning to write. All learning, including learning how to write, is also influenced by the learner's cultural and social contexts (Figure 2.7). Contextual networks branch off into sub-elements of social contagion (i.e., how attitudes spread within a group), and cognition (e.g., King & Mendoza, 2021), culture (e.g., Hammond, 2014), relationships (e.g., Sethi & Scales, 2020) and other environmentally induced, noncognitive influences on writing. For example, the ways reading and writing are used in society changes the value a student gives them, which is why homes with lots of books in them tend to produce students who have a higher likelihood of strong literacy skills (Puglisi et al., 2017). Furthermore, we know there is no cognition without emotion (Immordino-Yang, 2007). If a person experiences negative emotions such as fear, anxiety, anger, depression, or sadness, based on classroom relationships, including with the teacher, they will be hard pressed to learn to write. On the other hand, if they feel secure and experience positive emotions, like happiness, there is a higher likelihood of forming the new neural connections (Fong et al., 2018). Why? Because synaptic connections in the brain occur through neurotransmitters (chemicals). The combinations of neurotransmitters needed for the creation of new synapses are facilitated by the chemicals in positive emotional states and hindered in negative emotional states.

To make matters more complex, many students report feeling ashamed of their writing (Christensen, 2000), which is a negative emotion. This is why a teacher's purposeful design of an inclusive, mistake-tolerant environment can benefit learning. Each student comes to class with a unique set of prior experiences due to the contexts in which they were raised. Some of these serve as protective factors and speed up learning, and in other cases they are risk factors and

Figure 2.6. Neural Networks: Sensory Perception and Literacy

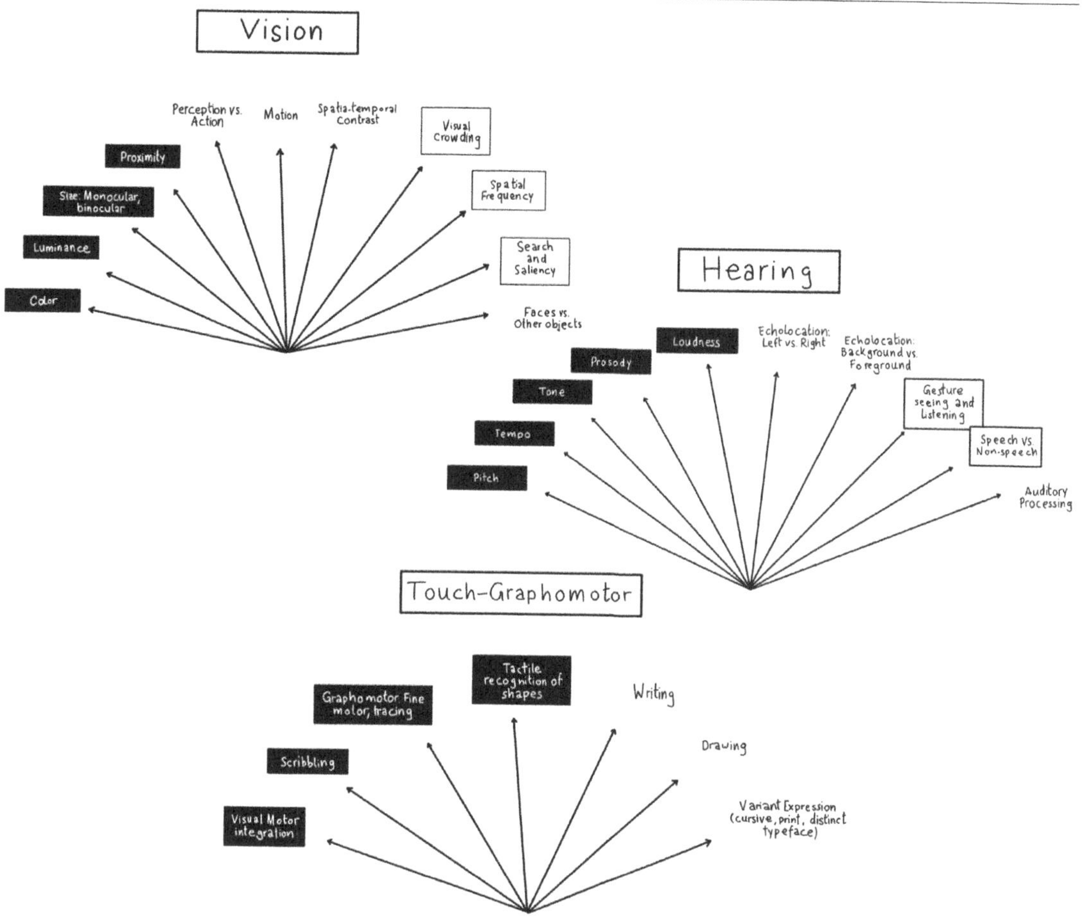

Artwork by Gabriel Espinosa Tokuhama for Tracey Tokuhama-Espinosa, 2019.

can slow strong literacy development. All the child's contextual conditions come accompanied by emotions, which have a direct impact on learning outcomes.

Humans are unique and there are no two identical brains. This explains one reason why educational interventions don't have a strong track record of replicability (Seah & Wong, 2019). Different cultural and social contexts make it hard to say what the "best" way to teach literacy is as it is nearly impossible to create identical conditions for literacy and compare them as people are different (Kim, 2019). It is hard to get a straight answer about the "best" writing interventions, not because the interventions aren't good but because a lot of available research does not take into consideration the range of learners and their individual contexts. What a student already knows, their level of motivation, and relationships with peers and teachers all influence learning outcome (Hattie, 2012). Aside from good curricular planning, strong methodologies and activities, a teacher also needs an appreciation of the social, cultural, and emotional contexts a student comes to class with in order to maximize each learner's potential.

Context and social interaction also have an influence on an individual's self-esteem and self-perception as a writer (Bottomley et al., 1997). A student's motivation to learn is directly related to the complex social interactions that occur in a classroom (Tokuhama-Espinosa & Borja, 2023). Teachers should know that no matter what level of motivation a student comes to class with, it is influenced, for better or worse, by the teacher (Ahn et al., 2021; Komarraju, 2013). Teachers who understand and can manage social contagion—changing the learning environment into a safe, positive place—have an edge in creating the right classroom environment.

Among the myriad of factors influencing literacy instruction, one factor appears to have the greatest influence, however, and that is the student–teacher relationships (Fisher et al., 2016). Strong, positive student–teacher relationships improve the rate, accuracy, and efficiency of learning in all topics, including writing (Kincade et al., 2020). Having a positive student–teacher relationship does not mean only giving positive feedback to make the student feel good; it is more dependent on the perception on the part of the student that the teacher cares (Chang, 2019).

Sensory and contextual networks are complemented by two kinds of cognitive networks in the brain, general and domain specific.

General Cognition Networks

A third category of networks for writing is called "general cognition," which refers to the general cognitive abilities of memory, attention, and executive functions (EFs) (Figure 2.8) (Tokuhama-Espinosa & Nouri, 2023). Memory and attention are the foundations of executive functions and together permit the opportunity to make choices. If the learner has strong self-regulation (an offshoot of strong EFs), then they can make good choices. Some of these choices involve a conscientious choice about where to "sustain" or hold attention and/or what to create a memory around. EFs and self-regulation are shown to have a stronger impact on learning outcomes than many other factors, including innate intelligence (Duckworth & Seligman, 2005; Moffitt, 2011). Memory, attention, and EFs are the basic cognitive functions that underpin all learning, academic or otherwise.

If a student has a problem in a general cognitive network, he will have learning problems in all subject areas, including writing. That is, problems with memory, attention, or executive functions will manifest in learning problems across the board. This is different from domain-specific neural networks dedicated to writing in the brain, which are specifically for literacy skills.

Figure 2.7. Neural Networks: Context

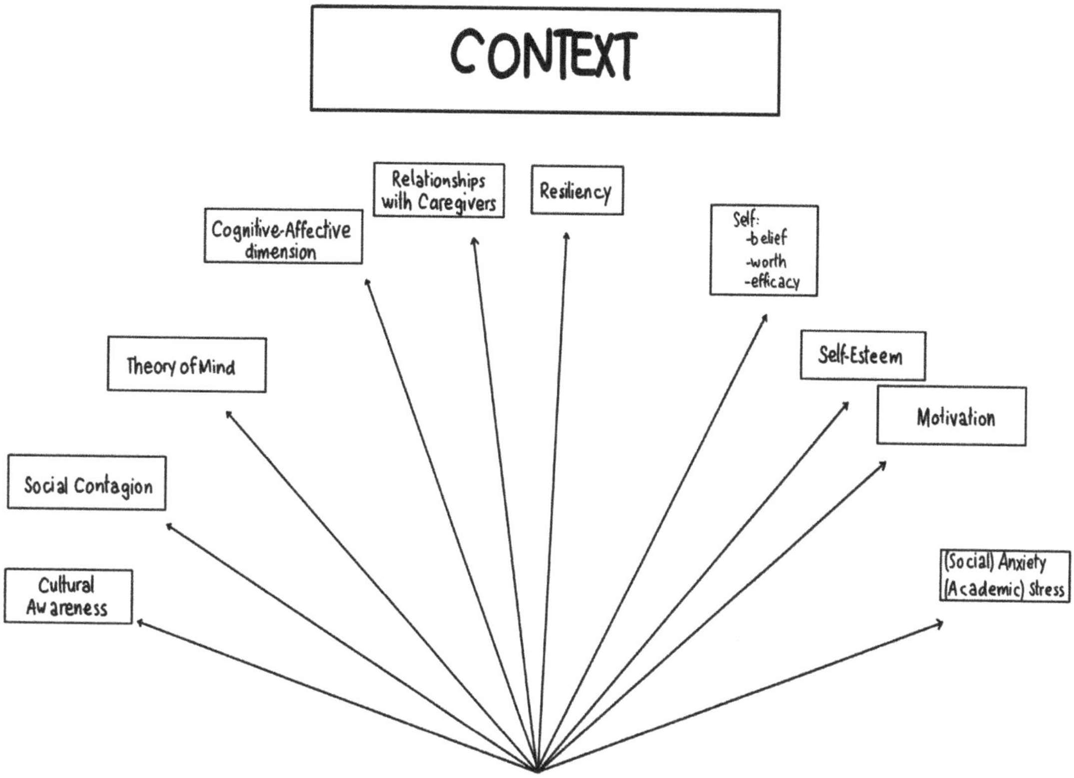

Artwork by Gabriel Espinosa Tokuhama for Tracey Tokuhama-Espinosa, 2019.

Domain-Specific Writing Networks

A fourth and final group of networks are the domain-specific networks. These are networks that organize domain-area knowledge, such as "language" in the brain (Figure 2.9). Writing depends on well-functioning domain-specific networks that underpin all the sub-elements of language, such as speaking, listening, reading, as well as writing itself. These abilities are in turn supported by understanding how innate language sense, symbols, patterns, order, categories, and relationships work (Tokuhama-Espinosa & Borja, 2023).

Many school psychologists are aware of specific language problems such as imperfect phonological awareness (Ruan et al., 2018). Phonological awareness is the ability to match a symbol, like a letter, to its corresponding property, like a sound (phoneme). What many school psychologists might not know, however, is that phonological awareness depends on multiple networks in the brain, including identifying letter symbols, recalling the name and property of the letter,

Figure 2.8. Neural Networks: General Cognition

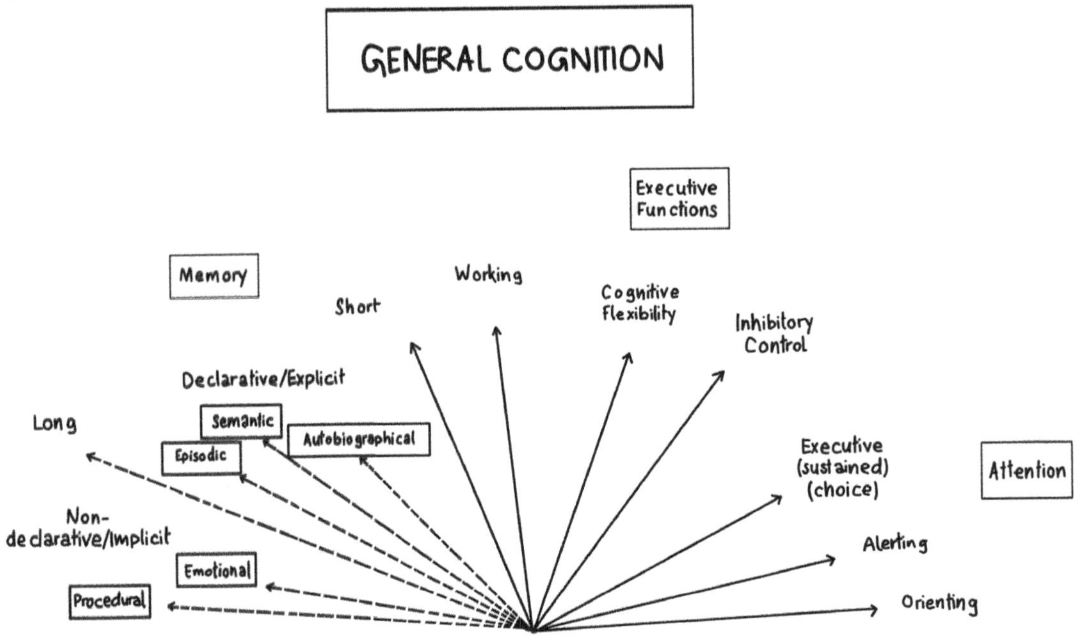

Artwork by Gabriel Espinosa Tokuhama for Tracey Tokuhama-Espinosa, 2019.

auditory memory networks to match the symbol to the sound, and so on, all of which are stimulated by different activities. This explains why labeling a language problem as a "phonological awareness difficulty" may not be enough to initiate an accurate intervention; the underlying networks involved should all be considered.

Additionally, kids are often labeled as having learning problems when the real problem may just be developmental. For example, some second-language learners make errors in writing because of *syntactic conservationism,* in which they get lazy and use the grammar of one of their languages in both of their languages. This is a normal phase of second-language learners (Fischer, 2002), and they can speed through it with the help of knowledgeable teachers who use good worked models (i.e., examples). Syntactic conservationism, like many language problems, is easily corrected once the patterning and ordering networks for the correct sentence structure have been rehearsed enough by the brain. Because this can be fixed so easily, it makes it clear that a good diagnosis is half the cure.

If we look at these four categories together, there are over 100 pathways underpinning these networks that must be triggered simultaneously for a person to be able to read (Tokuhama-Espinosa & Borja, 2023), and even more for writing due to the graphomotor coordination (Shah et al., 2013). All other cognitive functions use a fraction of these networks; there are more networks in the brain used to write that are active simultaneously than any other human activity! An appreciation of the complexity of writing in the brain also gives us access to more accurate diagnoses of writing problems. Rather than say a student has a "language problem," it is far more helpful to say they need to rehearse symbol-to-sound recognition, for example. Additionally, they help us teachers understand how easy it is to have problems along the path to better writing. This means that while the teachers think they are teaching *Romeo and Juliet*, the student is really negotiating new vocabulary, historical references, value differences, emotional intrigue, the genre of a play, Early Modern English, adolescent–adult quagmires, identifying key quotes that summarize core ideas, taking notes on what peers are saying, and a dozen other elements, simultaneously! This demand on so many neural networks at once puts a strain on the brain and helps us sympathize with the challenges the student is going through.

Working memory—the mental "desktop" on which one holds relevant information and procedures—is strained by writing. Pressure on working memory is aggravated when domain knowledge (such as the student's grasp of genre) is insecure or when the classroom culture is felt to be a poor fit by the student writer. The complexity of these writing networks helps explain why mastery of writing skills takes so much time, patience, and practice. The link between the reading and writing networks also underlines the importance of exposure to accomplished voices and building one's own expressive capacity.

To write, domain-specific networks—those just for writing—must work in tandem with general cognitive networks—memory, attention, and executive functions—as well as with context networks that connect the brain with the world—social, emotional, mentalizing about others, which is perceived through the senses. This is nothing less than awesome when seen in its smaller parts! The perfect coordination of all these different elements is what yields a solid, well-written sentence. Without purposeful attention to all these elements, as teachers we might attribute a student's writing difficulties or slowness to technical aspects of literacy, such as their inability to choose the right vocabulary word, or to a personality defect, such as laziness, when the real reason a student might be slower at writing well could simply be the lack of rehearsal of one neural network or another. Knowing the 16 networks (Figures 2.6–2.9) and how they need rehearsal before writing well becomes habituated should empower teachers and call attention to roadblocks and more accurate interventions. A detailed list of networks can be found in Table 2.1.

Figure 2.9. Neural Networks: Domain Specific for Literacy

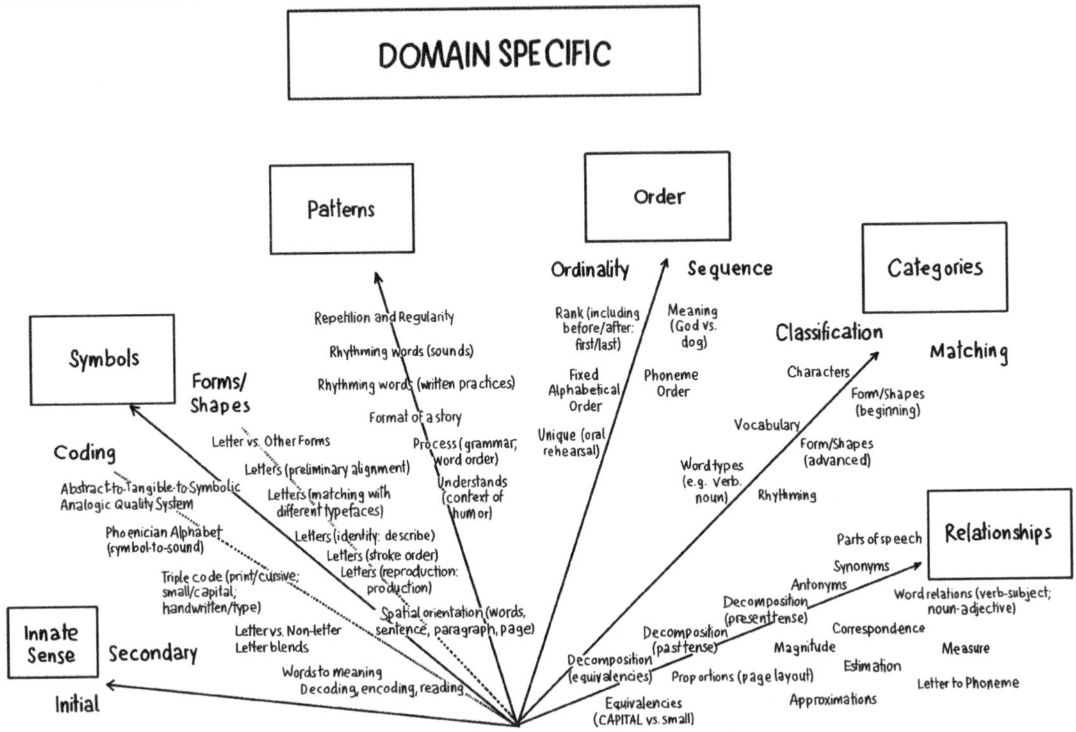

Artwork by Gabriel Espinosa Tokuhama for Tracey Tokuhama-Espinosa, 2019.

WHEN PROBLEMS OCCUR, DIAGNOSIS IS HALF THE CURE

It's important to remember that writing can be complex on a variety of levels, and part of being a great writing teacher is ensuring we have considered the physical, psychological, and general cognitive needs of students before presuming they have a language problem. Teachers post-pandemic are better than ever at recognizing that there are always exigent factors that can have an impact on student learning. To avoid the misattribution of the real problem, a good approach is to "scale up" interventions. First, as parents or teachers we should ask whether the visible behavior, such as the inability to write, is due to a physical cause, like the need for glasses, poor sleep, or a missed breakfast. If not, could it be a psychological cause? Is the student being bullied or are his parents divorcing? If not, do they have an identified learning problem with neurophysiological roots, like dyslexia? If not, can the problem be attributed to general cognitive issues of memory, attention, or executive functions (which would mean they have problems in all subject areas, not just writing)? If the cause of writing problems is none of these factors, then specific literacy-domain problems, such as poor vocabulary, second-language learner issues, or lack of genre knowledge can be considered.

Table 2.1. Neural Networks Involved in Writing

Sensory	Context	General Cognition	Domain Specific
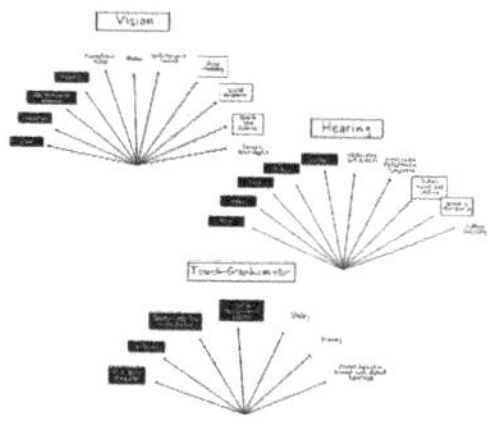	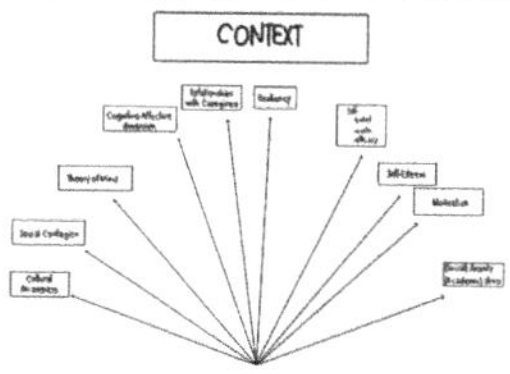	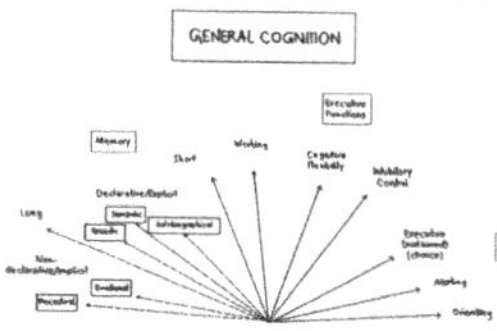	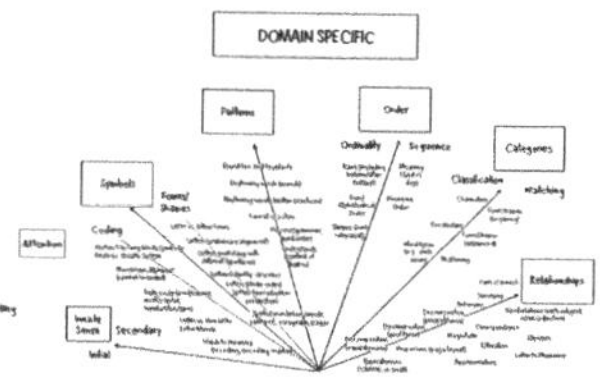
	Neural Networks		
Vision, Hearing, Touch/ Graphomotor	Cultural awareness, Social Contagion, Theory of Mind, Cognitive-affective dimension, Relationships, Resiliency, Self-concept, Social emotions, Motivation	Memory systems, Attention Systems, Executive Functions	Innate Language Sense, Symbols, Patterns, Order, Categories, Relationships
	Neural Pathways		
Vision: Proximity, Size (molecular), Size (binocular), Luminance, Color, Perception vs. Action, Motion, Spatial-temporal contrast, Visual crowding, Spatial frequency, Search and saliency, Faces vs. Other objects **Hearing:** Pitch, Tempo, Tone, Prosody, Loudness, Echolocation (left vs. right), Echolocation (background vs. foreground), Gesture, Speech vs. non-speech, Auditory processing	**Cultural awareness, Social Contagion, Theory of Mind, Cognitive-affective dimension, Relationships, Resiliency, Self-concept, Social emotions, Motivations**	**Memory:** Short-term, Working, Long-Term Procedural, Long-term Emotional, Long-term Episodic, Long-term Semantic, Long-term autobiographcal **Executive Functions:** Working memory, Cognitive Flexibility, Inhibitory Control **Attention:** Alerting, Orienting, Sustained, Executive	Innate Language Sense: Initial, Secondary **Symbols**: [Coding] Abstract to tangible, analogic quality system, Phonecian alphabet symbol-to-sound, triple code (print-cursive; small-capital; handwritten-typed), letter vs. non-letter writing symbols, letter blends, words to meaning, decoding-engaging-reading, [Forms/Shapes] letters vs. other forms, letters (primary alignment), letters (matching), letters (identity, description), letters (stroke order), letters (reproduction, sponteneous generation), spatial orientation

(continued)

Table 2.1. *(continued)*

Neural Pathways	
Touch: Visual-motor integration, scribbling, Graphomotor fine motor tracing, Tactile recognition, Variant expressions (cursive, print, distinct typefaces), Drawing, Writing	**Patterns:** Repetition and Regularity, Rhythming words (sounds), Rythming words (written practices), Form (e.g., of a story), Process (grammar, word order), Context (of humor) **Order:** [Ordinality] Rank (including before-after and first-last), Fixed (alphabetical order), Unique (oral rehearsal), [Sequence] Meaning (God vs. dog), Phoneme order **Categories** [Classification] Characters, Vocabulary, Word types (e.g., verb, noun), [Matching] Form(shapes (beginner), Form/Shapes (advanced), Rhythming **Relationships:** Parts of speech, Synonyms, Antonyms, Decomposition (present tense) Decomposition (past tense), Decomposition (equivalencies), Word relations (verb-sub-noun-adjective), Correspondence, Measure, Magnitude, Estimation, Letter-to-homonym, proportions (page layout), Approximations, Equivalencies (CAPITAL vs. small)

Source: Artwork by Gabriel Espinosa Tokuhama for Tracey Tokuhama-Espinosa, 2019.

Figure 2.10. Scaling Up Learning Interventions

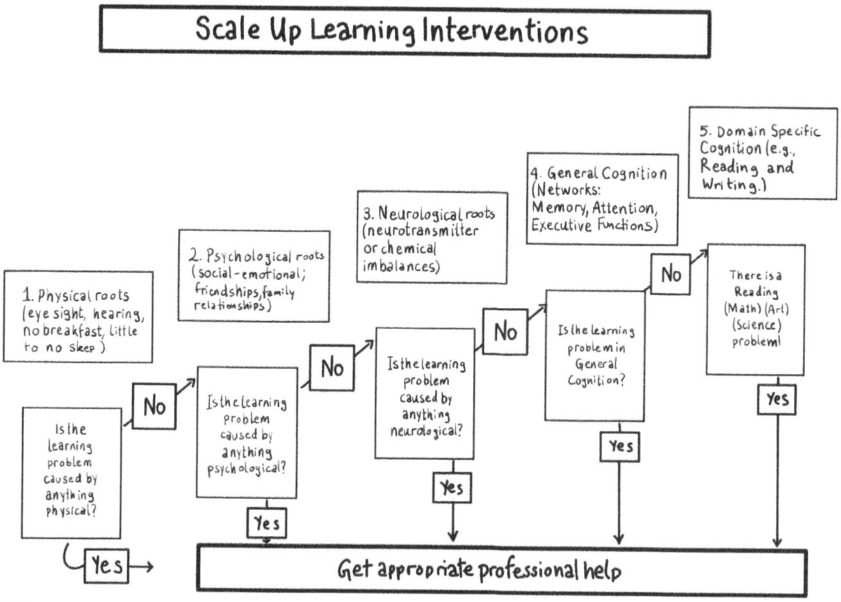

While most teachers have become very sensitive to noncognitive factors that can impact learning outcomes, it helps to constantly remind ourselves to scale up interventions (Figure 2.10).

THE HOLONS OF THE THINKWRITE MODEL

We built the ThinkWrite model with the knowledge that:

- "Thinking" is a multilayered system involving distinct stages (Dönmez et al., 2020);
- "Thinking" is related to the spectrum of consciousness involving both cognitive and affective (emotional) networks (Dolcos et al., 2020);
- Each thinking stage is subserved by different neural networks that are stimulated by different activities (e.g., Pujawan et al., 2022).

Some thinking stages, like mind wandering, can be identified with neuroscientific studies in a one-to-one correspondence (the default mode network in this case) (Poerio et al., 2017). Others, like reflection, are linked to the combination of neural networks for self-understanding (Ma et al., 2014), me-and-other references (Siegel, 2010), and semantic memory (Burianova et al., 2010), to name just

Table 2.2. The Stages of Thinking in Writing and Their Neural Networks

Writing	Stage of Thinking	General Cognitive Neural Networks	Research
Prewriting	Understand	Long-term autobiographical memory; long-term semantic memory; executive control; pattern knowledge; mentalizing	Syntactic comprehension (e.g., Sheppard, 2022); decoding comprehension (metalinguistic skills such as phonological awareness, orthographic skills, and morphological skills) (e.g., Feng et al., 2022); sentence comprehension (e.g., Kornrumpf et al., 2016); concrete vs. abstract word comprehension (e.g., Bucur & Papagno, 2021); metaphorical understanding (e.g., Schmidt & Serger, 2009); idiom understanding (e.g., Papagno et al., 2002); irony understanding (e.g., Bosco et al., 2017); evaluative and generative modes of understanding (Ellamil et al., 2012); eureka moments (Laukkonen et al., 2023)
	Know Things	Long-term semantic; consciousness; induced insight; transitive inference; autobiographical memory; episodic encoding	Self-knowledge (Tanguay et al., 2018); real-world autobiographical episodic and autobiographical semantic memory (Brown et al., 2018); induced insight (Kizilirmak, 2016); perceptual memory (Cohen et al., 2020); category knowledge (Fuhrmeister & Myers, 2021); mental schema (Brunamonti et al., 2016); domain-specific creativity (Boccia et al., 2015); bridging inference (Kim et al., 2012); category learning (Pérez-Gay et al., 2019); culture and emotion (Chen et al., 2019)
	Mind Wander	Default mode network; high and low rumination; reflective autobiographical memory	Self-reference, social cognition (Menon, 2023); conscious thought (Smallwood & Andrews-Hanna, 2013; Smallwood et al., 2021); internal and external attention (Scheibner et al., 2017); attentional networks (Wilf et al., 2019); mind-blanking (Kawagoe et al., 2019); semantic cue organization (Lanzoni et al., 2020); fast thinking networks (Gronchi & Giovannelli, 2018); task-focused attention (Sormaz et al., 2018): language systems (Gordon et al., 2020); reading (Zhang et al., 2021); memory networks (Lee & Xue, 2018); prediction (Dohmatob et al., 2020)

Table 2.2. (*continued*)

Writing	Stage of Thinking	General Cognitive Neural Networks	Research
	Reflect	Self-awareness; perception of others; semantic memory; reflective autobiographical memory; emotional memory; empathy; socioaffective mechanisms; metacognition	Self-understanding (Ma et al., 2014), me-and-other references (Siegel, 2010), and semantic memory (Burianova et al., 2010); mindfulness reflection (Semenov et al., 2020); different states of consciousness (Hanson & Grayout, 2022); brooding and rumination (Leutzinger & Philippi, 2021); self-referential processing (Yoon et al., 2019); self and other relationships (Long et al., 2020); self-correction through reflection (Schroer & Thomas, 2020); self-reflection (van Stee, 2022)
	Map and Connect	Long-term procedural memory; working memory; semantic memory; decision-making; categorical perception; lexical and sublexical processing; strategic memory; higher-order visual and spatial regions; transitive inference; episodic memory	Depths of comprehension (Caruso et al., 2022); false insights with semantic priming (Grimmer et al., 2022); enhanced connections with increased retrieval (Reilly, 2023); evidence accumulation (Liu & Pleskac, 2011); mapping problem to solution (Milovanovic et al., 2021); retrieval to strengthen connections (Van den Broek et al., 2016); visuospatial working memory and relational planning (Van Orden et al., 2001); visual working memory (Johnson et al., 2009); mental categorization (Pauen & Peykarjou, 2021); remote association (Ovando-Tellez et al., 2022); connectivism (Downes, 2022); bi-association (Benedek et al., 2020); categories and concepts (Miller et al., 2003)
	Outline	Procedural memory; inner voice; theory of mind; visual hierarchy; transitive reasoning; syntactic (lexical) reasoning; working memory; saliency networks; pattern recognition	Self-monitoring (Perrone-Bertolotti et al., 2014); creative cognition and executive functions (Hechtman, 2015); internal thoughts to visual imagery (Karapanagiotidis, et al., 2021); task prioritization (Liegel et al., 2022); task order (Steinhauser et al., 2021); semantic processing on task order (Hargraves et al., 2012a, 2012b); metamemory (Chua et al., 2009); brainstorming and story generation (Shah et al., 2013); intentional communication (Noordzij et al., 2010); theory of mind (Ho et al., 2022)

(*continued*)

Table 2.2. (*continued*)

Writing	Stage of Thinking	General Cognitive Neural Networks	Research
Writing	Plan	Working memory; long-term memory; forethought, ability to estimate time; attentional deployment; meaning-making; intrinsic motivation; affective processing; emotional regulation	Executive functions (Saylik et al., 2022); self-regulation (Larraín-Valenzuela et al., 2022); planning skills (Vriend et al., 2020); judgment and decision-making (Edgcumbe et al., 2019); memory for the future (Cieri, 2022); episodic and semantic memories (Alves, 2021); correlation between language and planning (Sun et al., 2019); planning and foresight (McKiernan, 2017).
	Research	Sustained attention; long-term semantic; working memory; mental schema processing; lexical understanding; inferential competence; perspective taking (intellectual empathy); social cognition; debiasing lexical choice	Critical thinking and executive functions (Li, S. et al., 2021); scientific problem solving (Tong et al., 2019); integrative inquiry (Ludvik, et al., 2016); grit and perseverance (Datu, 2021; Wang & Li, 2021); motivation (Morris et al., 2022); flow (Tan, 2021); language processing and sequential learning (Christensen et al., 2012); numerical semantic processing (Dunagan et al., 2022); body–object interaction (Hargreaves et al., 2012); context information vs. background information (van Moort et al., 2020); logic problem solving (Feng et al., 2021); reading comprehension (Perkins & Jiang, 2019).
	Draft	Working memory (visuo-sketchpad); long-term procedural memory; disinhibition; autobiographical memory; emotional memory; semantic memory; metacognitive skills; divergent and convergent thinking; graphomotor skills	Sentence-level processing (Wilson et al., 2014); reading comprehension (Moss et al., 2011); phonological processing (Powers et al., 2016); sublexical to lexico-semantic (Junker et al., 2020); nonlexical and semantic processing (Junker et al., 2023); working memory (Deldar et al., 2021); phonology-orthography-semantics (Graves et al., 2023); long-term memory (Yue & Martin, 2022); semantic context (Pino et al., 2022); homonyms and language ambiguity (Hoffman & Tam, 2020); spelling (Lebedeva et al., 2019); conceptual lexical representation (De Deyne et al., 2023); consistent and inconsistent orthography (Antalek, 2022); dysnomia and lexical retrieval (Aabedi et al., 2021); idea generation (Mastria et al., 2021); abstract to concrete words (Bucur & Papagno, 2021); syncopating comprehension (Hilton, 2020); serial order effect in divergent thinking (Wang et al., 2017)

Table 2.2. (*continued*)

Writing	Stage of Thinking	General Cognitive Neural Networks	Research
	Peer Exchange	Social cognition; social contagion; facial and voice perception; intellectual empathy; socioaffective networks; emotional memory	Narrative production (AbdulSabur et al., 2014); learning from the mistakes of others (De Visser et al., 2018); affective and cognitive mentalizing (Arioli et al., 2021); recursive thinking during interpersonal interaction (Zhen & Yu, 2021); social performance expectancy (Wilhelm et al., 2019); conformity (Minich et al., 2023); fear of negative evaluation (Li et al., 2022); social or group feedback (Rapp et al., 2021); anticipation and social anxiety (Topel et al., 2021); social acceptance (Weinberg et al., 2021); developmental patterns of social feedback acceptance (Dobbelaar et al., 2022, 2023); adaptive calibration to social feedback (Rudolph et al., 2021); persistent negative peer feedback and resulting aggression (van de Groep et al., 2021; 2022); prosocial behavior for friend or foe (Schreuders et al., 2018); error detection when listening to native vs. nonnative speakers (Sanders & de Bruin, 2022)
	Feedback and Feedforward	Self-regulation; long-term emotional memory; self-awareness	Inference (Bašnáková et al., 2014); feedback leads to improved prediction errors (Apps et al., 2015); team flow (Shehata et al., 2021); hyperscanning (Czeszumski et al., 2020); interbrain coupling (Chen et al., 2023); shared auditory attention (Stuldreher et al., 2020); interpersonal communication (Wilcox et al., 2020); errorless learning (Bertens & Brazil, 2018); feedback novelty (Ernst & Steinhauser, 2020)
Revision	Edit	Sustained attention; working memory; pattern recognition; novelty detection; procedural memory	Lexical stress and rhythmical well-formedness (Kandylaki et al., 2017); reading aloud (Timmer & Schiller, 2014); strategic reading comprehension (Moss et al., 2011); reading ability (Wang et al., 2019); visual acuity for fine text (Arnold et al., 2023); error detection (Di Gregorio et al., 2022); mindfulness, emotional stability, and error detection (Eichle & Stahl, 2017); error detection in complex tasks (Porth et al., 2022); choice and decision confidence (Rausch et al., 2020); semantics and syntactics (Schneider & Maguire, 2019); syntactic–semantic competition (Strotseva-Feinschmidt et al., 2019)

(continued)

Table 2.2 (*continued*)

Writing	Stage of Thinking	General Cognitive Neural Networks	Research
	Revise	Sustained attention; default mode network; metacognition	Eureka heuristic (Laukkonen et al., 2018); creative cognitive reappraisal (Wu et al., 2022); monitoring for errors through metacognition (Kirschner et al., 2021); cognitive flexibility and new evidence integration (Romero-Ferreiro et al., 2022); cognitive flexibility (Zühlsdorff et al., 2023); mindfulness to performance enhancement (Bondar et al., 2021)
	Proofread	Sustained attention; selective attention; symbols systems monitoring	Reading aloud (Cushing & Bodner, 2022); with and without homonym or morpheme spelling foils (Richards et al., 2017); effects of familiarity and type of encoding on proofreading (Pilotti et al., 2005); reading aloud reduced distractions (Halin et al., 2014); monitor and correct in the symbols systems arena of development (McCloskey & Perkins, 2012)
	Complete and Commence	Intrinsic motivation	Pride and joy (Jiang, 2021); enhanced sentence of competence (Matsuo et al., 2021); awareness and reward for self-regulation (Ludwig et al., 2020); celebrations for increased social support (Brick et al., 2023); intrinsic motivation (Reeve & Lee, 2019); sense of well-being and satisfaction (Maeda et al., 2021)

a few. This means that visible classroom behavior is normally broken down into much smaller parts for measurement in neuroscientific studies. We will give more concrete examples in Chapters 3, 4, and 5. For neuro-enthusiasts, Table 2.2 lists some of the many networks involved in writing.

As different networks are stimulated by different activities, knowing how the stages are related to the writing process can improve writing as teachers encourage different types of thinking for different types of problems that occur in writing. While more complex than other writing frameworks, ThinkWrite is about accuracy that compensates for the elaborate model. The precision in defining what comprises good writing in turn allows us as teachers to better diagnose where problems occur and what each person needs to do next to advance their writing. The next few chapters describe each of the 15 stages in the ThinkWrite model.

CHAPTER 3

The Holons of Prewriting

ThinkWrite: The Holons of Prewriting

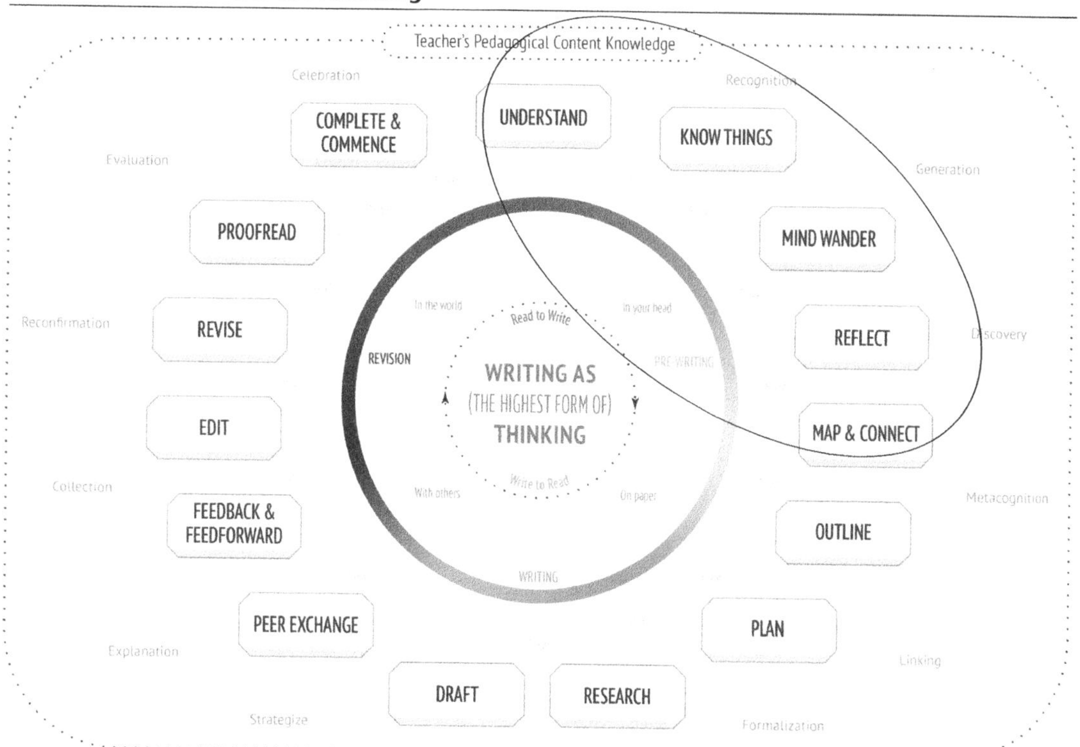

©Tokuhama-Espinosa, Nazareno, & Rappleye 2024

During what is traditionally called the prewriting phase, great teachers often support students in assessing and organizing their otherwise invisible thoughts. Prewriting includes ***understanding***, which involves multiple systems in the brain, including autobiographical memory, semantic memory, and other systems. Writers also need to ***know things*** or become aware of their own knowledge, existing knowledge in the world, relationships between things they know, and how these ideas connect to the writing project. At other moments in writing, students need to ***mind wander*** and let ideas just float around and come together in unexpected ways that would likely not occur during heavy task/goal-oriented work. Additionally, sometimes writers need to deeply ***reflect*** on how one idea relates to another or use focused attention to think about their growth, their own process or approach to projects, and their emotional connections. Reflection is also often promoted through some types of mindfulness meditation. At other moments, though, writers need to sketch out their thoughts and ***map and connect*** them together. Deliberative mind mapping and collective brainstorming are often used in writing classes to make visible the relational categories of concepts. Writers begin to classify and group ideas, establishing a framework to create and explore possible relationships between and among ideas and concepts. A strong mapping and connecting process can lead to a clear outline.

Outcomes of ThinkWrite Stages

- **Understand:** Writers ensure they build on their knowledge and write with a clear goal in mind to make a successful outcome more likely.
- **Know Things:** Writers value what they already know and need to know and are more likely to ground ideas in past experiences to produce authentic insights.
- **Mind Wander:** Writers take advantage of the brain's ability to freely connect ideas, leading to more creative insight.
- **Reflect:** Writers make more strategic decisions about how to execute the task and become more metacognitively aware.
- **Map and Connect:** Writers better organize their ideas and can visualize innovative links between concepts in their projects.

Each of the prewriting stages is explained below.

UNDERSTAND

Understanding ensures that writers build off of prior knowledge to construct the foundations for future learning.

To understand allows you to . . .

- □ Know the who, what, when, where, why, and how of your assignment or topic.
- □ Free the mind of doubt.
- □ Confirm success criteria for assignments.
- □ Have a strong foundation on which you can build higher-order thinking.

Figure 3.1 Bloom's Original and Modified Taxonomies

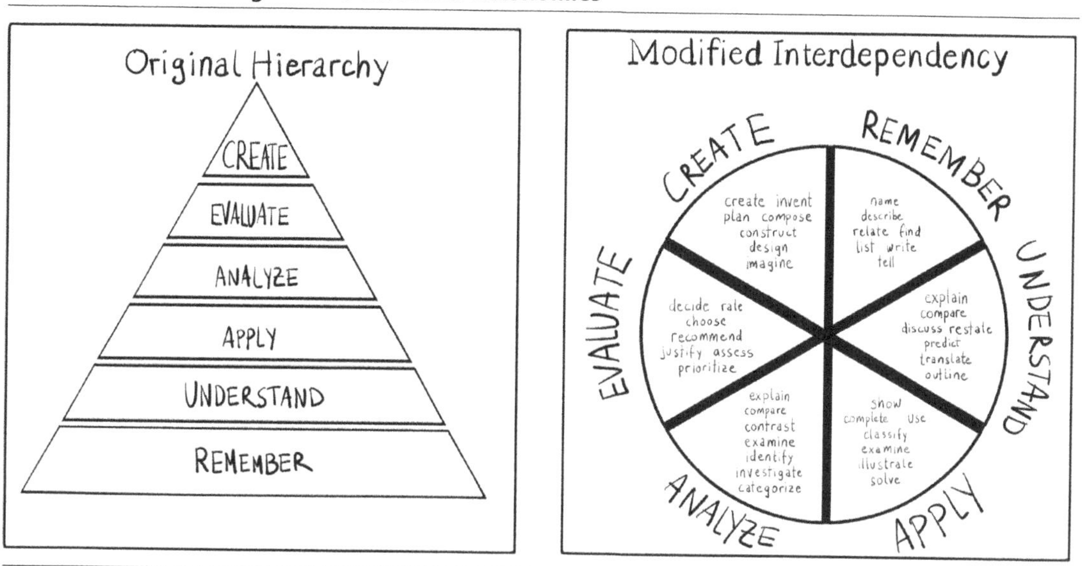

Artwork by Gabriel Espinosa Tokuhama based in part on Sosniak (1994).

As explained by Benjamin Bloom's classic hierarchy of cognitive activities, understanding is the basis for all learning. In Bloom's Taxonomy, "understand" is near the bottom of the pyramid and sustains all other knowledge, meaning it is fundamental, not that it is lower but rather of greatest importance because without it none of the other elements can exist (Bloom et al., 1956) (Figure 3.1). When looking at how the brain understands, it becomes clear that understanding relies heavily on memory systems in the brain, which is why Bloom recognized that remembering underpinned understanding. This is also why we say, "what you know influences what you can know."

All understanding depends on well-functioning memory systems in the brain. Memory is not located in a single place in the brain, but rather, memories are stored throughout the cortex (Gershman, 2023). Processing and encoding memories happens through networks that are slightly different from networks used to retrieve the memory—getting information out of your brain is not the same as putting it in. This makes identifying just how the brain "understands" more complex than one might initially expect, as it is linked to both memory and forgetting. We cannot understand if we do not have access to memories.

Sometimes we try to remember things by using neural pathways that might seem logical, only to find that we used a different kind of logic to structure the memory than what we are using to find it, meaning we forget. As teachers, we know memory is important for learning, but we should also know any given activity will create memories for some students but not for others. This is why the careful and purposeful repetition of key ideas helps learning; for a memory to become a part of understanding it must be linked to the meaning-making of that individual. Understanding depends on a clear path and access to memories. Humans move ideas and information into long-term memory (on which learning depends) when they are easily associated with things that are already known. This is why stimulating prior knowledge is a great pedagogical practice. A basic rule about memory and understanding is that it must be significant for the learner, or the memory might be created but not be accessible for retrieval at a later time. Moreover, habitual rehearsal of the retrieval process in performance-like situations is necessary to strengthen recall in the future during the actual test or performance situation. This is also why reviewing your notes is a less effective way to study than "dress rehearsal" which is generally a better way to prepare for the task. Also, mnemonic aids such as acronyms that "chunk" information and procedural order can help both in the encoding and retrieval of what is known and to be applied.

If understanding and memory networks are robustly supported in neuroscience, why haven't they reached teacher practice more broadly? Because most neuroscientific studies focus on very narrow bands of sub-elements of understanding and writing, while teachers look at the bigger picture. We'd like to recommend teachers examine the networks that make up understanding in order to better identify both teaching and evaluation interventions. Research in neuroscience (see Table 2.2) looks at how the brain comprehends (understands) syntactic structures—the correct order of words or phrases—in order to be as clear as possible in a meaningful expression (Sheppard, 2022); how the brain decodes letters (phonological awareness), how it learns to spell (orthographic skills), and how to structure the smallest units of language to change meaning (morphological understanding) (Feng et al., 2022). There is also a lot of neuroscientific research focused on how the brain pulls together all of these elements to finally understand or comprehend a complete word (Kornrumpf et al., 2016) or full sentences (Fedorenko et al., 2016), which includes rereading to be sure the "agent" or person in a sentence is labeled correctly as the subject or the object (Hirotani et al., 2011). A fascinating subcollection of research on understanding in the brain as it reads and writes is the way the brain comprehends metaphors (Schmidt & Serger, 2009), idioms (Papagno et al., 2002), irony (Bosco et al., 2017), and pseudo (fake) words (Barouch et al., 2022), or how it perceives and understands concrete words versus abstract ones (Bucur & Papagno, 2021). There are even complex studies that examine how two or more of these systems compete, as when the brain has to allocate resources between the role of syntactic understanding versus semantic understanding (Grisoni et al., 2017; Strotseva-Feinschmidt et al., 2019). Each of these sub-elements or holons of understanding have to be in place for good writing to occur, and they are triggered by different activities. One way to leapfrog understanding is with the use of worked models or examples.

A worked model is a finished product that exemplifies what a correct assignment might look like. Though they do not wholly eliminate the need for direct instruction, worked models can substantially enhance a student's ownership of and active engagement in the learning process and improve the ability to recall and apply that knowledge as they assimilate the form they will write in through their own senses, unique intelligence, and capacities to chunk down and internalize the form through their own filters.

We can learn a lot about understanding in the writing process by looking at dyslexics and bilinguals. In dyslexia, there is a debate as to whether poor handwriting, a typical sign of dyslexics, and poor spelling, another sign, are related causally, just correlated, or if they are independent (Gosse et al., 2022b). It seems that while both poor handwriting and poor spelling are signs of dyslexia, they are caused by a lack of stimulation to areas related to spelling and handwriting. This suggests a strong mutual dependence of input to output: You cannot write or spell correctly if you cannot read correctly as you have not rehearsed those networks. Bad spelling does not cause bad handwriting, and bad handwriting does not cause bad spelling; the two are separate networks in the brain. However, rehearsal of spelling networks can lead to more fluid writing because of less hesitancy (Downing & Caravolas, 2020). A cautionary note to teachers, however: Bad handwriting does not always mean dyslexia (O'Donnell & Colvin, 2019)! Other studies on dyslexics show that it is a natural strategy to replace phonemic awareness with whole-word memorization (Bub et al., 2017), which avoids neural networks for phonological awareness and depends on networks for semantic memory instead. This means dyslexics often use coping mechanisms such as swapping out weaker phonological awareness pathways for stronger semantic memory pathways, which is actually very clever!

In studies of bilinguals, there are additional hints at networks for writing. People's handwriting quality does not vary by the language they are writing, independent of the level of proficiency. For example, an adult with beautiful handwriting who starts to learn French will write French beautifully, not with childlike characteristics. This means that handwriting and other language skills are separate functions in the brain. This is the difference between understanding how to write versus understanding *what* to write.

"Understanding" in the bilingual brain depends heavily on vocabulary to strengthen semantic memory. Bilinguals often understand ideas in their native language, but they lack vocabulary to share this with others. The key? Teach vocabulary! More than any other aspect of language, including grammar and syntax, vocabulary is the key to understanding.

When it comes to writing, understanding requires automaticity of several subsystems linked to genre expectations. That is, understanding instructions on how to write a recipe or steps to tie your shoe is different than understanding how to write a haiku, sonnet, or other poetic subgenre, or understanding how to approach a research paper or lab report. Teachers can facilitate student understanding by remembering to stop at key junctions and ask explicitly if all is clear. To start, students need to understand what is being asked of them (the instructions). They then need to understand the elements of components of the prompt (vocabulary). This may result in checklists of activities or lists of definitions. To check for understanding, researchers like Robert Marzano (2007) suggest that offering students scaled response options from "full comprehension" to "completely lost" to gauge individual needs.

To increase understanding, teachers have a lot of different tools. On the left-hand column are things that are often recommended, and on the right are what we recommend to supercharge their impact. Teachers can check for understanding in the following ways.

Tools Often Used to Check for Understanding	Tools with Even More Impact
✓ Ask students to respond to an open-ended question about the topic.	✓ Write a 3-2-1 Reflection about the class (three things that were new, two that were interesting, one that might change your life).
✓ Ask for a thumbs-up or thumbs-down (use a five-finger rating).	✓ Turn to a partner and tell them if you understand and explain why or why not.
✓ Use technology to poll students about the self-assessment for understanding.	✓ Use technology to give a written response to a question that would confirm their understanding.
✓ Use exit tickets (short assessment activity to evaluate learning).	✓ Feedforward: Respond to the prompt, "what will you do better/differently tomorrow to improve your understanding?" Have students review their responses at the start of the next assignment.

Activities From ThinkWrite for Understanding

In Your Own Words

Objective: *To check for understanding*

1. Read the prompt or instructions for your writing assignment or goal.
2. Put the prompt or instructions into your own words, as if you are talking to a friend.
3. Share your work with a partner. Compare your ideas. Rewrite your response based on feedback.

What's happening in the brain: Among other things, "In Your Own Words" involves paraphrasing instructions: "activation was found in both executive control and comprehension areas, and furthermore, learning from text was associated with activation in the anterior prefrontal cortex (aPFC)" related to "coordinating the internal and external modes of thought that are necessary for integrating new knowledge from texts with prior knowledge" (Moss et al., 2011, p. 675).

Worked Models

Objective: *To understand the content and organization*

1. Find examples of successful work (i.e., the end product). Worked models may be provided by your teacher, from the Internet, or from an AI tool.
2. Review these models for content and organization.
3. Where do the worked models have content that you need to add or change in your own work?
4. How do the worked model's format and structure differ from your own paper?
5. Modify your work to incorporate any of the useful elements from the worked model you reviewed.

What's happening in the brain: "Worked Models" involves analogical thinking that reduces cognitive load for new writing by offering a template, which includes pattern knowledge and the ability to compare and contrast formats and content. This uses *semantic and visuo-spatial networks* (the left rostrolateral prefrontal cortex) (Hobeika, et al., 2016), among other things.

Pair-Think-Share (NOT Think-Pair-Share!)

Objective: *To clarify what you know and to broaden your ideas*

1. Pair means find a partner to broaden your ideas by listening to theirs.
2. Think means think about what you think you know about the topic.
3. Share means share your thoughts with your partner.
4. After you share, rethink what you now think you know about the topic taking into consideration your partner's ideas, and write a new response.

What's happening in the brain: "Pair-Think-Share" involves the ability to critically assess ideas and show intellectual empathy for others' ideas in oral communication, which includes the use of "knowledge sharing; turn-taking speech co-ordination; cooperation, problem solving and creativity; and naturalistic discussion paradigms. . . ." This involves among other things, active "alignment predominantly . . . in the *frontal and temporo-parietal areas*, which may reflect activation of the mirror and *mentalizing systems*" (Kelsen et al., 2022, p. 1249).

For more activities, see ThinkWriteMBE.com.

Maximizing a Student's Success in Understanding

Ask, how will you know if you are successful? Share example success statements:

- □ I understand the instructions when I read them more than once.
- □ I understand the text better by interpreting the author's thinking.
- □ I understand how to write a ____(genre) when I deconstruct its form.

Write your own success statement: "I realize I understand how to [insert verb here], when I [insert a different verb here]."

Encourage self-reflection:

- How often do I take the time to ensure I understand my assignment before I start?
- What do I normally do if I don't understand something?

Celebrate progress by checking off "I can" statements:

- ✓ I can define and use all the key terms needed for my writing project.
- ✓ I can tell you how I will know if I have done a good job.
- ✓ I can explain what I have to do to another person.

KNOW THINGS

By knowing things, writers make space for what they don't yet know, which is the path to insight.

To know things allows you to . . .

- □ Link new learning to prior knowledge.
- □ Make sense of new information through mental schema and frameworks.
- □ Connect and build meaning through analogical and metaphorical thinking.
- □ See similarities between otherwise unlike things.
- □ See differences between otherwise similar things.

"To Know Things" may also seem intuitive and a bit colloquial for a book on writing as "things" casts a wide net. To know things within ThinkWrite is a reminder that no matter how foreign the writing assignment, there is always something that the student already knows about it, even if this is not immediately obvious. The idea of knowing things might be best explained by the idea of six degrees of separation, made famous by *The Six Degrees of Kevin Bacon Game*. The idea is that any two people on earth can be connected to each other with fewer than six relationships (Leonsei, 2015). Similarly, we suggest any two ideas on earth can be linked to each other by realizing what you already know. For example, a 4th-grader might be told they have to research the life of a frog. They may feel they have no understanding of the topic at first, until they are reminded that they know about butterflies, which they studied in kindergarten. The metamorphosis of the butterfly can be paralleled to the frog's lifespan. This means that students can use what they already know about butterflies to begin to think about frogs. This is at the core of why using analogies is the very best way to teach a new concept if prior knowledge is not immediately available (Goel & Shu, 2015; Tokuhama-Espinosa, 2014).

Unsurprisingly, knowing things is also highly dependent on memory systems in the brain. A great deal of knowing things relates to the comparison of the new information to other things, which travels semantic memory routes in the brain (Kumar, 2021). Other types of knowing that have been measured in neuroscience are highly personal and relate to the neural correlates of self-knowledge (Tanguay et al., 2018), real-world autobiographical episodic memory pathways, and autobiographical semantic memory networks (Brown et al., 2018). The *aha!* moment that is felt when the 4th-grader sees the connection between butterflies and frogs is called "induced insight" (Kizilirmak et al., 2016) and is also part of knowing things. A lot of knowing things comes from the ability to frame new information or objects in the right way, or perceptual memory (Cohen et al., 2020), and depends on category knowledge (Fuhrmeister & Myers, 2021). All of this creates our personal mental schema about the world, which are the organizational structures we use to make sense of life (Brunamonti et al., 2016). Leveraging of mental schema is the key to knowing things. Teachers who can help students visualize their own categorization schemes of the world do this by helping them know what they already know about information. The key to unlocking mental schema for writing is to help students visualize how their mind catalogs the same piece of information in multiple ways.

For example, a person's mental schema (Figure 3.2) for a "dog" might be as a kind of pet, something soft and the reflection of loyalty. Students can be nudged to expand on this mental schema, however, and also think of breeds of dogs (German shepherds vs. poodles), stuffed versus real dogs, fictional dogs (Pluto vs. Clifford vs. Harry the Dirty Dog), and so on. The key to expanding schema is to know what already exists and what can be added. Once schemas are understood, analogies can be leveraged.

Figure 3.2 Mental Schema

Artwork by Gabriel Espinosa Tokuhama for Tracey Tokuhama-Espinosa.

This is why we say, "the more you know, the more you can know," which is true both in pedagogy and in neuroscience. Once you have the neural networks of a certain mental schema formed, that can be built on to form additional connections, just as the creation of new networks builds off existing ones.

The brain doesn't just know isolated facts, but rather these facts are connected to other information through autobiographical and semantic memory networks. To know things well is to know the larger context of those facts and their meaning within a particular domain, to know the frameworks and schema that explain how facts make sense or fit together. Teachers sometimes assume students have an equal capacity for such sensemaking once they have been exposed to "the facts" or data, but the capacity to abstract and organize facts is reliant on previous experience (Ganesh & Gabora, 2022), practice applying such mental schema (Ohki et al., 2023), and explicit instruction in using them (Rastle et al., 2021). Knowing things is further structured through our capacity to form meaningful analogies, and through such analogies, conceive of categories and form the capacity for abstract thinking (Bartha, 2013). The brain favors structuring complex knowledge, patterns, and processes as stories or narratives, which is basic to meaning-making (Thye et al., 2023). Conscious teaching of schema and frameworks encourages learners in developing their capacities for abstract thinking and making new information meaningful (Myhill et al., 2020). To borrow from a learning outcome, to know "the hero's journey" as a schema can allow students to make sense of the experience of characters in a story as well as their own experience and help them connect the character's otherwise distinct experience to their own. But students may need help in making such a connection to their own experience.

We do not just know *things* but also *procedures* that we have internalized, which differs between beginners and experts. In the expert's brain, knowledge is connected through functional relationships in ever more complex patterns due to the ability to abstract and see functional analogical patterns within the information (Dinsmore, 2021); there is an abstracted knowledge of procedures. Expert knowledge is not just a matter of degree—of simply knowing more facts than the beginner—but of being able to see how the patterns of one's domain of expertise (Boccia et al., 2015) and within one's own understanding connect to novel situations (Syrewicz, 2022). Experts have internalized procedural knowledge, genre and content and functional knowledge to a level of automaticity that can puzzle the beginner (Fadhly et al., 2023). While it can be helpful for a beginner to understand that such levels of knowing exist and are used by others, it is likely that the novice will find it more helpful in the short term to have such procedures broken down into more explicit steps.

Thinking is inevitable (Changeux & Ricoeur, 2021), but higher-order thinking depends on guidance from others, namely teachers (Meng et al., 2020). Metacognition is the ability to think about thinking and to learn how to learn. In practice, a teacher's ability to help students know what they already know about a new topic is key to higher-order thinking that permits them to know what they don't know. Researchers have shown that children begin to learn how to use "memory monitoring skills" to figure out the relationships to new information around the age of 4.5 years old (Liu et al., 2018, p. 34), but humans continue to perfect this skill throughout the lifespan and rely on others around us to do so (Heyes et al., 2020). As a recent thesis proclaimed, "you don't know what you don't know until you know it" (Newton, 2019). While this may be true, knowing the *process* of how to know what you know *can* be taught by teachers.

Like all stages of thinking, to know things in neuroscientific studies is not in a single area of the brain but rather involves multiple networks, including self-knowledge (Tanguay et al., 2018); real-world autobiographical episodic and autobiographical semantic memory (Brown et al., 2018); induced insight (Kizilirmak, 2016); perceptual memory (Cohen et al., 2020); category knowledge (Fuhrmeister & Myers, 2021); mental schema (Brunamonti et al., 2016); domain-specific creativity (Boccia et al., 2015); bridging inference (Kim et al., 2012); category learning (Pérez-Gay et al., 2019); and culture and emotion (Chen et al., 2019), to name a few. While many networks are involved, two primary areas include long-term episodic and long-term semantic memory.

Some breakthrough pedagogies in the past few decades based on these neuroscience findings have helped children know what they already know using culturally relevant pedagogies (e.g., Hammond, 2014). For example, hip-hop pedagogy has been used to "design curricula based on music and rhymes" (Adjapong & Emdin, 2015, p. 66), which stimulates distinct memory systems in the brain for retrieval. Significant memories are authentic. New pedagogies that are culturally relevant and easy for learners to relate to are those that require less cognitive load on the part of the learner because they are more natural due to rehearsal (Tanchuk, 2020). By tapping into diverse ways of encoding new knowledge, they aid in forming diverse memory pathways to aid in recall and application (e.g., Mendelowitz & Lazar, 2020; Murphy & Murphy, 2017; Wurdeman-Thurston & Kaomea, 2015).

One reason that *West Side Story* was so popular when it came out in 1957 and remains so today is because it turns Shakespeare's *Romeo and Juliet* (1595) into "known" ideas as the themes of love and family rivalry are put into familiar contexts without the cognitive load of unfamiliar vocabulary and syntax. The students might not understand the Early Modern English of Shakespeare, but they can relate to teen love. Culturally relevant pedagogies are a necessity because students grow up in different contexts and have different points of reference for information. To write an essay critiquing *Romeo and Juliet,* they need to know what they already know about the ideas in the book before they can explore what they don't yet know.

Teachers can check for what students know by doing the following.

Tools Often Used to Confirm Prior Knowledge	Tools With Even More Impact
✓ Graphic organizers	✓ Graphic organizers with oral presentation
✓ KWL (Know-Want to Know-Learn) Charts	✓ KWL chart in full sentences
✓ Think-Pair-Share	✓ Think-Pair-Share with written summary
✓ Brainstorming	✓ Group brainstorming

Activities from ThinkWrite for Knowing Things

Who, What, When, Where, Why, How

Objective: *To define the parameters of your work*

1. Think of the topic and then think about "who" it relates to.
2. Then think about "what" it means.
3. Then think about "when" it occurred or if it is time-bound in some way.
4. Then do the same for "where" the topic relates to.
5. Then think about "why" the topic occurs or exists.
6. Then think about "how" the topic came to be.
7. Circle any new ideas you generated in this process.
8. Compare your list with a classmate. What can you learn from their ideas? Add any new ideas you find valuable to your list. Revise and turn in your work.

What's happening in the brain: "Who, What, When, Where, Why, How" involves, among other things, the ability to frame the topic from different time and actor perspectives, which includes the use of the neural correlates of consciousness, induced insight, and transitive inference. This involves implicit and explicit knowledge tracts, including autobiographical memory, episodic encoding, and semantic memory, with "the amygdala evaluating the internal value (as an affective evaluation) of the suddenly comprehended information, and striatum-dependent reward-based learning" (Kizilirmak et al., 2016, para 1). Transitive inference involves the "hippocampus, prefrontal cortex (PFC), putamen, posterior parietal cortex (PPC), retrosplenial cortex (RSC), supplementary motor area (SMA), precentral gyrus (PreCG), and median cingulate cortex (MCC)" (Zhang et al., 2022, para 1).

Categories and Relationships

Objective: *To surprise yourself with how much you already know*

1. Think of what you know about the topic.
2. Think of as many different categories as you can in which the topic fits. (Consider all of your prior experiences including your understanding of the physical attributes, your personal experience with the topic, figures of speech, definitions . . .).
3. Name the categories.
4. Use a mind map, Venn diagram, or any other visual tool to show how the categories are related.
5. Compare your visual layout of categories and relationships with those of two other classmates. Now create one visual combining all of your ideas together.

What's happening in the brain: Among other things, "Categories and Relationships" involves the ability to group items by similar characteristics or associations, which includes the use of mental schemata to sort knowledge based on semantic representation dependent on "sensory, motor, spatial, temporal, affective, social, and cognitive experiences" (Binder et al., 2016, p. 130). This involves semantic, emotional, motor, spatial-tempo, and social memory retrieval, and includes "the default (precuneus and left angular gyrus; AG) and executive control (right intraparietal sulcus; IPS) networks" (Beaty et al., 2017, p. 163).

Parallel Ideas

Objective: *To use what we know to understand the unknown*

1. Make a list of similes or metaphors about the topic concepts.
2. Explain them to someone else.
3. Check for understanding.
4. Consider how a change of wording might improve the communication of the concept(s).
5. Consider how changing the metaphor changes your understanding of the topic.
6. What new questions does the new metaphor generate?

7. Compare your metaphors and similes with a classmate.
8. Make one list of all the metaphors and similes, combining your work.

What's happening in the brain: "Parallel Ideas" involves metaphorical thinking, as well as semantic understanding of similes and analogies (each a different neural network), which involves symbolic language, as well as a comparison of figurative and literal language processing. This includes the use of "left frontotemporal regions for idiom and metaphor processing," as well as large portions of the right hemisphere for novel metaphorical generation (Beaty et al., 2017; Bohrn, et al., 2012, p. 2669).

For more activities, see ThinkWriteMBE.com.

Maximizing a Student's Success in Knowing Things

Ask, how will you know if you are successful? Share example success statements:

- ☐ I realize I know things when I form networks between ideas.
- ☐ I realize I know things when I can categorize them together.
- ☐ To think about what I might already know about a new idea, I compare the new thing to things that look similar.

Write your own success statement: "I realize I know things when I can [insert a verb here]."

Encourage self-reflection:

- How much of knowing things is driven by heuristics and biases?
- Do you know more than you think?
- How can analogies help you expand your knowledge base?

Celebrate progress by checking off "I can" statements:

- ✓ I can explain what I know to someone else.
- ✓ I can apply what I know in novel situations.
- ✓ I can encode new information strategically and effectively.
- ✓ I can retrieve what I know when needed.
- ✓ I can find a way to make this assignment connect to my real-life outside school.
- ✓ I can use my good memory and strong imagination to connect ideas.
- ✓ I can connect anything to anything.

MIND WANDER

By doing Mind Wandering activities, writers take advantage of the brain's ability to freely connect ideas, leading to more creative insight.

To mind wander allows you to . . .

- ☐ Shift from effortful thinking, deliberate problem solving, or the external environment and attend to the arising of internal cognition (memory, fantasy, thinking about the future, daydreaming).
- ☐ Attend to the free flow of ideas to make unexpected connections among known concepts to achieve creative insight or resolve problems.
- ☐ Use daydreaming in problem solving, thinking, and creative processes.
- ☐ Disengage consciously from task/goal-oriented work for free associations.

Artwork by Gabriel Espinosa Tokuhama for Tracey Tokuhama-Espinosa.

Mind wandering is the most counterintuitive of all the writing stages. Though there have been guesses about the benefits of mind wandering in the popular press as early as 35 years ago starting with Claxton's book *Hare Brain, Tortoise Mind: Why Intelligence Increases When You Think Less* (1997), much of educational culture still celebrates focus and attention, not mind wandering. This means those whose minds wander are thought to be "lost" and often shamed.

Neuroscientific research on mind wandering considers multiple neural pathways, which relate to conscious thought (Smallwood & Andrews-Hanna, 2013; Smallwood et al., 2021), internal and external attention (Scheibner et al., 2017), attentional networks (Martinez-Pérez et al., 2023), mind-blanking (Kaufman et al., 2024), semantic cue organization (Shao et al., 2024), task-focused attention (Groot, 2023), language systems (Bernini & Fernyhough, 2022), memory networks (Wamsley & Summer, 2020), and prediction (Vékony et al., 2023). Mind wandering involves the default mode network in the brain as it is the brain's "go-to" place when it is not focused on the external environment or a demanding cognitive task. It is now also linked in neuroscientific studies to creative insight (e.g., Ogawa et al., 2018). Recent research in neuroscience has turned increased attention to the neural underpinnings of mind wandering, which continues to uncover the richness of this essential mental activity (e.g., Pachai et al., 2016; Smallwood & Andrews-Hanna, 2013). New research reveals that far from being merely the failed self-control of the idle daydreamer, mind wandering and the "default mode network" are the wellspring of some of the capacities that we most prize in one another: our ability for deep social connection (Mars et al., 2012; Li et al., 2014) and ethically rich empathetic engagement (Bzdok et al., 2015), perspective taking and moral imagination (Immordino-Yang et al., 2012), creativity and insight (Beaty et al., 2014, 2020), and recalling our past and imagining ourselves into the future (Yang et al., 2019; Østby et al., 2012). Mind wandering is a set of complex mental phenomena linked even to such deliberative actions as our ability to develop and maintain meaningful goals and motivation (Spreng et al., 2010; Xu et al., 2016).

Mind wandering taps into learners' capacities for "free thinking," the seemingly random thoughts, plans, and associations of ideas bubbling up within them spontaneously whenever their attention wanders "off task" or away from their immediate surroundings. The richness of mind wandering makes possible communication that is meaningful and creative, rich and insightful; it is an important source of a writer's distinctive personal voice and of innovation. Despite all these benefits, few teachers feel comfortable encouraging their students to mind wander. This literature shows that mind wandering is an umbrella term covering a great variety of internal mental activities. Researchers differentiate between a failure to control attention, that is, *mere* distraction, for instance, and rumination, the negative and obsessive internal narration, the rehearsing or rehashing of events that is common to anxious minds or those in depressive states (Nayda & Takarangi, 2021). A third broad category of mind wandering, and the focus of discussion here, contains positive and constructive experiences of mind wandering or daydreaming. Good teachers can help students understand these different mental behaviors by direct explanation and through examples that help scaffold emerging writers' capacities to engage in constructive mind wandering by helping them to observe and to think more precisely about their own thinking.

While mind wandering is commonly viewed as a failure of the brain's executive control over attention and a largely unintentional state, research further differentiates between *unintentional* mind wandering or lapses of cognitive control and *intentional* or deliberate mind wandering (Seli et al., 2016). At first glance, the idea of *deliberate* mind wandering might seem an oxymoron, but a little reflection might allow thoughtful teachers to recall some past experience in which they consciously chose to daydream, perhaps when engaged in a boring situation or undemanding task (doodling while in the staff meeting that leads to a new idea; daydreaming on a long drive that opens your eyes to an important insight). It is increasingly characteristic of the digital age that people often find themselves defaulting in such moments to self-soothing behaviors through engaging with digital devices. How much of that now habituated engagement with the algorithms that underlie the attentional economy is actually under one's own deliberate cognitive control is an open question, as is its long-term impact on the ability to mind wander freely and deliberately. There is growing consensus that technology interferes with the necessary, unencumbered, natural mind wandering state

(Oschinsky et al., 2019). These days, due to the company of the smartphone, people are rarely left alone with their thoughts (Khayretdinova, 2022).

In addition to intentional and unintentional mind wandering, "positive" mind wandering that is nonproductive or merely escapist with its positive ability to improve mood and provide a moment of mental refreshment should be distinguished from mind wandering that is positive and *productive* (Zedelius & Schooler, 2018). Both intentional and unintentional mind wandering can positively produce creative insights, the latter often after a period of deliberate concentration that has led to an impasse. One of the most famous examples of this is August Kekule's realization of the shape of the benzene ring, a realization he attributed to a vision of a snake swallowing its own tail that came to him while daydreaming after a bout of writing; the vision correctly resolved the molecule's proposed structure for him. Creatives, confident in the gifts of mind wandering, often purposefully put themselves in situations or engage in practices to produce and capture their mind wandering. While engaged on a large or difficult project, Thomas Edison was said to nap while sitting in a chair, holding metal balls or marbles in his hands below which he had placed pans so that, as he dozed off, he would drop the balls into the pans and awake. He would then note any insights that arose from his hazy hypnagogic state.

To learn to mind wander helpfully involves placing oneself into contexts that allow its emergence and cultivating the habit of capturing its insights; this is rather like learning to look off to the side of a dim star in order that its light falls on the cells in the retina more attuned to perception in dim light. Edison's example points to a key tool in making mind wandering productive: having a notebook or journal or another means of recording insights and ideas nearby to help capture the evanescent insights that arise for later use. Numerous writers have attested to the power of daydreams or similar free-flowing mental states, and cultivated them, during which they disengaged from the writing desk and task orientation, and got their blood and ideas flowing, some, like Joyce Carol Oates, through a habit of distance running. *Little Women* author Louisa May Alcott, far ahead of her time in this as in so many things, was a notable runner-writer, too. Studies have shown that for those who can, walking, particularly walking in a natural setting, stimulates the flow of creative ideation (Oppezzo & Schwartz, 2014). For others, time in an art gallery can be a productive arena to engage in mind wandering. In real-life classrooms, teachers rarely encourage their students to mind wander. This is changing. In many modern schools there are more flexible times and places where daydreaming is encouraged. For example, letting kids go to the pillow corner or to put their heads down on their desks for 5–10 minutes can yield better writing insights than an hour of intense, focused study.

Attention toggles between the external world and an internal world (Broyd et al., 2009). Cognitively and emotionally demanding external tasks, solving a difficult math problem on a test or navigating a physically threatening environment, direct attention outward, downregulating the default mode network and, hence, shutting down mind wandering. During restful moments in a safe environment, when bored, or doing routine tasks that make few cognitive demands—a run, leisurely hiking, or folding the laundry—the default network comes more fully online. The resulting collision of ideas and combinatorial possibilities of positive, constructive mind wandering can produce fresh phrasing, insights, hypotheses, fuel further inquiries, and generate motivation. This is the mental ground on which the creative leap takes place (Marron & Faust, 2018).

While such leaps and resultant divergent thinking are not the entirety of creativity, they are among its most distinctive features. There is a richness and originality of thought and voice to be found in mind wandering; the associations and the details that help make a writer's voice distinctive can also originate in this thinking mode. Juxtaposing diverse bodies of knowledge (e.g., staring at a cityscape, reading a cookbook, listening to a song, glancing at the titles on a bookshelf) while problem solving can provoke the brain to recall and begin to associate diverse ranges of knowledge and make unexpected connections with stimuli in the environment. Teachers may need to scaffold contextual knowledge to help students who have a narrower conceptual vocabulary and biographical memory to make sense of or contextualize their mind wandering, helping them to develop connections that are only latent in the students' present understanding.

Teachers can encourage mind wandering by doing the following.

Tools Often Used to Leverage Mind Wandering	Tools with Even More Impact
✓ Let kids daydream.	✓ Encourage problem-oriented daydreaming (frame the problem before letting go).
✓ Shutting eyes and putting your head down.	✓ Shutting eyes, putting your head down, keep track of new or important ideas in a journal.
✓ Put your phone down.	✓ Put your phone down and shut your eyes, attend to the ideas and thoughts that arise. After a few moments, record them.

Activities From ThinkWrite for Mind Wandering

Tuning Out to Tune In

Objective: *To be alone with your thoughts*

1. Close your eyes (and cover your ears).
2. Let your mind wander without distractions.
3. Jot down notes on new links between old ideas and new ideas born of these new connections.
4. Talk about your insights with a friend. How do their connections help you think of new ideas?
5. Compile your ideas and submit them.

What's happening in the brain: "Tuning Out to Tune In" involves purposefully giving yourself time to mind wander by shutting off stimuli from your eyes (and ears), related attention networks (Hobbis et al., 2019). This employs the default mode network, involving "a more comprehensive neuroanatomical model . . . including subcortical structures such as the basal forebrain, cholinergic nuclei, anterior and mediodorsal thalamic nuclei, and the thalamus and basal forebrain" (Alves et al., 2019, para. 1; Menon, 2023; Raichle & Snyder, 2007).

See the Voice in Your Head

Objective: *To listen to the voice in your head and make it visible*

1. While focusing on a specific topic, ask yourself, what connections do you see between different ideas? What are the relationships between different characters, scenes, themes, ideas, problems, solutions?
2. Record all associations you make between ideas. Do not edit. You do not need to write in full sentences.
3. Share your work with a classmate. How do your works differ and how are they the same?
4. Jot down any new ideas that come to you after sharing.

What's happening in the brain: "See the Voice in Your Head" involves, among other things, creating relationships between aspects of written work, which includes moving from surface to deep thinking, as well as *aha!* moments when ideas are linked. This involves "facial, emotional, and body language changes" (Berckley & Hattie, 2023, p. 439) triggered by "semantic priming" that results in changes "in bilateral anterior insulae" (Becker et al., 2020, p. 30), and other related networks.

Dream to Write

Objective: *To use sleep and dreaming to advance writing*

1. Remind yourself of the writing topic as you are about to fall asleep.
2. Go to sleep.
3. When you wake up, try not to get up immediately, but lie in the same position.
4. Think about what you dreamed.
5. Ask yourself if you have a new or different perspective on the topic.
6. Write down or record how your perspective has changed.
7. To guarantee you wake up remembering your dreams, drink a glass of water before going to bed. Have your notebook by your bedside.
8. Jot down any ideas that came to you in the middle of the night.

What's happening in the brain: "Dream to Write" involves productive sleep and lucid dreaming, which includes clarity and awareness about the meaning of the dream (Holzinger & Mayer, 2020, para. 6–7). Among other networks, this involves "prefrontal and parietal regions," as well as extended networks that relate to the "frontal parietal cortex; tempo-parietal cortex; precuneus; cuneus; prefrontal cortex (ventrolateral; dorsolateral); and the occipito-temporal cortex" (Baird et al., 2019, p. 30; Holzinger & Mayer, 2020).

For more activities, see ThinkWriteMBE.com.

Maximizing a Student's Success in Mind Wandering

Ask, how will you know if you are successful? Share example success statements:

- □ I know I have been successfully mind wandering when I have an unexpected *aha!* moment.
- □ I know I have been successful at mind wandering when I unconsciously link ideas together without knowing how I did it.

Write your own success statement: "I realize I have been mind wandering successfully when I [insert a verb here]."

Encourage self-reflection:

- What role has mind wandering served in your own experience as a thinker, writer, or person?
- How have you been taught to value or devalue mind wandering?
- How do you react when you find yourself or peers engaged in mind wandering?

Celebrate progress by checking off "I can" statements:

- ✓ I can understand and explain mind wandering and its value to thinking and writing to my teachers, parents, and fellow students.
- ✓ I can build the underlying social and emotional and environmental conditions for mind wandering to flourish.
- ✓ I can work with others to help them assess, strengthen, and value their mind wandering and use it to enrich their written work.

REFLECT

By doing Reflect activities, writers make more strategic decisions about how to execute the task and become more metacognitively aware.

To reflect allows you to . . .

- ☐ Use past experiences to continually improve.
- ☐ Use internal and external stimuli to change your perspectives.
- ☐ Track your learning by inquiring what you used to think, what you *now* know, and what you need to know.
- ☐ Understand your writing process.
- ☐ Acknowledge the role of emotions as a source of decision-making in the writing process.
- ☐ Become aware of your sense of self, your goals, and the congruence of your actions with those goals.
- ☐ See how your present task or situation fits into a larger whole, sense of meaningfulness, or greater purpose in life, and use that to motivate further action.

Artwork by Gabriel Espinosa Tokuhama for Tracey Tokuhama-Espinosa.

Unlike the free thought associated with mind wandering, reflection requires purposeful attention, from attending to the progress one makes from both successes and mistakes to attending to how one knows oneself as a writer and as a thinker. Many great teachers already observe the utility of reflection exercises, and research across disciplines reveals valuable ways that reflecting contributes to thinking.

When we tell students they should reflect on their work or prior mistakes, this sounds straightforward, but there are dozens of pathways in the brain that contribute to this ability. Good teachers recognize the layers of reflection that occur while writing, all of which make thinking and writing inseparable while also playing a role in supporting students' developing self-concept (Pesu et al., 2016). Students can reflect on what they think about their writing. They can reflect on whether their writing conveys what they were thinking. They can reflect on how writing changes their thinking. Reflection occurs with writing (e.g., what do I think about my writing?), across writing (e.g., does what I wrote match what I meant, and if not, what do I think I should do?), and after writing (e.g., what did I learn from writing about this?). Additionally, reflection can concern one's identity as a writer (e.g., how am I developing as a writer, how can my writing allow me to understand or cope with this better, what kind of writer am I, what are my strengths as a writer?). Students' reflections on their mindset toward themselves as writers or on their attitude and approaches to writing itself can awaken or fuel motivation for the task at hand. All these levels of reflection inform our students' knowledge of themselves as thinkers and as writers.

Some of the primary pathways are the ability to self-understanding (Ma et al., 2014), me-and-other references (Siegel, 2010), and semantic memory (Burianova et al., 2010). Also involved is mindfulness reflection (Semenov et al., 2020), different states of consciousness (Hanson & Grayout, 2022), and may include brooding and rumination (Leutzinger & Philippi, 2021). Reflection also involves self-referential processing (Yoon et al., 2019), self and other relationships (Long et al., 2020), and self-correction through reflection (Schroer & Thomas, 2020; van Stee, 2022). Reflection involves multiple networks, but primarily long-term autobiographical and emotional memory are involved (Pociunaite & Zimprich, 2023). Because reflection can involve consideration of nonpresent situations, it can also employ the default mode networks as when we think about our growth and development as writers and imagine our future self as a writer.

Reflection uses many hats in the classroom. Many skills valued in education require critical thinking (e.g., Yuksel, 2017), effective problem solving, and decision-making (e.g., Bialek & Pennycook, 2018; Pennycook & Ross, 2016); transferring learning across contexts (e.g., Novakovich, 2016); and even knowing oneself as a person (Moran, 2016; Vetter et al., 2017). The ability to reflect plays a role in the ability to make meaning of an experience (e.g., Franks, 2016; Nye et al., 2016), self-regulate (e.g., Mak & Wong, 2018), and self-assess (e.g., Bourke, 2016; Ratminingsih et al., 2018; Vasu et al., 2018). To reflect is to see oneself, not just through a mirror of the present but by also looking to the past to inform the future. Prior experiences inform all new learning (Tokuhama-Espinosa, 2014), though students may not always be consciously aware of how they continually construct themselves as writers.

Knowing oneself (or to "know thyself" as the Greeks would say) necessitates metacognitive awareness through reflection, a skill that can be developed through concrete feedback from teachers (e.g., Miller & Geraci, 2011). Reflection can feel like a lower priority or even a distraction from all the work to be done, an indulgence. One of the most important lessons of COVID-19, however, is that guided reflective practices are beneficial to both student and teacher. Taking the time to reflect in the middle of time-sensitive work can be challenging, though, as it often means that the person reflecting is not speaking or not "writing," creating what feels like an uncomfortable space or a space in which one worries they appear as unproductive. But this is the "space" needed for the internalizing of information. Reflecting on how meeting challenges is connected to our larger sense of purpose—to the big picture—can help us and our students be more resilient in the face of such stressors (Immordino-Yang & Knecht, 2020) and even help us develop an opportunity mindset and find greater success and happiness.

One way to make more time for reflection is to ensure it is habituated practice. That is, the more practice, the less instructions are needed to do well, meaning students can be prompted to get into a reflective routine quickly. The learners' brains will adapt to what they do most (Tokuhama-Espinosa, 2014). Traditional schooling has not prized time for reflection, so it is hard to feel comfortable acknowledging that it, too, needs more time in the busy school day. One way teachers can encourage and habituate reflection is to take time at the end of each class to write a 3-2-1 Reflection: three things you learned, two things you are now curious about, and one thing you will change. By carving out 5 minutes at the end of class to do this, teachers also help consolidate learning. If the 3-2-1 Reflections can be shared with the entire class, students can also cross-pollinate their reflections as well. The more students take the time to reflect, the more they anticipate and benefit from it. It is this change of pace—the toggling between stages of thinking—that bolsters creativity (e.g., Chrysikou, 2019). For some learners, the act of reflection may even be discomforting, revealing imperfect parts of themselves or emotions attached to previous experiences; nonetheless, such reflection may be necessary for growth. Great teachers build time into their plans to focus on this learning process. Reflection expands the concept of "prewriting" or "brainstorming" to include time to develop metacognition.

Reflection complements the time we spend doing with time for the often-neglected thinking processes that underlie more effective action. In fact, research reveals that thinking about a task while in a resting state (i.e., while not performing an action) is associated with increased connectivity of areas of the brain that would otherwise be active while performing the task itself (e.g., Gregory et al., 2016). The time spent thinking about writing is not necessarily less effortful than the time spent producing a written product and helps strengthen the neural networks needed to perform that task.

As all new learning requires well-functioning memory systems and well-functioning attention systems, some suggest that mindfulness, a type of focused attention, is beneficial to the reflection process (e.g., Farb et al., 2007). This is likely due in part to the neural networks underlying reflection (see Table 2.2). The way the brain processes information differs between when it is about the self or not (Moran, 2016) and is influenced by the heuristics a person uses to sort through the vast amount of data entering their mind from the world (e.g., Korteling et al., 2018). To reflect on an experience, one needs to have some memory of it, such that the learner's mind is connecting across long-term memory systems—episodic, semantic, procedural, emotional, autobiographical—while also sustaining attention long enough to move from past to present to future knowledge and avoiding distractions (Vecchi & Gatti, 2020). Like all skills, reflection improves with quality and frequency of practice (Evers, 2023). Additionally, toggling between the focused attention that reflection provides and the default mode or mind-wandering stages of thinking create conditions for creativity as well (Chrysikou, 2019). Mind wandering may even benefit from the habituation of reflection as a means to think about past experiences with free thinking and then turning that knowledge to help inform writing and growth.

Consciously taking time out to reflect can often advance the progress of writing more than "plugging away" without a focus. Reflection then complements drafting, for example, by shifting attention from the need to get words on paper to thinking (and rethinking) about the process of writing. By reflecting on the process, writers may be better able to plan out their approach to an assignment to meet expectations within their timelines. Writers could even find that reflection helps them to regulate their emotional reactions to feedback by reframing their past experiences with similar comments. Reflection on identity, self-concept, and mindset can influence motivation and our capacity for persistence in the face of challenge (Dweck, 2015; Green et al., 2012; Guay et al., 2010). In real-life classes, teachers have a myriad of activities that stimulate reflection from mindfulness meditation to journaling.

Teachers can improve reflection by doing the following.

Tools Often Used to Reflect	Tools With Even More Impact
✓ Mindfulness meditation	✓ Mindfulness meditation followed by discussion
✓ Journals	✓ Double-entry journals
✓ Time for self-reflection	✓ Time for self-reflection and a self-reflection scorecard
✓ Reflect on emotions	✓ Reflect on emotions (which are of the body) and feelings (which are of the mind).

Activities From ThinkWrite for Reflecting

Before and After

Objective: *To value and document how and why thinking evolves*

1. Think about your project.
2. Consider how you got to where you are now.
3. Use the prompt "I used to think . . . now I think . . . because . . ."
4. Reflect on the many ways you can fill in this prompt.
5. Celebrate where you are with your writing project.
6. Talk to one or two other people in class about their "I used to think . . . now I think . . . because . . ." statements.
7. What additional reflections do you have now that you have talked with others?
8. List all reflections you have come up with.

What's happening in the brain: "Before and After" involves self-reflection and the ability to compare and contrast the present to the past, which includes autobiographical memory, autobiographical reflection, and metacognition. This involves "activation in the medial temporal lobe . . . during autobiographical recall" (Fuentes-Claramonte et al., 2019, p. 1). "At the neural level, the lateral parietal cortex and . . . left-lateralized activations of the angular gyrus are also found during self-referential processing" (Mizrahi & Axelrod, 2023, p. 219). The metacognitive processes also include the dorsal medial prefrontal cortices (Shoko et al., 2019), which is key to reflection.

How Do You Feel?

Objective: *To identify and use your feelings to self-assess your work*

1. Reread your work.
2. Identify the positive feelings you have for your work. Record where they occur in the writing.
3. Identify the negative feelings you have for your work. Record where these occur.
4. Note how the sections that elicited positive emotions about your writing differ from the ones that elicited negative emotions about your writing.
5. Identify ways or strategies to make the negative positive.
6. Rewrite the sections that elicited negative feelings.
7. Show your original paper and your revised paper to a friend. Do they feel the same about the paper sections?
8. Discuss.
9. Reflect on additional edits.

What's happening in the brain: "How Do You Feel" involves emotional intelligence and self-reflection, which includes empathy and emotional regulation and "socioaffective brain mechanisms underlying putative EI [emotional intelligence] constructs" (Stoica, 2021, p. vi). This involves the "salience (SN), default mode (DMN) and central executive networks (CEN)," which relates to "ACC—Anterior Cingulate Cortex, mPFC—Medial Prefrontal Cortex, PCC—Posterior Cingulate Cortex, dlPFC—dorsolateral Prefrontal Cortex, IPL—Intraparietal Lobule" (Stoica, 2021, p. 7), among other areas.

3-2-1 Reflection

Objective: *To take stock of what you learn, find interesting, and want to know more about*

1. After you learn something about your topic, think of three things you did not know before. Record your response.
2. Think of two things you are now curious about related to the topic. Record your response.
3. Think about one thing you will change due to what you have learned. Record your response.

4. Upload your reflection to a digital whiteboard where everyone in class can read each other's 3-2-1 Reflection.
5. Reflect how different people took away different ideas from the same assignment.
6. Summarize your takeaway ideas.

What's happening in the brain: "3-2-1 Reflection" involves personal, autobiographical reflection; the ability to self-reflect; and metacognitive awareness, which includes self-awareness about one's knowledge (Terneusen, 2023; Terneusen et al., 2023; Terneusen et al., 2024) related to personal semantic, general semantic, episodic memory (Tanguay et al., 2023), and self-reflection. This involves among other things, the "left angular gyrus during autobiographical memory retrieval" (Mizrahi & Axelrod, 2022, p. 219), and metacognitive ability is triggered by the lateral prefrontal cortex and medial prefrontal cortex (Fleming & Dolan, 2012).

For more activities, see ThinkWriteMBE.com.

Maximizing a Student's Success in Reflecting

Ask, how will you know if you are successful? Share example success statements:

- □ I reflect by taking time to contemplate the important ideas in the passage.
- □ I reflect by dissecting each part of the dialogue I am going to write.
- □ I reflect by assessing how my work looks compared to a worked example [the instructions].
- □ I reflect by being mindful of my choices.

Write your own success statement: "I realize I have been successful reflecting when I [insert a verb here]."

Encourage self-reflection:

- What role has reflection served in your own experience as a thinker, writer, or person?
- How have you been taught to value or devalue the time for reflection about how your thinking has evolved?
- How do you react when a peer is engaged in reflection when a different task is assigned?
- What do I already know about reflection, and what have I learned that is new?
- What do I still need to know (and what do I know I need to know) to move forward with this project?

Celebrate progress by checking off "I can" statements:

✓ I can center my focus and attention.
✓ I can identify my own feelings.
✓ I can see my strengths as a writer.
✓ I can explain my conception of myself as a writer to another.
✓ I can mindfully acknowledge spaces for improvement.
✓ I can focus attention inward.
✓ I can focus attention outward.

MAP AND CONNECT

Mapping ideas helps the learner understand the relationships between them. Connecting ideas creates a logic that can be used to write the outline of written work.

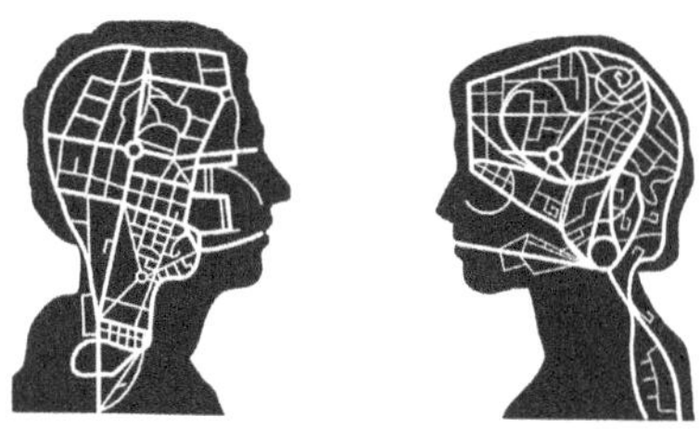

To map and connect allows you to . . .

- ☐ Successfully visualize how concepts are related.
- ☐ See how distinct ideas can often share characteristics.
- ☐ Learn to categorize analogous ideas.
- ☐ Develop abstract thinking abilities.

Artwork by Gabriel Espinosa Tokuhama for Tracey Tokuhama-Espinosa.

Once the writer understands what's expected of them and knows what they still need to know to put words on paper, they can often be faced with what can be described as a lot of loose ends, all related to the topic but not yet related to each other. To advance in the writing process, at this stage the writer must stand back at a macro level and link, categorize, and group ideas by describing the connections between them. Some writers begin with the end in mind; they know how they want the reader to feel at the end of the reading but have no idea how to start. Others have an idea about how one concept relates to another in a linear fashion but not how they all link among themselves. Mapping serves to get from one place to another. Connecting serves to make explicit links between ideas. "Mapping and connecting" is some of the most complex thinking that goes into writing, primarily because its success depends on a shared vision. If the writer feels certain ideas belong together but the reader can't understand why, then the student's organization might not be accepted. One way to make thinking visible around mapping and connecting is through "mind mapping" itself. Made popular by Tony Buzan in the 1970s, mind-mapping tools have become highly popular and often-required writing tools (Buzan, 2018). Before digital versions, some of the authors of this book remember the glorified doodling that serves as a mind-mapping precursor. To use a mind map to help develop and understand connections deliberately and logically in the stage of mapping and connecting is distinctly different from the use of a mind map to freely associate and capture the "random" personal associations that might occur in mind wandering. Venn diagrams can also be a useful tool in mapping similarities, points of connection, and differences between things.

To map and connect ideas and concepts through written words, the brain uses dozens of pathways (see Table 2.2). Some studies focus on the way the brain assesses depths of comprehension (Caruso et al., 2022) or might experience false insights with semantic priming (Grimmer et al., 2022) that need correcting before shared understanding can occur. Others review how there are enhanced connections with increased retrieval (Reilly, 2023), or evidence accumulation (Liu & Pleskac, 2011). The research also maps a problem to its solution (Milovanovic et al., 2021) and the retrieval to strengthen connections (Van den Broek et al., 2016). Mapping and connecting research also involve visuospatial working memory and relational planning (Van Orden et al., 2001), visual working memory (Johnson et al., 2009), and mental categorization (Pauen & Peykarjou, 2020). Studies in this field also look at how remote associations are formed (Ovando-Tellez et al., 2022), how heuristics develop (Rubaltelli, 2023), and how many involve connectivism (Downes, 2022), bi-associations (Benedek et al., 2020), and an understanding of categories and concepts (Miller et al., 2003). Studies of working memory illuminate the key role it plays in mapping and connection via both the visual sketchpad and phonological loop to enhance relational planning (Da Vita et al., 2021).

In real-life classrooms, teachers have become accustomed to mapping ideas through mind-mapping tools and connecting them through think-alouds or group brainstorming. We suggest doing these things together and using the maps to write up an outline. Some digital tools allow one to toggle from the mind map into an "outline" format whereby the information can be further sorted into visual hierarchies and sequences. Sometimes the speed of handwriting can best capture the flow of ideas, but moving into a different format or organization can be more laborious. This extra labor is not necessarily a bad thing as active engagement increases the time on task as one works to manipulate and incorporate the map into a new form, which can lead to greater understanding and memory formation. Sometimes in the process of mapping and connecting we discover that there is more than one criterion by which things can be connected, and we have to consider which connection is the most meaningful given the task at hand. Flexibility in connecting ideas can be a sign of mature executive capacities and a source of creative insight.

Teachers can map and connect by doing the following.

Tools Often Used to Map and Connect	Tools With Even More Impact
✓ Word mapping	✓ Word mapping and connecting by relationships
✓ Idea mapping	✓ Idea mapping and connecting by relationships or categories
✓ Concept mapping	✓ Concept mapping and connecting by hierarchy
✓ Concept mapping	✓ Spatial or temporal mapping of ideas

Activities From ThinkWrite for Mapping and Connecting

Connecting Big Ideas

Objective: *To create as many flexible relationships among your ideas as possible*

1. Get paper Post-its, index cards, or your favorite digital note-taking tool to record your responses.
2. Make a separate note of each idea/thought.
3. Move and regroup the ideas in as many ways as you can to show different kinds of logical relationships.
4. Document each configuration.
5. Show your favorite combinations to a classmate, and explain your logic. Do they see what you see?
6. Use their feedback to make any further modifications to your groupings.

What's happening in the brain: "Connecting Big Ideas" involves, among other things, categorical perception (Pérez-Gay Juárez et al., 2019) through spatial and temporal organization (Teghill et al., 2022), which includes semantic knowledge, as well as lexical and sublexical processes (Murphy et al., 2022) and strategic memory retrieval (Joubert et al., 2004). This involves "activity in higher-order visual regions, including the fusiform gyrus, the lingual gyrus, and the cuneus" for spatial relations, and "the globus pallidus and the thalamus was relatively enhanced when subjects used a temporal-associative structure" (De Rover et al., 2008, p. 1068). "The lexical condition engaged primarily an area at the border of the left angular and supramarginal gyri. . . . Both sublexical conditions elicited significantly greater activation in the left inferior prefrontal gyrus" (Joubert et al., 2004, p. 9).

Generate-Group-Sequence-Elaborate

Objective: *To show the relationships between different categories of ideas*

1. Generate lists of ideas on the topic.
2. Group the ideas into categories.
3. Create a sequence or give a hierarchy to the ideas within each category.

4. Give each category a hierarchy.
5. Elaborate on the ideas.
6. Name each category.
7. Share your hierarchical design with a classmate. How do your groupings differ? How are they all the same?
8. What changes will you make to your own work based on what you have discussed?

What's happening in the brain: "Generate-Group-Sequence-Elaborate" involves mental schema and hierarchies of conceptual grouping, which includes transitive inference (Zhang et al., 2022). This involves the prefrontal cortex, which "contributes to the construction and use of a mental schema to represent premises" (Brunamonti et al., 2016, p. 1223).

Building Relationships

Objective: ***To translate visual connections into written notes***

1. Generate a mind map.
2. Look at the connections between ideas.
3. Set your timer for 5 minutes.
4. Without stopping, freewrite notes on the connections you find in the ideas in your mind map.
5. Don't erase anything you've written.
6. If you pause during the freewriting, remember to return to your mind map.
7. Review your elaborated descriptions next to each idea.
8. Do they change the way you would map the concepts now? If so, modify your map to reflect your new thinking.

What's happening in the brain: "Building Relationships" involves mind mapping (to identify relationships through one's own cognitive ontology [Khalidi, 2023]), which includes episodic memory linking feeling of knowing (Irak et al., 2019) and cognitive, heuristic biases surrounding an individual's mental schema. This involves "emotional episodic memory retrieval . . . activations . . . in the medial temporal lobe (bilateral amygdala, left hippocampus, and left entorhinal cortex and perirhinal cortex), visual processing regions (bilateral occipital cortex and right middle temporal gyrus), prefrontal cortex (bilateral orbitofrontal cortex, bilateral inferior frontal gyrus, bilateral precentral gyrus, left middle frontal gyrus, right frontal pole) and . . . the left hemisphere including the temporal pole, insula, putamen, angular gyrus, and parietal opercular cortex" (Dahlgren et al., 2020, p. 107495).

For more activities, see ThinkWriteMBE.com.

Maximizing a Student's Success in Mapping and Connecting

Ask, how will you know if you are successful? Share example success statements:

- □ When I map and connect, I can join and link my thoughts.
- □ To map and connect, I find bridges between concepts.
- □ To map and connect, I can show how ideas crisscross and overlap.

Write your own success statement: "I realize I have mapped and connected successfully when I [insert a verb here]."

Encourage self-reflection:

- What mapping tools do I already use?
- How many ways can information be connected logically?
- How much time do I dedicate to mapping and connecting ideas?

Celebrate progress by checking off "I can" statements:

- ✓ I can show the natural relationships between ideas.
- ✓ I can both draw and write out categories of ideas.
- ✓ I can map and connect ideas to create a strong outline from written work.

Prewriting involves some of the most complex thinking, yet it is rarely celebrated in a classroom with the time it deserves and is often given no weight in the gradebook because it is primarily based on thinking, not writing. The mental processes involved in the understanding, knowing things, mind wandering, reflecting and mapping and connecting concepts lay the foundation of all good writing assignments and products; without good thinking during prewriting there is no good writing, period. We'd like to motivate teachers to think creatively about how they could elaborate the prewriting thinking stages in their own classrooms. Barriers to implementation are often superficial and hinge on the time needed for classroom activities. We have found that the time to do the prewriting stages of thinking pay off in time saved during the writing and revision stages.

We now turn from prewriting to writing.

CHAPTER 4

The Holons of Writing

ThinkWrite: The Holons of Writing

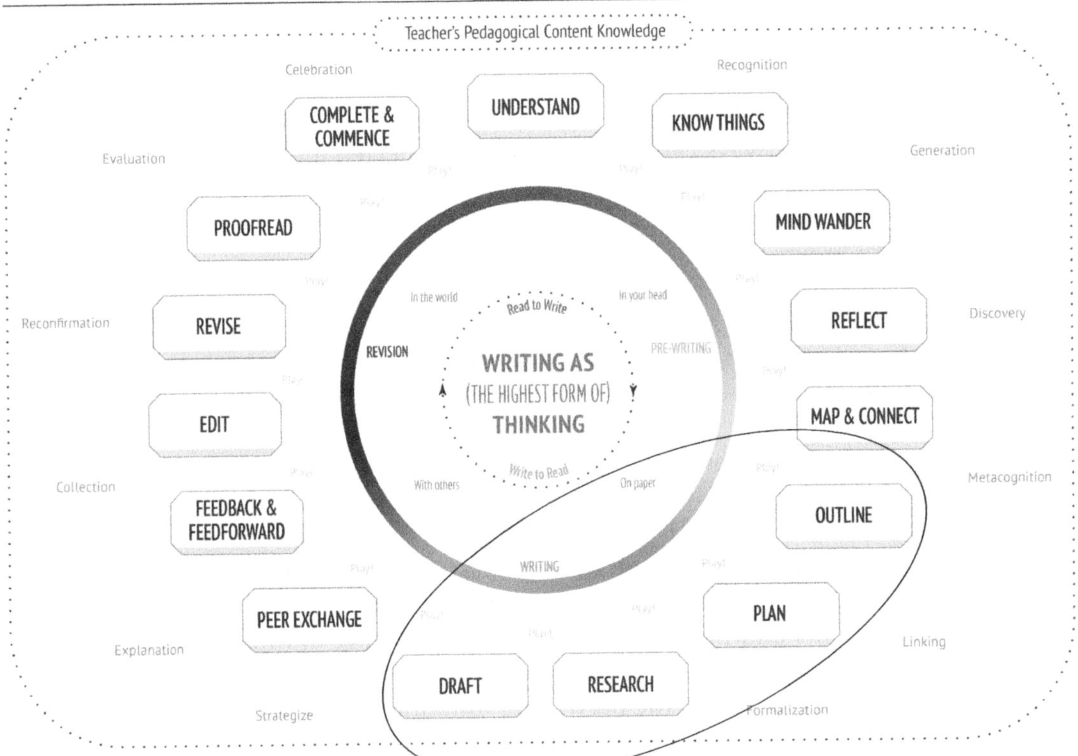

© Tokuhama-Espinosa, Nazareno, & Rappleye 2024

In the writing phase, work completed by learners tends to be more readily visible to others. They move from making sense of connecting loose ideas to formally developing an ***outline*** of what they will write. They structure the written work, assign order, balance competing ideas, check if one concept transitions to the next or what they might've been missing. Attention and tasks shift from more free-form associations, connections, and insights to establishing a more linear, logical, and sustained rhetorical structure. During the actual writing itself, students might need to ***plan*** each step in their process and manage or optimize their time to get things done in accordance with their personal goals. Sometimes they need to stop and ***research*** to fill in gaps in understanding, rethink their methodology and revisit their topic or question, and figure out how to get information and evaluate it. Sometimes writers just need to take the time to write and rewrite ***drafts*** of what will become their final work. Drafting is an iterative process where students learn to work at both the micro (words, sentences) and macro level (structure of project, order of ideas, genre), and must find routines and modalities that work for them. Skilled drafting often involves aspects of editing and revising "in the moment," making this a particularly complex mental stage. Sometimes in drafting, students gain confidence and allow themselves the space and opportunity to dare to err and explore new ideas. Throughout these stages of writing and thinking, the writer must imagine the audience's existing knowledge, concerns, and questions, honing and applying their "theory of mind" to intellectually empathize with their reader's needs.

Outcomes of ThinkWrite Stages

- **Outline:** Writers find a logical order and determine a hierarchy of concepts for their ideas. By establishing a blueprint for the content, they can then focus more of their mental energy on the writing process and remember all their great ideas.
- **Plan:** Writers make their processes more visible and manage their time and energy better.
- **Research:** Writers gather and analyze materials and evaluate sources to expand their knowledge with multiple perspectives, and appeal to readers by using authentic, contextualized evidence.
- **Draft:** Writers begin to formalize, externalize, visualize, and connect their thinking processes, giving their writing its "public" shape in words, sentences, paragraphs, or lines and stanzas.

OUTLINE

If you have a good outline, the paper writes itself. A good outline ensures all the important parts of a paper are included in the right places.

To outline allows you to . . .

- ☐ Structure and nest ideas.
- ☐ Give a hierarchy to concepts.
- ☐ Order thinking.
- ☐ Free up cognitive load during the drafting process.
- ☐ "Beta test" the completeness or rigor of your thinking or idea.

One of the first graded assignments in writing projects is often the outline in which the writer exposes the mental hierarchies of ideas they have been working on. A natural product of the mapping and connecting process is to create a written outline, but there is a big mental leap from one process to the other. Before you bought this book, it is highly likely you flipped to the table of contents to see if your expectations, created by the book title, met or surpassed expectations of content. The outline to written words also shares the author's style. It lets the reader know if the work is framed analytically, or has fun twists, if it aims for punch lines or for conclusions, if the tone is friendly or formal.

Outlines differ by genres and are often skeletons of worked models that writers can use as comparative blueprints for their own work. Outlines for short stories, novels, instructional manuals, infographics, screenplays, ad copy, book reports, poems, and shopping lists all have their unique structures, distinct formats, and levels of formality. The more technical the writing, the stricter the outline. For example, peer-reviewed academic articles are usually very rigid in their outlines, whereas the structure of a science fiction novel is far less so.

Form versus content. Many school curricula recommend or even require certain literary works be read and then written about. In some cases they do this because these works are considered exemplary of their genre. While most teachers understand how to teach each book, novel, play, short story, or infographic, few leverage these "worked models" by using them to explain outlining. To help students understand the structure of these exemplary works better, and to learn about outlining specifically, teachers can spend more time "backward engineering" their design. For example, most young children in the United States have heard of "Goldilocks and the Three Bears." Why not have students reverse engineer the story to learn how to write an outline for a children's book? This might include an introduction of the main characters, the setting, the problem, and the resolution, followed by a moral. Outlining a story they know can help students see patterns in different literary genres.

Many Common Core guidelines identify the important role of understanding the difference between outlines of lab reports and narrative essays, but these are not often taught explicitly side by side. One way to facilitate students' understanding of different literary genres is to outline them. Asking students what they see as the "typical structure" of historical fiction novels versus the screenplay of the same novel can provide deep insights into the role of different genres in shaping distinct messages depending on the objective.

In the brain, outlining forces a consideration of the contextually apt principles of ordering hierarchy and of the "logic" of relationships, calling to mind and reinforcing which schema to apply in the writing situation (e.g., chronology, cause and effect, strongest to weakest argument) depending on the genre and rhetorical situation (see Table 2.2).

Similarly, in outlining, the writer begins to consider and anticipate the potential reader's needs in constructing meaning from the writer's ideas as presented in linear form. In many situations, outlining requires the writer to break an idea into its constituent parts, to relate various levels of abstraction, and to connect abstract concepts to specific examples. This requires self-monitoring (Perrone-Bertolotti et al., 2014), creative cognition and executive functions (Hechtman, 2015), and bringing internal thoughts to visual imagery (Karapanagiotidis et al., 2021). Outlining also requires task prioritization (Liegel et al., 2022), understanding task order (Steinhauser et al., 2021), and semantic processing on task order (Hargraves et al., 2012b). To outline, one has to use multiple memory pathways and metamemory (Chua et al., 2009), apply brainstorming and story generation (Shah et al., 2013), frame intentional communication (Noordzij et al., 2010), and leverage theory of mind (Ho et al., 2022) to ensure the reader will understand the logic with which information is structured. Templates and graphic organizers can be a helpful means for keeping hold of these nested relationships in mind, relieving some of the cognitive load for the writer by chunking the relationships as the budding writer's build facility in these skills. As in all stages of thinking, templates and organizers provide models to facilitate the writing process. This will vary by individual, but there may be times such as working in a new genre or when students return to writing after a lengthy break where all students can benefit from such scaffolding.

We often underestimate how little rehearsal the neural networks that support writing get, assuming that once a student has done something well once or twice, perhaps months ago, the skill is permanent. It is not! Skills need rehearsal to become easily retrievable. Students often achieve a level of proficiency in one grade level or in one task and then experience a long delay and the subsequent lack of rehearsal that can result in a discernible falling off since there have been no behaviors to strengthen the underlying neural networks in the meantime. The key with templates and organizers is to frame their use in such a way as to get students thinking about the function and relationship of the parts of the framework and final writing project. Outlining, which makes considerable demands on the students' ability to understand and apply levels of abstraction and the relationship to concrete examples, for instance, can be one of those areas. Scaffolding outlining tasks helps. Eventually, the ideal is to bridge to where the student can take on more and more of the skills themselves, but teachers should be aware of the need for students to rehearse and build these activities in the first place. Just because a student was able to outline successfully in one assignment does not mean they can do it in the next, primarily because they have had little rehearsal in between writing assignments. This is another reason why it is helpful to break the phases of writing process down into the underlying stages of thinking, and to consider the complexity within each of those stages and finally the need to strengthen the developing writer's neural networks through a thoughtful sequence of rehearsal.

To create an outline for a written piece of work, the brain has to think of logical beginning-middle-end parts of the paper as well as the audience. This involves neural pathways related to self-monitoring (Gómez-Andres et al., 2022), creative cognition and executive functions (Luchini & Beaty, 2023), prospective thoughts (Girardeau et al., 2022), task prioritization (Liegel et al., 2022), and task order (Perone et al., 2021),. This also involves metamemory (Li et al., 2024) and brainstorming (Barr et al., 2023), as well as story generation (Rastelli et al., 2024) and results in intentional communication by considering what the other is experiencing through our writing using theory of mind (Hauptman et al., 2023).

A note about flexibility. Outlines are often the first graded work in a writing assignment and as such, are seen as a contract of what will be submitted. Some of the best teachers we know encourage *evolving* outlines that mature as the student's thinking devolves around the paper. We see it is not uncommon for the drafting stage to reflect a different outline from the original as students grow in their understanding.

While teachers already use templates for paper outlines with an introduction, a body, and a conclusion, or follow the structure of accepted forms like a five-paragraph essay, we recommend extending these tools.

Tools Often Used to Outline	Tools With Even More Impact
✓ Templates for essays or research papers	✓ Backward engineer a worked model.
✓ Generate an outline	✓ Use mind maps of the topic, assign a hierarchy, and order the groupings to create an outline; indicate transitions on the outline (use Table 7.5 as a guide).
✓ Interview your audience for expectations.	✓ Create an outline and then interview your audience and add things to meet their expectations.
✓ Use an outline template downloaded from the Internet.	✓ Condense your narrative into a single sentence and compare it with your outline.

Activities From ThinkWrite for Outlining

Mind Map to Outline

Objective: *To leverage a mind map to develop an outline*

1. Generate a mind map.
2. Review the categories and connections on your mind map.
3. Use the categories to assign an order to the ideas.
4. Assign headers to the different levels of ideas.
5. Create an outline.
6. Compare your outline to another student's.
7. Identify similarities and differences.
8. Ask yourself what the differences in the outlines are based on.
9. Rethink your own outline. Modify if needed.

What's happening in the brain: "Mind Map to Outline" involves deciding on an order and hierarchy of concepts based on a clear narrative toward completion (beginning, middle, end) of a project, depending on the genre of writing, which includes reducing cognitive load through mind mapping (Nesbit & Adesope, 2006) and by making invisible thinking more visible by committing to a visual hierarchy. This ordering of ideas is based in part on transitive reasoning, which is changed by the relationships determined by word order (Prado et al., 2013). This involves "spatial representations in the posterior parietal cortex (PPC)" as well as "verbal processing regions of the left inferior frontal gyrus (IFG)" (Prado et al., 2013, p. 499), to then leverage working memory to organize the relationships in an outline (Oberauer, 2020).

From Worked Models to Template

Objective: *To use a worked model to create a template for your work*

1. Review the worked model to understand the outline of your writing genre.
2. Create a template to make sure you are organizing your work in a way that conforms to the worked model you just read.
3. After your finish writing your outline, compare your work with the worked model's outline.
4. Make any revisions necessary.

What's happening in the brain: "From Worked Models to Template" involves using an ideal outcome (worked model) to develop an outline, which can then be compared with your own work to backward engineer the outline by determining the format, including key headers and the order of sections, which includes using a macro view of the worked model's format and structure to create a parallel format for the writing assignment. This means seeing salient information in headers as well as seeing patterns in structure depending on the writing genre (Jiang et al., 2023). This involves "two saliency formulations—CRF Saliency and Discriminant Saliency, for predicting salient patches, which can correspond to different types of annotations" (Pandey & Harit, 2021, p. 1).

Checkpoint

Objective: *To ensure you have a complete outline*

1. Develop an outline.
2. Check your outline against any previous list, notes, or other writing you have generated on this topic.
3. Review the instructions for your writing project.
4. Ask yourself, have I covered all of the bases? or have I missed anything?
5. Revise your original outline.

What's happening in the brain: Among other things, "Checkpoint" involves reviewing instructions, rubrics, and other requirements and comparing them to your outline. It also involves rereading and assessing notes and guidance received in class, which includes visual working memory systems and conceptual comparing and contrasting. This involves the "left medial frontal gyrus, left precentral gyrus . . . [as well as] activation across the PFC, fusiform gyrus, parietal cortex, and parts of the cerebellum" (Emch et al., 2019, p. 1).

For more activities, see ThinkWriteMBE.com.

Maximizing a Student's Success in Outlining

Ask, how will you know if you are successful? Share example success statements:

- ☐ To outline, I first make a thumbnail sketch of all my ideas to ensure I didn't forget anything important.
- ☐ To outline, I make an inventory of all the pieces that need to go into my paper based on the instructions, rubrics, and other guidelines.
- ☐ To outline, I enumerate all the main points in the right order using logical structures typical of this genre.

Write your own success statement: "I realize I have mapped and connected successfully when I [insert a verb here]."

Encourage self-reflection:

- Do I always write an outline before starting a writing project? Why or why not?
- Do I see how a good outline guarantees a strong opening and closing to my paper?
- How flexible am I in creating multiple outlines as a project evolves?

Celebrate progress by checking off "I can" statements:

✓ I can use a variety of tools to visually map ideas.
✓ I can write a clear outline that covers all major ideas.

PLAN

A good plan ensures the achievement of proposed goals.

To plan allows you to . . .

- ☐ Avoid missed deadlines.
- ☐ Pace your writing calmly.
- ☐ Have the satisfaction of achieving small victories on the road to completion.

Writing a good outline helps assure the content of your written work responds to the expectations of the assignment and the readers of your work. This means very little if you are not able to complete your writing in a timely way, however. Some people write amazing outlines only to realize they are way too ambitious given the time frame available. Others begin working on time but halfway to the deadline realize they don't have the materials (the research, the information, the physical tools like paper and printer, and so on) to complete the work. Yet others see each stage of writing as equal in time and effort, only to find that they should have given far more time to deciding the research question before launching into the data gathering because they now know the question has already been answered by someone else, or that they have developed a story around a main character who is really secondary and have not taken enough time to develop the true main character. Planning means realistically organizing time and resources to achieve a writing goal.

Planning goes beyond the individual and into consideration of other actors in the world. It depends on conditions and resources involving things like "life happening" and catching a cold the same week you need to present your paper. Or living conditions in which parents are fighting and keeping a student from sleeping well so they cannot concentrate as they normally would. Or weather conditions in which a hurricane or high temperatures or fires keeps the school library closed for days, or the Internet is down, preventing the ability to complete the assignment. Resources include things like pen, paper, computers, other people's willingness to help, and most of all, time. The ability to plan well is a far more complex task than the ability to outline, as the outline can become an empty promise and list of good ideas if it is not accompanied by the ability to execute.

Planning involves the executive functions that support awareness and estimation of time and the ability to estimate the effort necessary to complete the task, and is dependent on the degree of awareness of the subject area knowledge, genre, or specific writing task involved. Awareness in these arenas is built by repeated experience and explicit reflection on previous experiences as well as the ability to consider other tasks and time demands that may impinge on one's ability to complete the task. Checklists (derived from understanding the task activities), timelines, and calendars are useful tools in the planning process, and habituating record-keeping and reflection on the accuracy of one's past planning processes are other means by which temporal awareness can be built up. Timely reflection can therefore support the future growth of one's planning abilities. These activities depend on executive functions (Saylik et al., 2022), self-regulation (Larraín-Valenzuela et al., 2022), planning skills (Vriend, et al., 2020), and involve judgment and decision-making (Edgcumbe et al., 2019). Planning also involves memory for the future (Cieri, 2022) and episodic and semantic memories (Alves et al., 2021), which involves a correlation between language and planning (Sun et al., 2019) and planning and foresight (McKiernan, 2017).

Planning is a higher-order skill that is not innate and must be developed with practice. It is an executive function that relies on other, "lower" executive functions—working memory, inhibitory control, cognitive flexibility—functioning seamlessly (Diamond, 2013). Working memory is the bridge between short- and long-term memory and involves managing processes to execute tasks. For example, listening to what the teacher asks you to do and then walking back to your desk to actually do what they ask involves working memory. Inhibitory control is the brain's ability to block out unwanted stimuli and focus on what is important. For example, when you are tempted to watch the game on TV but you ignore that stimuli to stay focused on the homework until it is completed. Cognitive flexibility is the brain's toolbox of options and is the ability to bend, not break, when new demands are made, and to task switch when appropriate. For example, if the teacher says students have to each write about a different animal and someone else chooses lions before you can, your ability to switch to a new animal shows cognitive flexibility. In addition to core executive functions, planning depends on other cognitive abilities, like self-regulation, judgment, decision-making. Planning also involves neural pathways of self-referential knowledge, which is why episodic and semantic memories also come into play, as does the correlation between language and planning. Teachers can help students develop good planning skills by attending to the sub-elements of planning (see Table 2.2), like activities and exercises that enhance working memory (e.g., playing a game of concentration with a deck of cards), inhibitory control (e.g., mindfulness meditation), and cognitive flexibility (reminding them to use all of their metacognitive awareness tools, such as asking themselves if they have all used all of the resources at their disposal).

Teachers can help students plan by doing the following.

Tools Often Used to Plan	Tools With Even More Impact
✓ Use a calendar.	✓ Backward engineer the project due date to the present.
✓ Set a deadline.	✓ Set goals.
✓ Make a to-do list.	✓ Make an I-get-to-do list.
✓ Identify resources.	✓ Think of friends, family, and tools that can support you.

Activities From ThinkWrite for Planning

Reverse Engineer the Plan and the Product

Objective: *To use a worked model and then tweak it*

1. Look at the end product of a worked model.
2. Ask yourself, what do I need to do to produce something similar?
3. Do a gap analysis of where you are and where you want to be.
4. Decide what you need to do to get to the end product.
5. Write out each step and adjust to ensure you meet the deadlines.

What's happening in the brain: "Reverse Engineer the Plan and the Product" involves comparing your evolving product with a worked model to plan next steps, which includes working memory comparison of written passages and long-term memory systems. This involves "various cognitive, phonological and motor processes [that] are executed through working memory; whereas long-term memory provides the knowledge that will be recovered during textual production. Proper functioning of these memory systems—and neural substrates such as hippocampus and temporal cortical areas—are related to effectiveness of composing a text" (Moreno & Tabullo, 2023, p. 1).

You Are in the Driver's Seat!

Objective: *To stay motivated and define a plan that is meaningful and achievable*

1. Understand the overall objective of the writing project.
2. Decide why this project is meaningful to you. Find one reason that is practical and at least one that is personally meaningful.
3. Remember that you make progress in small steps. Split your project into minigoals (divide and conquer).
4. Establish the steps you can take to accomplish each minigoal.
5. Celebrate each time you reach a minigoal.

What's happening in the brain: Among other things, "You Are in the Driver's Seat!" harnesses meaning-making and the sense of achievement to self-motivate by making a writing project enjoyable, which includes improving a sense of well-being (Cruyt et al., 2023) and even enjoyment for the complex writing task. This involves "brain areas . . . [that] were generally related to emotional and affective processing, motivation, and reward" (Cruyt et al., 2023, p. 1) and is based on "the activation in the ventral striatum/pallidum" based on "task enjoyment. These results suggest that people are intrinsically motivated to challenge a nearly impossible task, but only when the task requires certain skills and extrinsic rewards are unavailable" (Sakaki et al., 2019, p. 1).

Want Versus Need (Micro)

Objective: *To choose the next tasks for your writing process*

1. List everything you can think of that is related to tasks in your writing project.
2. Ask yourself, what are the tasks in my writing process that I want to do? Why? Identify them as the "want" category.
3. Then ask yourself, what are the tasks in my writing process that I need to do? Why? Identify them as the "need" category.
4. Now make a choice. What will you do next? Remember to think about how much time is needed for each task.
5. Write up a plan that orders all of your wants and needs activities in a way that allows you to meet your deadline.

What's happening in the brain: "Want Versus Need" helps students create priority lists to advance toward the completion of the writing project, which includes acknowledgment of wants (enjoyable), which can trigger positive emotions, and needs (required and not necessarily enjoyable), which can trigger negative emotions. This involves, among other things, "Attentional Deployment, Cognitive Change, and Response Modulation" during positive emotions, underpinned by "the prefrontal cortex (PFC) and anterior cingulate cortex (ACC). Region of interest analysis revealed greater activation of the ventral striatum during positive emotion regulation" (Tsujimoto et al., 2022, p. 1).

For more activities, see ThinkWriteMBE.com.

Maximizing a Student's Success in Planning

Ask, how will you know if you are successful? Share example success statements:

- ☐ I know I made a good plan when I organize my time so as not to feel pressured.
- ☐ To plan my writing, I lay out all the tasks before I start so I can see visible milestones.

□ I am sure I have a good plan when I timetable a complete to-do list and achieve it.

Write your own success statement: "I know I made a good plan when I [insert a verb here]."

Encourage self-reflection:

- Before launching into a writing project, do I make a timeline for completion?
- Are my plans always reasonable? Why or why not?
- Do my plans depend too much on factors I can't control?

Celebrate progress by checking off "I can" statements:

✓ I can use a variety of planning tools.
✓ I can meet my deadlines by following a plan.
✓ I can set realistic goals with good planning.

RESEARCH

Good research ensures your writing is original, based on facts, and builds on our existing knowledge rather than repeating it.

To research allows you to . . .

□ Ensure accuracy.
□ Avoid erroneous information.
□ Know who else agrees with you and who might disagree and why.
□ Learn from others and stand on the shoulders of giants.

"Re-search" literally means to search again. The idea of strong research is to ground your work in evidence and is what some scholars argue propels humanity forward. Research is a means of satisfying people's innate curiosity to know more and involves a process of discovery of ideas that in turn can shape who we believe we are in the world both individually and collectively. Research is the ability to identify quality sources of information, even if (especially when) they contradict our current beliefs, ideas, and understandings. This means that the ability to research requires both an open mind and a scrutinizing brain that can recognize its own biases about the information and overcome the temptation to invest lower cognitive load into heuristics.

While we think of research often in terms of seeking out secondary sources (what someone found out about a topic or question), some research may involve simply looking more closely at a primary source with a critical eye (what they failed to report or highlight about what they found). The idea of scrutinizing sources is especially important in an age of ready access to information on the Internet, which can contain both evidence-based as well as made-up ideas. Rigorous research is a different set of tasks and distinct neural networks from engaging in confirmation bias, which requires far less energy (cognitive load) and effort (Martín & Valiña, 2023). Quality digital literacy habits are needed now more than ever and are every teacher's responsibility (Phippen et al., 2021). The goal of research is to expand and critically review our knowledge base, which requires the prerequisite state of mind of being open to new ideas and coaching on how to have these (Rodriquez et al., 2019). Many people find it hard to research because the information they find contradicts what they would like to believe, so they reject it. There are no right and wrong answers in research, just the weight of the evidence. The trait of "openness" means being willing to question your own thinking and to doubt some of the belief statements we make, according to Bertrand Russell: "In all affairs it's a healthy thing now and then to hang a question mark on the things you have long taken for granted." Being open means asking rather than stating.

Research is at the heart of problem solving. Research is not only needed in academic and scholarly writing, but it is just as important when writing fiction and placing the character in the right environment (the ability to allude to the right song of the time period or describe the fashion of the day). Research is also about anyone who wants to remain up-to-date with the world. Keeping current in areas of interest is something that we all do naturally, which makes authentic research into personal areas of interest a great place for students to start rehearsing these skills. A simple question that can be used to start to teach research skills is to ask, *What do you want to know?* We have found in our cases that it is a surprisingly difficult question for people to answer (people who have not yet learned the joys of discovery involved in research often answer this question by saying they want to know how to get an A on the assignment!). By starting with an authentic base of interest, many students are intrinsically motivated to dive into the information to search for answers.

Staying up-to-date with information is another way of helping to know what kinds of problems have already been solved and what things still need solving. For example, if you are interested in helping the environment, a good place to start is to research the other successful initiatives around the world. This way you don't begin from scratch or make the same mistakes as others; you can stand on the shoulders of giants (the researchers who came before you) and build something even better. When teaching research, in addition to sharing sources and databases (*where* information can be found), it is helpful to teach research strategies (*how* to research) and to gain an overview of a domain before narrowing one's search (*what* is being researched). This will help developing writers make use of best practice research before speculating too much on one's own findings.

Research can be used by anyone who wants to have a better idea about what is out there, including things like knowing if you are getting a good deal on the car you want to buy or the bananas from one store to another (comparative shopping is research!) or figuring out whether your recycling practices are really making a dent in climate change. Research is used in all forms of business to identify the competition and to determine "norms" or "the average" rates of things from how much sleep people get to how often they ride bikes versus take public transportation.

Research is also extremely useful in building up credibility. Statements proclaimed as facts are just opinions unless they are supported by evidence. Nonfiction authors who write ideas without providing support from research evidence raise red flags in academia. Their counterparts in fiction who provide those extra details from research to embellish descriptions are rewarded by more believable prose. There is nothing more powerful than evidence to build credibility, which is why research skills help protect us from salespeople or politicians who are out to scam and make the difference between a possible description in the work of fiction to a probable context for storyline.

Perhaps most importantly, the better the researcher you become, the better discernment you have for judging situations, and therefore the better decisions you will make in life. The ability to research involves, above all things, critical thinking and executive functions (Li, S. et al., 2021), scientific problem solving (Tong et al., 2019), and integrative inquiry (Ludvik et al., 2016). To stick with the process, other researchers look into the role of grit and perseverance (Datu, 2021; Wang & Li, 2021), motivation (Morris et al., 2022), and even flow when done right (Tan, 2021). Researching involves sophisticated language processing and sequential learning (Christensen et al., 2012), as well as numerical semantic processing (Dunagan et al., 2022). In some research, body–object interaction (Hargreaves et al., 2012) is important, as is context information versus background information (van Moort et al., 2020). All research relies on logic and problem solving (Feng et al., 2021) as well as strong reading comprehension (Perkins & Jiang, 2019).

There are specific neural pathways related to scientific problem solving (Tong et al., 2021), logic problem solving (Feng et al., 2021), integrative inquiry (Ludvik et al., 2016), and expository text comprehension (Keller et al., 2024). These more technical aspects of the thinking involved in research are complemented with other neural pathways for grit and perseverance (Wang & Li, 2021), motivation (Ng, 2024), and if lucky, flow (Alameda et al., 2022).

Teachers can improve student research skills by doing the following.

Tools Often Used to Research	Tools With Even More Impact
✓ Explain how to evaluate resources.	✓ Practice or model evaluating sources.
✓ Have a conversation about your topic with a friend.	✓ Converse with friends, then broaden out by conversing with a well-regarded chatbot like ChatGPT, and then share your ideas with your friend again.
✓ Research online in Google.	✓ Identify keywords and research in Google Scholar or other respected database.
✓ Takes notes and compile information.	✓ Take notes and compile information, and then create digital files with annotations.

Activities From ThinkWrite for Researching

Worked Models to Learn About Genres

Objective: *To learn how to research writing models*

1. Identify the genre of your writing project.
2. Research examples of successful models in this genre. A successful model is the end product. Research tools include the Internet, your instructor, friends, or guidance from a librarian or other resources.
3. If using the Internet, type in "examples of" + "the name of the genre."
4. Look at a minimum of three different models from three different pages.
5. Select the best worked model you can find.
6. Justify why you chose this model.
7. Ask yourself what it will take for your work to look like the worked model.

What's happening in the brain: "Worked Models" are exemplary works that either can be provided by teachers or can be found through student research, which includes Internet tools, and then comparing and contrasting findings with their own writing. To do this, learners must know the name of the genre of writing they are being asked to complete, involving among other things, semantic memory to correctly use definitions through inferential competence involving the "bilateral posterior-parietal lobe and ventrotemporal cortex, including fusiform gyrus" (Garbarini et al., 2020, p. 1).

Step Inside

Objective: *To explore a different perspective in a fiction writing project*

1. Ask yourself what you think is the point of view of a particular person or object in the literature.
2. Be that person or object.

3. Think about what that person or object perceives.
4. Think about what that person or object knows.
5. Think about what that person or object cares about.
6. Identify as many perspectives (values, beliefs, likes, dislikes) as you can.
7. Ask yourself, what are some doubts or open-ended ideas you need to tighten up related to your knowledge?
8. Jot down any new ideas or questions that you want to research.

What's happening in the brain: "Step Inside" requires empathy to perceive distinct perspective taking, which includes intellectual empathy and leveraging social cognition to know what your reader knows and to address other audience presumptions about your topic. This involves "convergent activity within the ventrolateral and dorsomedial prefrontal cortex as well as temporal regions . . . emotion regulation and empathy were related to highly similar executive and internally oriented processes" (Morawetz et al., 2022, p. 1).

Confirmation Bias

Objective: *To reduce confirmation bias in your research*

Confirmation bias means we tend to migrate toward research that confirms what we already believe.

1. To reduce confirmation bias, when researching, use neutral words related to your topic. Avoid descriptions that show your bias ("how does X benefit Y?"), and use more neutral words ("how does X influence Y").
2. Make a list of those words.
3. Consciously choose to review sources you might disagree with.
4. Make a list of those sources that you will now include in your research to reduce confirmation bias.

What's happening in the brain: "Confirmation Bias" can be avoided by first being aware of biases, and second, to consciously mitigate our use by selecting neutral words during research, which includes awareness of heuristics and the brain's shortcuts due to lexical choice. Word choice changes perception and decision-making. Neutral words are less stimulating than emotional words (Sylvester et al., 2021), which is why we use them less. This involves "debias[ing] these word-level embeddings" (Liang et al., 2020, p. 1), including "semantic and syntactic components, [which] are encoded in the inferior frontal gyrus (IFG), superior temporal gyrus (STG), posterior superior temporal sulcus (pSTS), middle temporal gyrus (MTG), inferior temporal gyrus (IFG), precuneus (Pcun), cingulate gyrus (CG) and angular gyrus (AG)" (Zhang et al., 2022, p. 11727).

For more activities, see ThinkWriteMBE.com.

Maximizing a Student's Success in Researching

Ask, how will you know if you are successful? Share example success statements:

- □ I know I researched completely when I have considered (included) viewpoints I don't agree with.
- □ I am sure I have done complete research when I examine every source of information.
- □ I know I did good research when I interview lots of different people.
- □ I know my research is thorough when I can discern good information sources from fake ones.

Write your own success statement: "I am sure I have done complete research when I [insert a verb here]."

Encourage self-reflection:

- Do I know how to identify quality information?
- Do I acknowledge my own biases before beginning to research?

Celebrate progress by checking off "I can" statements:

- ✓ I can use a variety of sources (people and technology) to research.
- ✓ I can spot fake news.
- ✓ I can conduct unbiased research.

DRAFT

As the first public viewing of your thinking, drafting helps visualize ideas into words, making your internal mental process available to coaching and feedback.

To draft allows you to . . .

- □ Begin to see your thinking as others will view it.
- □ Have something concrete on which you can get feedback.
- □ Compare the genius of your insights with actual concrete words.
- □ Move from idea generation to idea perfection through rewriting.

Artwork by *Gabriel Espinosa Tokuhama for Tracey Tokuhama-Espinosa.*

When one drafts a paper, they put their ideas out for public view for the first time, which can be scary. The very first time we share our ideas with others we can be defensive, apologetic, and worried that what we meant to convey is not coming across well. This means that teachers can play a powerful role in reducing the potential anxiety around drafting. Classroom environments that have a high tolerance for errors composed of students and teachers who have been trained how to give good feedback to each other can go a long way in making drafting a fun and exciting process rather than one to dread.

Great writers normally write multiple drafts. This is an excellent opportunity to embed formative evaluation (e.g., Wiliam, 2011) into feedback that can later be used to further improve the manuscript. Unfortunately, many institutional deadlines give little time for multiple drafts, and often only timetable for one opportunity. This can be remediated through teacher planning or by student planning. For example, rather than have due dates for the outline, draft, and final paper, teachers can create multiple micro due dates in between that give the students the chance to learn and refine their work through multiple drafts. For example, in one of our courses we have a semester-long research paper. To nurture the drafting process, we have nine small assignments that lead up to four bigger submissions that culminate in a final paper (see a full example in Chapter 7). By piecing together each of the smaller elements, students begin a dialogue of feedback on their work that evolves over time. This also means that the teacher can nip problems in the bud by catching errors in research earlier on. Finally, this benefits the teacher who, granted has more assignments, but they are all short. This also ensures that once all the pieces are put together after having gone through multiple drafts, the final papers are of exceptionally high quality. Best of all, the students themselves go through the experience and benefit of writing multiple iterations of their work, helping them understand their own thinking process along the way. Students can also create multiple drafts, even if teachers don't require them. Many writers make the mistake of writing up until the last minute and then submitting the latest version of their drafts just as the clock runs out. This is a mistake. Because the brain needs time to process, consolidate, and retrieve memories, we know that students who let the ideas percolate for a day or two can often improve their work dramatically. This means that students need to allow enough time in their planning between writing and submitting to ensure their drafts are as good as possible.

While its primary purpose may be to transform the outline into sentences and paragraphs, drafting typically also involves the brain in different levels of thinking. One is not only assaying diction, sentences, and phrasing but reconsidering, proofreading, and discovering. Drafting makes considerable demands on our executive functions, and our ability to see our work in near-final form at last allows us to evaluate our plan and outline anew. The ability to draft and arrive at a facsimile of the final version of a text can deceive many developing writers. Seeing our thoughts formatted in something like the final form can cause us to disengage from further critical grappling with our thinking, believing that we are saving time with a single draft. Great writers, however, view their first draft as the starting place in the writing process, and novice writers benefit from explicitly identifying the thinking stages that underlie the writing process and using metacognitive reflection to build up their developing awareness of the diverse thinking strategies involved in writing (see example in Chapter 7).

Drafting involves numerous neural networks related to a range of skills (see Table 2.2). There is research that considers neural pathways for the technical aspects of writing, such as sentence-level processing (Grisoni et al., 2017), reading comprehension (Lee & Stoodley, 2023), and phonology-orthography-semantics (Graves et al., 2023). There is also research on how the brain accesses just the right word to express the right meaning through sub-lexical to lexico-semantic networks (Gauthier & Levy, 2023), and nonlexical and semantic processing (Junker et al., 2024), which involves planning (Junker & Grünbaum, 2024). Furthermore, drafting also incorporates homonyms and language ambiguity (Rodd, 2020), conceptual lexical representation (Lai et al., 2020), consistent and inconsistent orthography (Antalek, 2022), and anomia and lexical retrieval (Snyder et al., 2023). Most importantly, drafting generates idea generation (Mastria et al., 2021), abstract to concrete words (Villani et al., 2024), syncopating comprehension (Hilton, 2020), and serial order effect in divergent thinking (Bai et al., 2021).

Teachers can help students draft by doing the following.

Tools Often Used to Draft	Tools With Even More Impact
✓ Get feedback on your draft from your mother.	✓ Use a shared online document like a Google doc to share your draft with several people in your class.
✓ Write a draft.	✓ Make a storyboard and explain it to your peers.
✓ Read a model writing project for inspiration.	✓ Rewrite the model paper with your own information and fill in gaps.
✓ Brainstorm.	✓ Brainstorm with a story map and visuals.

Activities From ThinkWrite for Drafting

Freewriting

Objective: *To jump-start your draft, write not right!*

1. Focus on your topic.
2. Think about what you know about the topic from your own experience.
3. Think about what you know about your topic from your research.
4. Put a sticker in front of you that says, "Write not right" to keep you from hesitating.
5. For a set amount of time (5–15 minutes), write about your topic nonstop. Do not stop. If you are stuck and don't know what to write, you can write things like, "I don't know what to write . . ." or any other thoughts that come into your head.

6. Do not judge the content or quality.
7. When the time is up, read what you have written.
8. Mark the sections you like and the sections that need changing.
9. Rewrite the draft.

What's happening in the brain: "Freewriting" creates a format for disinhibition and for the free and natural connection of ideas, which includes a documented structure for implicitly and explicitly linked ideas. This involves multiple memory systems, including autobiographical, semantic, and emotional memory, as well as metacognition complemented by mindfulness practices. This involves "connectivity [which] decrease[s] in the visual-temporal and parietal regions, in relation to increased levels of DT [divergent thinking]. Link-level analyses showed higher local connectivity within visual regions was associated with lower DT, whereas projections from the precuneus to the right inferior occipital and temporal cortex were positively associated with DT" (Orwig et al., 2021, p. 499).

Mimic the Masters

Objective: *To consciously make your written voice consistent with genre expectations*

1. Pick a passage from a known writer in the genre.
2. Read this person's writing aloud.
3. Consider the stylistic choices that define or are unique to the genre.
4. Read a passage from your own draft aloud.
5. Compare your own work and the other person's work side by side.
6. Make a checklist of how they are similar and different in terms of voice.
7. Draft or revise your own work in comparison with the checklist.

What's happening in the brain: "Mimic the Masters" involves listening to experts' voices and replicating them, which includes auditory memory, in which, among other things, shadow reading (De Guerrero et al., 2013) helps learners gain intellectual empathy and pattern recognition, and the ability to compare and contrast one's work with others (Ahern, 2013). This involves the strengthening of working memory's phonological loop and implicates the "subcortical structures, particularly the *basal ganglia (caudate)*, and of widespread right hemispheric regions" (Deldar et al., 2021).

Cover Up

Objective: *To create a visual representation of your writing project*

1. Design a cover page. Consider using illustrations, photos or word clouds. Include purposeful use of lines, textures, color, space, shapes, forms, and patterns. Also choose an appropriate lettering style (typeface, font). Remember to think of framing,

balance, and saliency. Consciously decide how to integrate symbols, patterns, order, categories, and relationships.
2. Pretend you are talking to your audience and explain the inspiration for your cover. Revise as necessary.

What's happening in the brain: "Cover Up" involves metaphorical thinking and a shift from mental to verbal to visual thinking, which includes how an individual's personal semantic memory (Tanguay et al., 2023), combines with attentional saliency, and semantic symbol-to-visual connections, and some hypothesize a call on synesthetic (cross-sensory modality) development to achieve the visualization of written information. This involves mental representations of multimodal information and includes "increased engagement of cerebellum, thalamus, left parietal cortex, right superior frontal, left prefrontal and paracingulate/cingulate regions, such that activation in the cingulate and left prefrontal cortices negatively influenced task performance. Further, using parametric fMRI analysis, increasing subjective difficulty ratings for drawing the word engaged higher activations in the left pre-frontal cortices, whereas higher expert-rated creative content in the drawings was associated with increased engagement of bilateral cerebellum" (Hong et al., 2015, p. 1).

For more activities, see ThinkWriteMBE.com.

Maximizing a Student's Success in Drafting

Ask, how will you know if you are successful? Share example success statements:

- □ In my first draft, I always run through the big ideas before adding details to ensure I have given space to the most important ideas.
- □ I am successful in drafting if I have experimented with the order of my thoughts.
- □ I know I have a good draft if it approaches the worked model shown in class.

Write your own success statement: "I know I have a good draft if I [insert a verb here]."

Encourage self-reflection:

- Do I always plan for one or more drafts in writing assignments?
- Do I flexibly modify my outline when the draft seems like it's missing something?
- Do I treat each draft as if it were a final paper (spell-checked; review instructions)?

Celebrate progress by checking off "I can" statements:

- ✓ I can get my ideas out into words in draft form.
- ✓ I can use the outline and template to write a strong first draft.
- ✓ I can balance the content to get the right effect.

The bookends of prewriting and revision frame the savory center to the writing process, and each of these stages has a special role in developing thinking. The writing process itself is particularly important in terms of thinking of others: *How do others think about my thinking, how does putting my written words out into the world feel, how much self-efficacy have I developed in this process?* As the first public viewing of our work, writing plays a vital role in shaping our projects. Some have suggested that without a solid base, we would be stymied in reaching our final writing goals because it is on this base that we can then revise. Indeed, some have gone so far as to say all writing is really revision (or revision *is* writing), which we turn to next.

CHAPTER 5

The Holons of Revision

ThinkWrite: The Holons of Revision

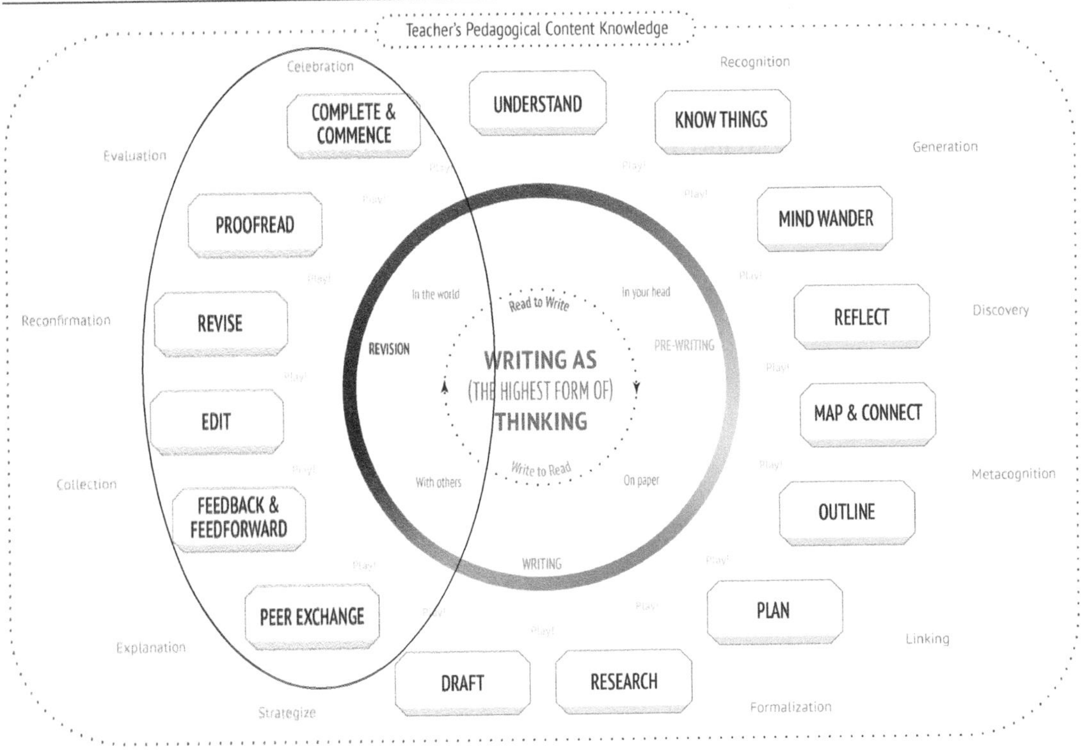

After drafting, we enter what is traditionally called the revision phase of writing. In closer detail, here students may be lucky enough to have a ***peer exchange*** to test their skills in perspective taking, to check if their view of the topic or subject is shared by other people, and to have another perspective to learn from. The bouncing off of ideas helps to clarify the writer's thinking. Other times the process of giving someone else feedback results in examples and ideas a writer can apply as they edit their own work. Both sides of peer review help develop the writer's sense of an audience and of the reader's needs for the next draft and the next writing task beyond that. Getting students to engage meaningfully with feedback, to see patterns in it and to learn from it for future work, can be a challenge in a grade-oriented school culture. We like thinking of feedback more as **feed*forward*** in which students learn to habituate a growth mindset around what they will improve in the future. The social aspects of feedback necessitate the development of social skills from both partners, and the emotional context helps the brain remember to anticipate and attend to the reader's needs in the next draft and in the next writing task.

The revision phase of writing includes editing. ***Editing*** requires students to unify the many choices they make about how their ideas are presented, evaluate the various responses of their test readers and strategize to reach clarity of organization and precision in the mechanics of language used to communicate to their audience. This is different from when a writer needs to ***revise*** or "see once again" whether what they wrote meets their goals once they have edited the work. The thinking stage of revision involves stepping back to see the new whole of one's work and often leads to refining ideas or considering new or different ways to meet the original objectives (or assignment goals). In the revision stage, the learner may need to ***proofread*** their work to find errors like careless misspellings as a courtesy to their readers and as a means of establishing the credibility of the written work. In this stage, it helps when students know how to identify and correct errors, and what tools or modalities help this process. In these steps, the writer's work becomes public in a new way, and the theoretical reader of the outlining and drafting phase takes flesh. Consequently, the social and emotional demands of this stage bring other parts of the writer's brain into play.

Ultimately, there are the steps involved to ***complete*** the work—submitting, publishing, sharing the "finished" product—but even this is a provisional stage, as one may look at the work as a whole and ask of it and oneself, "what's next?" When we carry forth what we have learned from one writing project to the next or imagine ways in which our writing can be differently structured in a new genre, we ***commence*** the next round of thinking and writing. Writers benefit from the emotional engagement of authentic assessment (Leong, 2022), which can lead them to metacognitively assess the relationship of one assignment to the next or to imagine how they might recast what they have produced in a new genre. Extending the life of a writing project in this way increases the likelihood of the skills and content "sticking" in memory, enhances awareness of the role of the unique rhetorical appeal of different genres, and of how genres reveal different aspects of content. This iterative process continues to engage the writer emotionally with the material, further deepening encoding and strengthening recall.

Outcomes of ThinkWrite Stages

- **Peer Exchange:** Writers will gain better insight into themselves and their writing by knowing others' perspectives.

- **Feedback and Feedforward:** Writers will know how to improve their work as well as listen to and manage feelings about assessment.
- **Edit:** Writers unify decisions about word choice, audience, syntax, and intonation, along with understanding the order of ideas.
- **Revise:** Writers revisit their goals, reconsider the order of and type of information being presented, and refine their ideas (or generate new ones).
- **Proofread:** Writers use different modalities and tools to check their work for errors and to make their product clear to understand for their readers.
- **Complete and Commence:** Writers celebrate completion of their product, consider what they've now learned, and turn their work into the beginning of a new idea.

We begin the discussion about the continual improvement of writing with peer exchange.

PEER EXCHANGE

Good peer exchange gives you the opportunity to improve writing by hearing how others perceive it and enhances intellectual humility as the writer learns from others in age-appropriate language.

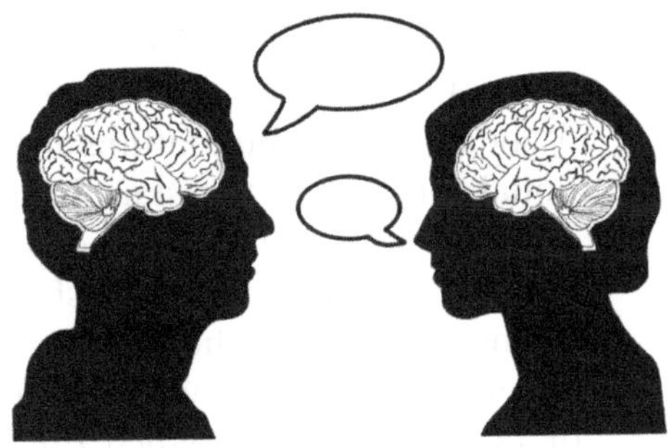

A peer exchange allows you to . . .

- ☐ Gain new perspectives on your work.
- ☐ Hear how someone other than yourself understands what you have written.
- ☐ Gain new approaches to your paper.
- ☐ Understand the need to communicate to a specific audience.

Artwork by Gabriel Espinosa Tokuhama for Tracey Tokuhama-Espinosa.

When we ask students to talk to each other about their written work, it may seem like an uncomplicated request. However, the truth of the matter is that this can be one of the most highly emotional asks we can make in a school setting; inviting students to critique each other's work can cause even the strongest people to feel vulnerable. One way teachers can assist is by delineating the boundaries of the conversation, and when important, matching students. Boundaries around the peer exchange means delineating a clear focus in the conversation and an expected product outcome. For example, a teacher can tell students they need to read another student's work quietly and then reflect and share three sentences with their partner: "I see . . . , I think . . . , I wonder. . . ." As each pair of students needs to bring back the same formatted statements, it is easy to keep the group focused and the outcomes measurable. This also helps set ground rules for what is and is not acceptable sidebar conversation.

Matching students means the teacher selects who gives peer feedback to whom. While the free choice of partners to give feedback can be helpful in some contexts, peers who already know and like each other will often avoid critiquing work in a serious way. Students may openly say they feel bad critiquing a classmate's work; in such moments it is worth explaining the role of a "critical friend" in the writing process, one whose ability to act as a devil's advocate or to find mistakes in our work is ultimately serving the purpose of our greater success. Teachers can sweeten the pot by telling students that anything corrected by their peer review will not be counted against them. Sometimes, rather than risk their feelings over a comma splice or unclear passage, friends may be tempted to tell one another that everything about their writing is great; remind them that that critical friends won't let us get away with such errors. Outside of classroom structures, people can also benefit from nonschool peers, like pen pals, parents, or even writing to experts in their genre. Often, feedback from someone who knows the genre of writing is even more important than feedback from a social peer.

An important aspect of feedback is that both giver and receiver are changed by the process. Learning to give feedback requires perspective taking and intellectual empathy for others, and it reminds us of our own vulnerabilities as writers. Sometimes harsh observations can be softened by the right choice of words, and in the opposite case, sometimes relatively unimportant criticisms can be perceived as doomsday warnings, depending on the framing. It is easier said than done, but emerging writers often need to develop thicker skin, or distance from their work, in order to fully benefit from peer exchange.

A look into brain research shows us the complex neural underpinnings of peer exchange (Table 2.2). This involves narrative production (AbdulSabur et al., 2014), learning from the mistakes of others (De Visser et al., 2018), and affective and cognitive mentalizing (Arioli et al., 2021). Peer exchange also depends on neural circuits for social or group feedback (Rapp et al., 2021). Research on peer feedback illustrates developmental patterns of social feedback acceptance (Dobbelaar et al., 2022, 2023). Done well, good peer feedback can encourage prosocial behavior for friend and foe (Schreuders et al., 2018). Furthermore, students need to employ recursive thinking during interpersonal interaction (Zhen & Yu, 2021) and take into consideration social performance expectancy (Valle et al., 2015; Wilhelm et al., 2019). There is also substantial research showing that a student's desire for conformity (Minich et al., 2023) or fear of negative evaluation (Li et al., 2022) in the context of social or group feedback can lead to anticipation and social anxiety (Topel et al., 2021). Additionally, some studies show that all students seek social acceptance and may be working through different developmental patterns of social feedback acceptance (Weinberg et al., 2021), meaning there is a need to continually fine-tune adaptive calibration to social feedback on the part of the learner (Rudolph et al., 2021). Furthermore, there is also research that shows that persistent negative feedback can result in aggression (van de Groep et al., 2022). Taking time to openly address our expectations and the social-emotional context of such exchanges can help students regulate and negotiate these emotions profitably. "Networks in the brain that process social cognition as well as sensory perception for facial expressions and voice intonation influence the ability to conduct good peer exchange (Beaudoin & Beauchamp, 2020). Finally, some teachers find that peer exchanges are improved when the class develops a rubric together before sharing ideas.

Teachers facilitate peer exchange by doing the following.

Tools Often Used to Conduct Peer Exchange	Tools With Even More Impact
✓ Students swap essays and discuss.	✓ Students swap essays and have discussion on "I see . . . I think . . . I wonder . . ." comments.
✓ Peer presentations	✓ Peer discussions around a focal point
✓ Pair for discussion	✓ Before grouping, remind students to have a two-way conversation, be empathetic, offer constructive feedback.
✓ Pair for discussion	✓ Before looking at each other's work, share what each finds hard about the writing project and what they like about the it.

Activities From ThinkWrite for Peer Exchange

I See-Think-Wonder

Objective: *To focus peer review on a few concrete suggestions*

1. Find a partner and exchange drafts.
2. Look over your partner's writing project. Think about what the writing says.
3. Record three sentences: "I see . . . ; I think . . . ; I wonder. . . ." Be as precise as possible.
4. Exchange ideas with your partner.
5. Decide what to do with the information you now have about what your peers think of your writing.

What's happening in the brain: "I See-Think-Wonder" involves observation, reflection, and projection conducted in an intellectually empathetic way, which includes comparing and contrasting one's own work to peers' work for peer learning and to the instructions for the assignment; careful word choice; keeping an eye on other's feelings; and prediction and projection of areas for improvement. This involves, among other things, "the mesolimbic dopaminergic pathway during social interaction" and implicates a process by which "the production of dopamine reinforces the desire to continue the interaction, and heightens feelings of anticipation for future peer-learning activities . . . cooperative learning and problem-solving interactions [which] can bring about the 'intrinsic' motivation to learn" (Clark & Dumas, 2015, p. 1).

The One-Minute Talk

Objective: *To improve your writing by getting feedback on a synthesis of your topic from a peer*

1. Compose a 1-minute talk that synthesizes your topic.
2. Find a partner.
3. Share your 1-minute talk with your partner.
4. Have your partner finish the sentences "I see . . ."; "I think . . ."; "I wonder. . . ."
5. Use your partner's responses to identify ways to develop your topic further.
6. Make a list of the ideas you will pursue.

What's happening in the brain: "The 1-Minute Talk" involves the synthesis of ideas in concise and precise wording based on knowledge of what the audience already knows and needs to know, which includes conceptual synthesis, semantic retrieval and meaning-making, and emotion-attention interactions (Dolcos et al., 2020), including spontaneous theory of mind (Boccadoro et al., 2019). This involves discourse between individuals ("language in the wild") that depends on word frequency, surprisal and entropy, semantic features, embodiment, combinatorial and compositional processing that jointly employ the anterior temporal lobe, angular gyrus, precuneus, and posterior cingulate related to semantics and discourse (Riccardi & Desari, 2022).

Diamond in the Rough

Objective: *To frame peer exchange around strengths*

1. Find a partner.
2. Have your partner read their writing aloud to you.
3. As your partner reads, take notes on the best ideas and/or strongest elements that you hear.
4. After your partner finishes reading aloud, think about the potential of the writing.
5. Tell your partner what you think are the strongest elements of their writing and its potential.
6. Discuss how these strengths can be extended to the rest of the paper.
7. Document the discussion. Change roles.

What's happening in the brain: "Diamond in the Rough" involves sentence comprehension, the ability to discern meaning, and the imagination to reenvision something, which includes summative skills and anticipatory feelings related to prediction (Stefanova et al., 2020) mediated by "context-induced semantic predictions" (Grisoni et al., 2017). This involves among other things, "future-oriented cognition [which] is mediated by two distinct networks: the Default Network and the Salience Network. The Default Network is mainly active in supporting future thinking, whereas the Salience Network is primarily involved in prospective memory and delay discounting" (Cona et al., 2023, para. 1).

For more activities, see ThinkWriteMBE.com.

Maximizing a Student's Success in Peer Exchange

Ask, how will you know if you are successful? Share example success statements:

- □ I know I gave good feedback when my partner feels supported.
- □ I know I have a good peer exchange about my writing if I can give reasons for my comments.
- □ I know we have a good peer exchange if we understand each other.
- □ I know we have a good peer exchange when we can have conflicting ideas and still learn from them.
- □ I know we have a good peer exchange when I learn something new about the impact of my writing on another.

Write your own success statement: "I realize I have had a good peer exchange when I [insert a verb here]."

Encourage self-reflection:

- What is hardest thing about getting peer feedback?
- How do others' ideas about my writing make me feel?
- How could I learn to enjoy peer feedback more?
- What can a peer exchange bring to me that teacher feedback does not?

Celebrate progress by checking off "I can" statements:

- ✓ I can be intellectually humble.
- ✓ I can be open to new ideas.
- ✓ I can learn from others' perspectives.
- ✓ I can use ideas from others to feed*forward.*
- ✓ I can use peer exchanges as a lesson in writing.
- ✓ I can be aware of and regulate my emotions during peer feedback to both give and take in necessary information.

FEEDBACK AND FEEDFORWARD

People who are open to learning from their mistakes learn faster.

To feedback and feedforward allows you to . . .

- □ Learn to ask yourself what you will do better in the future.
- □ Gain perspective on how to improve.
- □ Prioritize revisions.
- □ Realize when your writing is strong and effective or weak, and how to fix the weaker parts of the work.
- □ Move beyond viewing feedback as a list of corrections to be done to improve a grade at a superficial level and towards deeper thinking about the writing process itself.

Artwork by Gabriel Espinosa Tokuhama for Tracey Tokuhama-Espinosa.

Learning means figuring out what you don't yet know and then learning it; this is expedited by quality feedback (Darling-Hammond, 2015). Feedback can come from one's personal reflection, but most feedback comes from people outside of the individual and takes place in school settings, which means the teacher is usually involved. Teacher feedback is also one of the most important elements impacting student motivation in a classroom (Gentrup et al., 2020). While most teachers understand feedback's crucial role in nurturing student learning, it is one of the most time-consuming elements of teaching (Gray, 2021). Preparing to teach, teaching, and evaluating student work do not take equal amounts of time. In our personal assessments of the literature, we have found that most teachers agree that they do not spend time equally between these three aspects of teaching (1:1:1) but more like 3:1:3. That is, for 1 hour in front of students, teachers spend 3 hours preparing and 3 hours evaluating. As one of the most time-consuming aspects of teaching, the feedback process should be optimized by remembering a few key ideas.

First, while teachers often think that the feedback they give is limited to the explicit moments they offer it, students take just about everything a teacher does as feedback, from the way the teacher says good morning to them to how they looked at them when asking a question. This means that every interaction we have with students can shape the way they think of themselves, including how they think we think about their writing skills. Teachers should be aware that neuroscientific studies show that how a person perceives the feedback often carries a different message from what is said. For example, a teacher's tone of voice and facial expression may convey one message (anger, contempt), while the words may carry another (kindness, happiness). Hearing "You are doing just FINE!" from a face brimming with disdain and in a harsh voice tells the student they are anything but fine. This means *how* something is said and the emotional weight it carries are more influential on a student than the actual words used during feedback. Sarcasm is best avoided, even when intended playfully, as it can be confusing to students who are still developing their social and emotional skill set and who are self-conscious and unsure of their standing with the teacher.

Second, getting feedback from a teacher is different from peer exchange. Whereas social contagion reins in peer exchange, feedback from the teachers primarily involves networks related to self-regulation (Gan et al., 2021), long-term emotional memory (Schwab et al., 2022), and self-awareness (Mograbi et al., 2024). Research on the neural correlates of feedback involve inference (Basnálova et al., 2014), improved prediction errors (Apps et al., 2015), and the way the brain pays more attention to feedback novelty (Ernst & Steinhauser, 2020). If perfected, great feedback looks like errorless learning (Bertens & Brazil, 2018) in which feedback loops are so rehearsed that mistakes are not perceived as negative and therefore learning advances more quickly. Feed*forward* works similarly to feedback with a future-focused framing.

Third, feedback is typically used to structure formative evaluation and entails one person—usually the teacher—giving another person—usually a student—a critique of their work. The power relationship between student and teacher brings with it stress, mainly on the part of the student, though teachers can experience negative emotions as well (Yu et al., 2021). Students unaccustomed to receiving a lot of feedback may become stressed when it is given in large quantities, even if it is positive and full of praise! (There is a composition professor at one of our institutions who prefaces the return of papers by saying, "Words are love!" to lower their angst at seeing so many comments on their papers.) Teachers can reduce student stress by telling them they hope to have a dialogue around the feedback, suggesting that teacher comments are not the final word but rather the start of a conversation. Feedback has been studied under different conditions, including team flow (Shehata et al., 2021), hyperscanning (Czeszumski et al., 2020), and interbrain coupling (Chen et al., 2023). Feedback recruits networks for shared auditory attention (Stuldreher et al., 2020) and interpersonal communication (Wilcox et al., 2020). (Bertens & Brazil, 2018).

Good feedback is timely, precise, and either encourages the student (positively motivates) and/or includes action items for improvement. The use of elaborate (descriptive) rubrics facilitates feedback, but it does not replace the individualized messages that summarize areas for improvement. That is, the use of a rubric should not replace the personalized message that will bring students closer to understanding how they need to begin to improve their work (Dirkx et al., 2021).

A key idea is that the best feedback is often framed in a question form because it leads to stronger metacognitive development. Rather than tell students what they need to do, why not ask them what they could do better to improve? These questions become the student's own inner dialogue as they deal with subsequent writing challenges. This means that offering questions about the student's thinking behind the writing throughout the paper can often deliver more guidance than a rubric. For example:

school communication, trust, and understanding. Parent engagement with the school and school communication with the parent is widely considered to be beneficial for the students. If the parents and school (encompassing teachers,

> "This is a great idea! Would it help narrow in on the focus better to begin your paragraph with this statement?

Getting students to engage with feedback with their higher cognitive processes is a persistent challenge; questions are one means of engaging them to do so. Activities that cause them to pause, consider options, or reflect and find patterns can also be helpful in this regard. There is a proverb that if you give a man a fish, he eats for the day, but if you teach a man to fish, he eats for a lifetime. Telling students what they need to do is different from guiding them on how to think about their writing. While formulating questions initially takes more time on the teacher's part until they get used to this, the payoffs are almost immediate. Students approach the revision of their work less like a checklist for improvements or corrections (with minimal thinking and engagement) than as a process of improving their own thinking. Helping students think about their choices in writing and how the reader perceives them can force a level of reflection on the part of the writer that leads to changes in the next writing assignments. That is, feedback in the form of questions about thinking results in a faster learning curve than just listing the needed changes and has greater long-term effects on learning.

Teachers can help students use feedback by doing the following.

Tools Often Used to Give Feedback	Tools With Even More Impact
✓ Tell students to use the rubric.	✓ Develop the rubric with the students and then create a checklist of questions based on the rubric criteria and instructions.
✓ "Sandwich feedback" with good, bad, good comments.	✓ First get students to self-assess and then add teacher's observations.
✓ Do a line-by-line correction of conceptual thinking.	✓ Do line-by-line correction of conceptual thinking, AND give feedback in question form.
✓ Give feedback.	✓ Embed feedback in instruction.

Tools Often Used to Give Feedback	Tools With Even More Impact
✓ Critique the work.	✓ Focus on the learning intentions and success criteria.
✓ Tell students what to fix.	✓ Help student identify what can't be done YET, and suggest next steps in thinking stages or activities.
✓ Tell students what to fix.	✓ Ask Socratic questions to help the student identify their own areas of improvement.

Activities From ThinkWrite for Feedback and Feedforward

Quantity vs. Quality

Objective: *To develop criteria about when quality is more important and when quantity is more important*

1. Feedback can come from different people, such as from friends, family, teachers, former teachers, colleagues, your boss, social networks, your community groups, or thought leaders on the topic. Feedback can come from experts and nonexperts alike as well as people you know well or don't know well. Feedback can be in person or virtual.
2. Determine the agenda of where the feedback is coming from. Rank the authority of your sources for your writing project.
3. Think about the difference between *quantity* of feedback, whether positive or negative, and the *quality* of feedback, based on the critic's expertise, whether positive or negative.
4. Decide which is more important to your writing project and why. Explain.
5. Think about how you can get more quality feedback on your writing assignments.
6. Take steps to secure this.

What's happening in the brain: "Quantity vs. Quality" involves perspective-taking and an evaluation of sources of feedback, which includes mentalizing about others' motives as well as theory of mind and values assessment (Knupsky & Caballero, 2020), followed by a decision of which feedback is best. This involves the neural correlates of doubt in decision-making in which conflicting variables make a clear choice difficult, manifested in the fact that "high doubt exhibited increased activation in the bilateral inferior parietal lobule (IPL)" during decision-making (Naaz et al., 2021). Interestingly, "honesty-based trustworthiness mediates choice about who to work with in the future and is represented in the posterior cingulate cortex, dorsolateral prefrontal cortex and intraparietal sulcus" (Bellucci et al., 2019, p.1).

Accentuate the Positive

Objective: *To understand what would happen if you only received positive feedback*

1. Find a partner.
2. Ask your partner to find those areas of your work that merit positive feedback.
3. Note the qualities of your work that were praised by the reader.
4. Notice how you feel when your writing is praised.
5. Direct your attention to the areas of your work that didn't receive positive feedback.
6. Describe how you might alter these other areas of your work to match the writing in the areas that did not get good feedback.
7. List these differences on a piece of paper and keep them in mind as you revise.

What's happening in the brain: "Accentuate the Positive" means using the qualities of good work as a model or goal that guides editing, which includes the ability to compare and contrast as well as assess the importance of others' perspectives based on the positive emotions that are experienced. This involves among other things, upregulating positive emotions (Grosse et al., 2019), which individuals can self-regulate to enhance positive emotions based on activation of "emotion-related brain regions including insula, amygdala, anterior cingulate cortex, and dorsomedial prefrontal cortex" (Li et al., 2016, p.3575).

Reframing

Objective: *To intentionally reframe your perspective when you feel negative about the feedback you have received*

1. After you receive feedback, decide if it has merit for your work.
2. Describe how you feel.
3. Take any negative thoughts and feelings, and intentionally replace them with positive ones by asking yourself: Is there another way I could think about this feedback? What could I possibly learn from this feedback? How can my writing project be improved thanks to the feedback?
4. Record your responses.
5. Describe what you are feeling and thinking now.
6. Write a thank-you note to the feedback provider indicating what you learned from their feedback.

What's happening in the brain: "Reframing" places a situation in a new light based on a change in perspective, which includes what positive psychology calls "reframing" or "reappraisal" of a situation (Goldin et al., 2019). This involves an important network in the brain including, among other things, "the amygdala, the presupplementary motor area (preSMA), the ventrolateral prefrontal cortex (vlPFC), dorsolateral prefrontal cortex (dlPFC), and ventromedial prefrontal cortex (vmPFC)" (Steward et al., 2021, p. 961).

For more activities, see ThinkWriteMBE.com.

Maximizing a Student's Success in Feedback and Feedforward

Ask, how will you know if you are successful? Share example success statements:

- □ I know how to feedforward when I think of the evaluator as my critical friend who is out to help me.
- □ I know how to use feedback to feedforward to inspire myself to work harder.
- □ I know I understand how to feedforward when I get advice use it to and feel motivated.
- □ I know how to feedforward and feel spurred into action.

Write your own success statement: "I realize I have been successful at using feedback to feedforward when I [insert a verb here]."

Encourage self-reflection:

- Am I open to feedback?
- In what format do I most appreciate feedback (written, face-to-face, direct, question form, etc.)?
- Who am I most open to receiving feedback from about my work (a parent? a teacher? a peer?)?

Celebrate progress by checking off "I can" statements:

- ✓ I can use feedback to learn about the strengths and weaknesses of my writing.
- ✓ I can be open to feedback.
- ✓ I can use feedback to improve.
- ✓ I can understand rubrics as well as written feedback.

EDIT

Perfect the formatting, visual structure, and presentation of your written work.

To edit allows you to . . .

- ☐ Refine the technical aspect of your writing.
- ☐ Critically evaluate patterns in the feedback received and strategize for a next draft.
- ☐ Improve the structure and organization of ideas.
- ☐ Become more detail oriented.
- ☐ Look at the parts and wholes of a written assignment (holistic thinking).

Artwork by Gabriel Espinosa Tokuhama for Tracey Tokuhama-Espinosa. All rights reserved.

Editing requires a great deal of thinking mainly because it demands the ability to get into both the reader's and writer's heads and marry needs. What is the message trying to be communicated? Who will receive the message (audience)? Is this expressed as clearly and eloquently as possible? As one edits, one is "drafting again" and creating a new version of their work. To edit written work means to adjust the form and/or content of the work. Editing can be used to shorten or lengthen sections to arrive at the current balance of ideas. Editing can also mean fine-tuning for the appropriate voice and its consistency in the work. Some people self-edit by rereading their work out loud, while others rely on the feedback they have received from others to hone in on typical errors or specific punctuation troubles (and others do both!). Some find editing the definitive task in the process of writing as it means putting the meat on the bones of a draft. Editing is such an important part of writing that there exists the profession of "editor." Editors are people who help writers sharpen their focus and affirm the writing content matches promised goals. "Copy editors" review the more technical aspects of the paper and confirm that the formatting and grammatical conventions are adhered to. Some people who believe "editing is writing" often keep their multiple iterations of the work to remind themselves of the needed corrections and to preserve any key material that might be cut during a first edit but deemed important for a later time, place, or project.

Sometimes editing is simply a hack job when the writing is too long and is completed by prioritizing what should be kept and what should be dropped. Other times editing requires imagination to determine what is missing to trigger the desired emotions. And at yet other moments, editing steps back to look at the whole of the written work to see how each comma and word fits into the larger sentence, which fits into the paragraph, which fits into the story. Such an assessment can mean changes at any and all levels of punctuation, words, sentences, and whole paragraphs.

Sometimes editing involves our ability to look at our work's impact from an outsider's perspective. Other times we can give ourselves enough distance from our writing to allow time to trigger a "strategic forgetting," through which we can more easily separate in our mind what we meant to say from what we wrote and to correct our course. Sometimes having our work read to us by another can help enhance this distancing effect.

To successfully edit a writing project requires numerous neural pathways, many of which relate to a strong detail-oriented ability, especially for semantic and syntactic error detection (see Table 2.2). When editing, a person needs to use their visual acuity for fine text (Arnold et al., 2023) to measure lexical stress and rhythmical well-formedness (Kandylaki et al., 2017), as well as comprehend semantics and syntactics (Schneider & Maguire, 2019), and syntactic-semantic competition (Strotseva-Feinschmidt et al., 2019). Reading ability (Wang et al., 2019) and techniques such as reading aloud (Timmer & Schiller, 2014) are shown to increase strategic reading comprehension and editing. Error detection (Di Greggorio et al., 2022; Moss et al., 2011) in complex tasks (Porth et al., 2022) through attention to detail is improved with mindfulness and emotional stability (Eichle & Stahl, 2017). Additionally, confidence to correct errors varies based on the amount of practice they have had in the past (Rausch et al., 2020). Editing requires a great deal of sustained attention and depends on extended working-memory abilities (Olive, 2021).

Teachers help students edit by doing the following.

Tools Often Used to Edit	Tools With Even More Impact
✓ Do a line-by-line grammar correction.	✓ Use digital tools to catch grammatical mistakes.
✓ Use the feedback received from teachers and peers.	✓ Assess the feedback that's been received and then prioritize points for change.
✓ Use style guides.	✓ Use digital style guides to highlight technical errors with explanations.
✓ Use the rubric to confirm expectations.	✓ Use a student-generated rubric and feedback to create a checklist of stylistic components.
✓ Do a read-through out loud.	✓ Do a read-through for bigger ideas and then a careful review, line by line.
✓ Create the assignment in one sitting.	✓ Correct for each element separately (e.g., first, followed instructions; second, content; third, form).

Activities From ThinkWrite for Editing

Compare Documents

Objective: *To see how your writing has evolved and improved between drafts of your work*
This activity requires you have two Microsoft Word files of your work, one an early draft, and the other the current version.

1. Click the Review tab on the ribbon.
2. Look for the "Compare" button and click on it.
3. Choose the two documents for comparison.
4. Review each of the changes, which will include all the additions, deletions, and formatting modifications since the last version.
5. If you are happy with the changes, congratulations! If not, modify the current version as needed.

What's happening in the brain: "Compare Documents" involves the technical ability to generate a document with tracked changes that compares past and current versions that can be assessed, which includes reviewing changes and evaluating the choices made in the past for future work, forcing a "revision decision" (Anderson & Dean, 2023). This involves, among other things, neural networks for decision-making based on a writer's justification for the changes (Mutta & Johansson, 2018), including those related to word selection in which "results demonstrate how subtle differences [in words] can be accumulated and amplified along the cortical hierarchy" (Yeshurun et al., 2017, p. 9475).

Correct Punctuation

Objective: *To become more sensitive to finding your own punctuation errors*

1. Think about feedback you have received in the past.
2. Make a list of punctuation errors that commonly occur in your writing (e.g., do you typically overuse commas?).
3. Choose a page from your current writing project.
4. Highlight the punctuation marks about which you are unsure.
5. Run your page through a grammar checker.
6. Compare your list of punctuation errors with those identified by the grammar checker.
7. If your list of punctuation errors coincides with the grammar checker, congratulations! This means you are improving your sensitivity to punctuation errors. If not, note the errors you missed, and make necessary corrections.
8. Adjust your list of punctuation problems. Make a new list of common errors you want to remember in the future.

What's happening in the brain: "Correct Punctuation" involves syntactic accuracy and symbol understanding as well as the role of punctuation in writing, which includes distinction between letter and nonletter symbols in writing, which are distinct in the brains of literate and illiterate people (Dehaene et al., 2015). This involves, among other things, the "integration of cognitive and motor skills, specifically language functions, executive functions, and graphomotor output" (O'Donnell & Colvin, 2019, p. 59), and the brain's ability to distinguish yet combine letter and nonletter symbols in written language and that shows different "responses to written characters [which] are increased in the left occipito-temporal sulcus" in literate populations (Dehaene et al., 2015, p. 234).

Audience and Vocabulary

Objective: *To use appropriate vocabulary for your audience*

1. Read your draft. Remind yourself of your primary audience for this written work by thinking of one real person who embodies the audience.
2. Circle key words in your writing.
3. Would your audience use the same words? Is this typical/correct vocabulary for your audience?
4. Review other writing examples (blogs, Internet recommendations, publications) meant for this audience. Are you using the same vocabulary?
5. If yes, congratulations! If no, make a list of the vocabulary you want to integrate into your draft. Integrate additional core vocabulary into your draft where appropriate.
6. Rewrite sentences in your draft using the new words.

What's happening in the brain: "Audience and Vocabulary" involves an awareness of your audience that changes how you communicate. This includes intellectual empathy about language levels and preferences, as well as the neurolinguistics of discourse (Zacks et al., 2018). This involves predictive processing, segmentation, embodied language effect, and theory of mind. Predictive processing involves a range of brain regions in a complex network (Ficco et al., 2021): "These mechanisms have been identified in a large set of brain areas, including the primary sensory and motor cortices, motor association cortices, dorsal and ventral prefrontal cortices, parietal cortex, anterior cingulate cortex, insula, hippocampus, amygdala, basal ganglia, thalamus, hypothalamus, cerebellum and the superior colliculus," (Ficco et al., 2021, para.3).

For more activities, see ThinkWriteMBE.com.

Maximizing a Student's Success in Editing

Ask, how will you know if you are successful? Share example success statements:

- □ I know I did a good job editing when I can harmonize the voices of the different sections of my work.
- □ I know I did a good job editing when I spell-check the paper before submitting it.
- □ I know I did a good job editing when each sentence is as crisp as possible.
- □ I know I did a good job editing when I can trim down unnecessary words.

Write your own success statement: "I know I did a good job editing when I [insert a verb here]."

Encourage self-reflection:

- Have I reflected on the quality of feedback I have received and chosen what to prioritize in my editorial changes?
- Have I decided whether to fix problems from a content level or a form level first, or will I go line by line and do this simultaneously?
- Do I use all the tools available to correctly edit my paper (spellchecker, grammar check, templates)?

Celebrate progress by checking off "I can" statements:

- ✓ I can pay attention to details (catch spelling errors, grammar and punctuation problems).
- ✓ I can identify macro editing concerns like organizational problems.
- ✓ I can ensure my primary audience will like the voice and style I used.
- ✓ I can prioritize corrections and address them efficiently.
- ✓ I can clearly understand the reasoning behind my edits and explain them.
- ✓ I can take the time to read my work out loud to edit it accordingly.

REVISE

Revision is the opportunity "see again" and make any final changes for improvement.

To revise allows you to . . .

- □ Step back and view the written product as a whole (holonic thinking).
- □ Narrow in and view the micro image of the paper as a whole (holonic thinking).
- □ Be sure your project responded to all its goals as expressed in the instructions and the rubric.
- □ Reassess choices about examples, placement, words, and organization.

The revision stage of writing means rereading the work once the edits have been made and assessing any further changes needed to perfect the work. Editing is not enough; editing changes the final product, so going through it once again to see the completed work, now with edits included, may lead to further insights. Seeing new possibilities even in the midst of the commitment to words already formed and in print, as in editing, involves a mental "stepping back" and an openness to change in the midst of that commitment. For example, after editing for a consistent voice, or moving one paragraph from the introduction to the conclusion, a writer may regret the decision and need to revise once again. As with editing, revision is often most successful after significant time has passed (several days) to allow the writer to read what they wrote with fresh eyes. By permitting time to have its effects on the written product, the author is likely to see things they had missed during the first edits. Writers can often focus heavily on one element to the detriment of others during editing, but these can be caught during revision. A fresh set of eyes can be very helpful at this stage of writing; ask someone you trust to read through (1) the instructions or goals and then (2) your work to ensure you have fulfilled the promises made at the start of the project.

When revising written work, the brain does not just make mechanical changes in grammar or word choice but also often has important *aha!* moments about concepts, ideas, and relationships including Eureka heuristic (Laukkonen et al., 2018). At the least, the brain monitors for errors through metacognition, but in the best cases, revision involves creative cognitive reappraisal (Wu et al., 2022). Revision includes monitoring for errors through metacognition (Kirschner et al., 2021), cognitive flexibility, and new evidence integration (Romero-Ferreiro et al.,

2022). If a student truly has learned through the editing process and continues to grow as a writer through the revisions, this demonstrates cognitive flexibility (Zühlsdorff et al., 2023) and allows the integration of new evidence. Teachers should remember that one way to facilitate these new insights during revision is to consider mindfulness for performance enhancement (Bondar et al., 2021). Revision networks in the brain hopscotch from sustained attention to the default mode network and involve metacognition.

Teachers can help students revise by doing the following.

Tools Often Used to Revise	Tools With Even More Impact
✓ Think of *what* needs to be revised.	✓ Think of *why* something needs revision.
✓ Revise line by line.	✓ Revise for one conceptual change at a time throughout the paper.
✓ Rewrite based on peer exchange.	✓ Begin by asking what was good and bad about the draft, and consider if feedback is pointing to some larger issue that might require larger creative solutions.
✓ Rewrite based on teacher feedback.	✓ Revise by looking at a worked model alongside the current draft.
✓ Revise based on teacher feedback.	✓ Revise by looking at the original teacher feedback alongside the current draft.

Activities From ThinkWrite for Revising

Writing With Scissors

Objective: *To ensure that any repetition in your paper is purposeful*

1. Print out your writing.
2. Cut up the paper by sections or by paragraphs.
3. Scatter or shuffle the cutouts.
4. Reorder the cutouts in the best logical order for the writing project.
5. Highlight similar ideas in the same color, and decide if they should be revised.
6. Eliminate cutouts or sentences that are unneeded and/or add repetition for emphasis.
7. Revise your work.

What's happening in the brain: "Writing With Scissors" involves tricking the brain into seeing parts instead of the whole, which includes ordering and sequencing of a narrative, and categorizing of conceptual knowledge, as well as deconstructing and constructing meaning from wholes to parts (Baicchi, 2015). This involves holonic thinking about the parts and whole of the written work and involves a conceptual hierarchy of ideas that result in weaving a story (Assouline & Mendelsohn, 2023). Among other things, this involves "the neural mechanisms that underlie coherent narrative construction of causally connected information . . . [including] two separate networks that discerned between coherent and incoherent narrative conditions: a network associated with information processing, consisting of primary and high-order association cortices that showed increased functional connectivity among themselves, as well as a distributed fronto-parietal network" (Assouline & Mendelsohn, 2023, p. 1).

Review Expectations

Objective: *To make sure you have met the expectations of your writing project*

1. Aside from the explicit instructions, what other expectations are there for your writing project?
2. Make a checklist of your audience, the genre, and the person who assigned the work.
3. What kinds of expectations do your audience, genre, and person who assigned the work have?
4. Go through your completed project and confirm you have met all of the expectations for the audience, the genre, and the person who assigned the work. If you have, celebrate! If not, revise as necessary.

What's happening in the brain: "Review Expectations" involves understanding the instructions, the audience, and then comparing them to your written work, which includes semantic understanding, meaning-making, and stepping back to compare your writing with macro and micro expectations. This involves, among other things, a process in which "searchers review documents to gather information relevant to their information need" and assessing the degree to which you realized a successful search, including "the psychophysiological manifestation during the moment of satisfaction [of a good search] . . . the right insula and superior frontal gyrus as well as the left anterior cingulate and posterior cingulate cortex" (Paisalnan et al., 2021, p. 8).

Let the Clouds Clear

Objective: *To check your writing for repetition or frequency*

1. Upload your writing into a word cloud program.
2. Review the word cloud. What is your reaction to the most frequently used words?
3. Notice the words that were repeated the most. Notice if there are any unexpected words that stand out. In your opinion, what are the most important words that are missing?
4. Discover the reason why certain words have been repeated. Remember: Frequency is not equal to importance, but their prevalence influences the reader's understanding. Ask yourself, does this represent the intended priority of your thinking? Does this show the need to expand vocabulary or show your favorite words? Or is there another reason for the repetition?
5. Revise as necessary.

What's happening in the brain: "Let the Clouds Clear" involves quantitatively comparing word concepts with the conceptual purpose of your written work, which includes comparing and contrasting semantic (word meaning) and lexical sequencing (word placement) dominance and evaluating it against expectations. This involves reconciling word use frequency with the purpose of the writing project and a reflection as to whether the visualization of word frequency reflects content importance as it does salience and ease of recall (Gregorová et al., 2023). Feng and Hirsch (2023) used ERP to index "the expectancy of certain target words in a preceding context" and found that people have biases toward emotional interpretations and that different combinations of words trigger different emotional states for different people.

For more activities, see ThinkWriteMBE.com

Maximizing a Student's Success in Revising

Ask, how will you know if you are successful? Share example success statements:

- ☐ I know my revision was successful when I have responded to all the feedback I received.
- ☐ I know I did a good job revising because I regrouped all the similar ideas into one paragraph.
- ☐ I know I did a good job revising because the reorganized sections show improvement.
- ☐ I know I did a good job revising because I added in a lot of missing details.

Write your own success statement: "I realize I have been successful revising when I [insert a verb here]."

Encourage self-reflection:

- Have I gone back to the instructions to ensure I'm submitting the right assignment?
- Have I taken into consideration all the feedback received?
- Have I added visual representations to facilitate understanding?

Celebrate progress by checking off "I can" statements:

✓ I can confirm my work is complete by reading it from start to finish.
✓ I can confirm I have incorporated all feedback I found useful.

✓ I can confirm the thinking and emotions I wanted to trigger are conveyed effectively.
✓ I can confirm that I have considered alternative organization, examples, and vocabulary.

PROOFREAD

Proofreading crystallizes your written presentation as clearly as your thinking.

To proofread allows you to . . .

- ☐ See the final, polished version of your work.
- ☐ Hear yourself think.
- ☐ Avoid careless errors.
- ☐ Show respect for your reader.

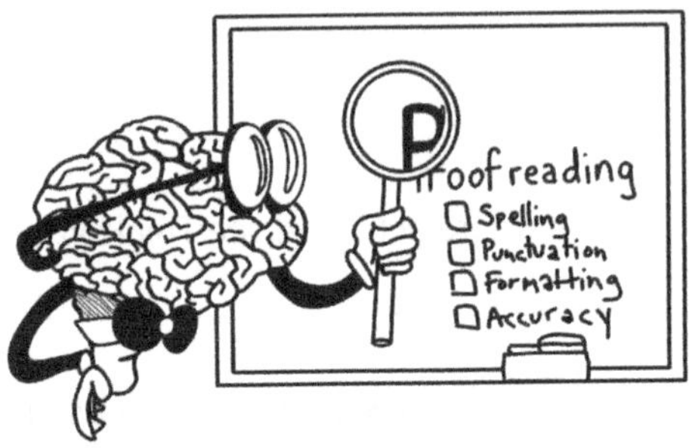

Artwork by Gabriel Espinosa Tokuhama for Tracey Tokuhama-Espinosa. All rights reserved.

Proofreading is the penultimate step in the writing process and is therefore often exhausting. Luckily, there are a number of digital tools that can help ensure that what is submitted is the best version of your work. Because proofreading means reading something for a second, third time, or tenth time, the brain must remember to pay specific attention to things it might gloss over quickly with a presumption of meaning. It is also clear that there are the effects of familiarity and type of encoding on proofreading abilities. Technically speaking, the brain must also read with and without homonym or morpheme spelling foils and correctly infer meaning. This is why the research indicates that successful proofreading depends on reading work aloud (Cushing & Bodner, 2022). One reason reading aloud helps is because it helps protect against distractions (Halin et al., 2014) and can help identify errors (Cushing & Bodner, 2022), including those in the symbols systems arena of development (McCloskey & Perkins, 2012). Some neuroscientists study how the brain manages to detect spelling errors with and without homonym or morpheme spelling foils (Richards et al., 2017). Research shows that there are effects of familiarity and type of encoding on proofreading (Pilotti et al., 2005).

A final look at the whole writing project from a macro view is often helpful but sometimes not completed before submission because it is not required by the teacher or students don't think they have time. The good news is that students using word processors can quickly zoom out on their final submissions independent of the format—be it a novel, a screenplay, an advertisement, a book report—by just making the document smaller. Rather than looking at the writing in 100%, try reducing it to 25%, which will highlight the titles, body text, and subtitles to show how consistently the format used to break up the text has been applied. If the work is an academic paper, it may also benefit from using the Word Styles to create a table of contents that lays out the order of the main parts. The student can then compare this zoomed-out outline with a worked model or exemplary writing piece in the same genre to see how closely they match. If there are significant differences, the writer should dig back into the proofreading details of spelling and punctuation. Finally, a small but important reminder to students that proofreading also means the assignment cover page itself. The authors have all had their own names, or the name of the assignment, misspelled or mislabeled, which pricks at our sensitivities as readers. Remember to spell-check all elements of the paper for accuracy, including cover pages and references, before submitting.

Proofreading requires knowledge of "rules," the ability to recognize their violation, and the correction of them. As with other steps in the "revision" phase of writing, familiarity with the intended meaning can interfere with one's ability to spot and correct such errors. One can reduce this familiarity by disrupting expected patterns by reading the work at a smaller level of meaning aided by such techniques as reading each paragraph backward (last sentence first, first sentence last) to attend to sentence sense and punctuation more readily.

Teachers can help students proofread by doing the following.

Tools Often Used to Proofread	Tools With Even More Impact
✓ Read the paper through and correct line by line.	✓ Proofread one paragraph at a time. Correct for spelling. Then correct for grammar. Then for formatting. Then for word choice and accuracy.
✓ Read the paper silently.	✓ Read the paper out loud.
✓ Check for proper punctuation.	✓ Overemphasize the effects of punctuation when reading aloud.
✓ Read the paper on the computer screen.	✓ Print the paper out in a different font and read it out loud.
✓ Read the paper as soon as you finish it.	✓ Leave the paper for a few days to give your brain a break from what it anticipates it will see.
✓ Review the headers.	✓ Use Word Styles to see your headers as a table of contents.
✓ Use a spellchecker. ✓ Use a grammar checker.	✓ Use an editor function that checks for spelling, punctuation, and grammar simultaneously.

Activities From ThinkWrite for Proofreading

Peer Ears

Objective: *To proofread for errors by reading to someone*

1. Find a partner.
2. Read your writing aloud to your partner.
3. As you read, have your partner interrupt you when something does not sound right or when your ideas are not clear.
4. Each time you stop, mark those passages.
5. After you finish reading aloud, go back to the markups.
6. Revise your work.

What's happening in the brain: "Peer Ears" involves comparing what is read to what is heard by others, which includes auditory accuracy and semantic memory, sense-making, and perspective taking. This involves, among other things, meaning-making networks, most importantly "three of the brain's major networks: affective salience, effortful attending, and broader reflection" (Immordino-Yang & Knecht, 2020, p.4), which must override prediction networks in the brain (Ryskin & Nieuwland, 2023).

Read Backward to Move Forward

Objective: *To shift your attention to word-level details by reading in reverse order*

1. Read your writing aloud one word at a time, from the end to the beginning. This means to start with the very last word and then work your way backward.
2. Pause after each word.
3. Ask yourself, is this the best word? Is this word spelled correctly? Is the punctuation correct (if the word has a punctuation mark)?
4. Revise as needed.

What's happening in the brain: "Read Backward to Move Forward" at the word level involves visual acuity, spelling, semantics, and syntactic accuracy, which includes vocabulary choices, accurate spelling, as well as lexical decisions. This involves, among other things, neural networks for both semantic retrieval and spelling, which then must be placed into the context of sentence reading: "Reading a sentence entails integrating the meanings of individual words to infer more complex, higher-order meaning. This highly rapid and complex human behavior is known to engage the inferior frontal gyrus (IFG) and middle temporal gyrus (MTG) in the language-dominant hemisphere . . . [suggesting a] "distributed, dynamic computation across the frontotemporal language network" (Woolnough et al., 2023, p. 583).

Impressing Words

Objective: *To prepare your writing for another person to read*

1. Choose someone you would like to impress with your writing.
2. Have a copy of your writing in front of you. To prime your attention networks, print a physical copy of your writing or change your screen view or font.
3. Read every single word aloud, imagining the person you want to impress.
4. Listen for anything that does not sound right.
5. Make a note next to passages that sound like they need to be rewritten.
6. Revise your text.
7. Share your writing with the person you want to impress, and gauge their reactions and register their comments.
8. Rewrite as necessary.

What's happening in the brain: "Impressing Words" involves the reflection of appropriate vocabulary for the audience, which includes attentional networks to audience levels and appropriate vocabulary choice that then compare inner speech "hearing" with external speech. This involves auditory attentional networks (Huang & Elhilali, 2020) and lexical retrieval (Lopopolo et al., 2020) for accurate intonation (Kurumada & Roettger, 2022) and includes, among other things, "lexicality [which] is encoded earliest in mid-fusiform (mFus) cortex, and precentral sulcus, and is represented reliably enough to allow single-trial lexicality decoding. Word frequency is first represented in mFus and later in the inferior frontal gyrus (IFG) and inferior parietal sulcus (IPS), while orthographic neighborhood sensitivity resides solely in IPS" (Woolnough et al., 2022, p. 5438).

For more activities, see ThinkWriteMBE.com.

Maximizing a Student's Success in Proofreading

Ask, how will you know if you are successful? Share example success statements:

- ☐ I know I did a good job of proofreading when there are no misspelled words.
- ☐ I know I did a good job of proofreading when there is no repetition.
- ☐ I know I did a good job of proofreading when I can hear my own voice come through.
- ☐ I know I did a good job of proofreading when I read it out loud and it sounds like one clear narrative.

Write your success statement: "I know I did a good job proofreading when I [insert a verb here]."

Encourage self-reflection:

- Have I read my paper aloud to proof my work?
- Have I asked someone else to read my paper through to see if it makes sense?
- Have I read my paper out loud to someone else?
- Have I done an editor check (spelling, grammar, and punctuation)?

Celebrate progress by checking off "I can" statements:

✓ I can hear my own voice in the paper.
✓ I can ensure each word is well chosen.
✓ I can write a well-organized and error-free paper.
✓ I can use tools to facilitate proofreading.
✓ I can get up the courage to read my work aloud in front of others.

COMPLETE AND COMMENCE

Successfully completing a project gives a sense of closure and permits the commencement of new offshoot projects. This allows you to consider what you learned that might apply in the future.

To complete and commence allows you to . . .

- ☐ Bring the ideation process full circle.
- ☐ Fully experience the positive emotions and completion and the intrigue of expectations.
- ☐ Extend your possible audience and continue to rehearse your learning.
- ☐ Strengthen your identity as a writer.

Artwork by Gabriel Espinosa Tokuhama for Tracey Tokuhama-Espinosa.

While it is true that some students only feel relief that the writing assignment is finished, teachers can still make a difference about how the students view writing in the future. When a student completes an essay, a research paper, a poem, or a newspaper article, one of the best things we as teachers can do to encourage further writing in the future is to celebrate that accomplishment and suggest ways to extend writing. Rather than being rewarded by a sigh of relief, once a writing project is submitted, it should be celebrated for all new doors that open in terms of new writing projects. One of the best ways to teach about writing genres, to get more traction out of all the effort of writing, and to expand your audience is to use the base of the current, completed writing as a jumping-off point for a new and possibly even more exciting project. Many have heard of how a short story turned into a screenplay and movie, but there are other examples, such as how a research paper converts to an infographic or a book report becomes a blog. All genres of writing have the potential to morph information into others.

Even if the student did not enjoy the process, celebrating the tough journey together ("what doesn't kill you makes you stronger!") can give positive closure. Different teachers have different ways of celebrating the completion of a writing assignment. Some hang the work up around the room for public viewing during Open House. Others include it in the students' portfolio and share it with parents. Some write notes to their students telling them what they liked most about their process and product. Others publish the work in a school newspaper or go even further and submit it to a state or national writing competition. All these actions are more than token gestures or extras; they are the mainstay of what the student will use as the basis for intrinsic motivation in the next assignment. When we think of a work, the role of authentic audience comes to mind. So much of what students write is artificially limited to an audience of one, the teacher.

Consideration of audience cues motivational circuits throughout the writing process and can energize the attainment of competencies in writing that come with a sense of well-being and satisfaction (Maeda et al., 2021). Once a paper is submitted, we often think of the writing as "finished." Calling to mind the audience for any writing project reminds the writer of the social context of the task. Repurposing what one has learned in a new genre provides yet another opportunity to rehearse the content knowledge and makes the writer aware that different audiences and different forms may require a different "voice" as well as restructuring that knowledge, requiring cognitive flexibility and further developing the writer's awareness of genre and reader expectations. Completing a writing project should be leveraged to motivate future writing and to shape the students' self-image as a writer. A simple closing assignment that can cement this for students is to ask them to finish this sentence: "As a writer, finishing this assignment makes me feel. . . ." This reaffirms their identities as writers and explicitly labels the typically joyful feelings they have on accomplishing such an important task (Jiang, 2021).

We are reminded by many writing experts that changing our mindset from one of *completion* to one of *commencement* opens new possibilities. Just like graduation from high school signifies something has ended (K–12 education), it also, more importantly, points to what is possible next. The brain experiences many contradictory emotions when a writing project ends (see Table 2.2). The research for the neural correlates related to completing and/or commencing includes studies on an enhanced sense of competence (Matsuo et al., 2021). There is also a recognition and awareness and reward for self-regulation (Ludwig et al., 2020). In some cases, students join in group celebrations and are thankful for increased social support (Brick et al., 2023), all of which results in intrinsic motivation (Reeve & Lee, 2019) and a sense of well-being and satisfaction (Maeda et al., 2021). Finally, social emotions of gratitude can also be mixed with personal emotions of pride and joy. Celebration of completed work can instill a new motivation to continue improving the work.

Teachers can help students complete and commence by doing the following.

Tools Often Used to Complete and Commence	Tools With Even More Impact
✓ Congratulate the students in class.	✓ Congratulate the students by inviting an audience to hear their work.
✓ Tell each student what you liked about their written project.	✓ Get students to tell each other what they liked about their written projects.
✓ Conduct an awards ceremony.	✓ Identify the awards categories and ask students to call out their peers.
✓ Create an archive of student work.	✓ Publish the work and share it in the school library, the Internet, or on the class blog.

Activities From ThinkWrite for Complete and Commence

Gratitude Letter and Visit

Objective: *To thoughtfully express gratitude to someone involved in your writing process*

1. Name a person who was supportive in your writing process.
2. Write a letter to this person expressing your gratitude. Consider how this person is important to your writing process, progress, or product. Focus on sharing what this person did, why you are grateful, and how this person affected you.
3. If you are willing to, deliver and read the letter to this person aloud.
4. Note how this letter and their reaction made you feel.

What's happening in the brain: "Gratitude Letter and Visit" involves reviewing all the stages of your writing project, the feedback you received along the way, and appreciating how this contributed to your improved writing process, which includes emotional memory, autobiographical memory, emotional intelligence, and the ability to express this in written form. Gratitude generation includes, among other things, the "relationship between regional gray and white matter volume (rGMV/rWMV) in the medial prefrontal cortex (MPFC) and trait gratitude . . . [and] Voxel-based morphometry analyses found that trait gratitude was associated with smaller regional gray matter volume and regional white matter volume in the medial prefrontal cortex (MPFC) implicated in social-cognitive processes, consistent with the behavioral findings reporting the social functions of gratitude. Importantly, structural variations in the MPFC related to trait gratitude also significantly predicted life satisfaction, and this association was fully mediated by trait gratitude" (Kong et al., 2020, p. 917).

End to Start

Objective: *To extend the life of your ideas by exploring different genres*

1. Review the Genres of Writing list (Figure 1.5) for inspiration.
2. Identify your project genre on the list.
3. Imagine all of the different genres that could come of your finished product (e.g., videos, drawings, podcasts, journals, essays, short stories, books, social media posts) and how the message is modified by the change in genre.
4. Identify the key characteristics of this new genre.
5. Create a prototype of your work in this new genre.
6. Explain how your ideas will be changed by using this new genre and this new audience.

What's happening in the brain: "End to Start" involves imagination and knowledge of different forms, modalities, and genres of writing, which includes comparing and contrasting similarities and differences of writing genres. This involves, among other things, neural networks for identifying structural and content differences between writing genres based on the brain's ability to imitate the structural patterns from one genre to another (Clark, 2022). The brain then categorizes genres, according to the "theory of literary comprehension that assumes distinct literary processing modes and incorporates text categorization as an initial processing step," (Blohm et al., 2022, p. 1). The rehearsal (familiarity) with genres indicates the speed with which a person can distinguish variances.

Writing Exhibition

Objective: *To share your thinking and writing journey (process)*

1. Select key pieces or milestone work from your draft documents. Consider including some of your worst mistakes as well as your best triumphs.
2. Design a museum presentation and create a one or two-sentence narrative of the exhibit. This can include displaying the different writing artifacts along the hallway, making a video that walks through each stage of your thinking, a book that documents your process, or a mobile app or any other creative documentation of your process.
3. Share your work with others.

What's happening in the brain: "Writing Exhibition" involves creatively reflecting on your writing process, which includes acknowledging both positive learning steps and hard/difficult stages of the writing process, followed by the ability to self-assess. This involves neural networks for self-assessment (Beer & Harris, 2019), autobiographical memory, and creative reconstruction, as well as self-evaluation with others in mind (Van de Groep et al., 2021). The neural correlates of "self and other evaluations" across adolescence show "brain activity within the dorsal medial prefrontal cortex (dMPFC) and right temporal parietal junction (TPJ) showed a quadratic change from early to mid-adolescence, with a peak in activity at the second measurement when evaluating the self, the similar and dissimilar peer" (von Buuren et al., 2022, para.1), suggesting that this activity will have different success rates with different age groups, depending on their general level of self-awareness.

For more activities, see ThinkWriteMBE.com.

Maximizing a Student's Success in Complete and Commence

Ask, how will you know if you are successful? Share example success statements:

- ☐ I know I have successfully completed a writing project when I can articulate the steps in my own writing process.
- ☐ I know I finished a writing assignment successfully when I feel fulfilled as well as excited about things to come.
- ☐ I know my sense of achievement is well merited when I hear others' praise for my process.
- ☐ I know I have successfully completed my work when I want to commence. . . .

Write to your own success statement: "I know I successfully completed and commenced when I [insert a verb here]."

Encourage self-reflection:

- Have I taken the time to think about how this work potentially leads to new work?
- Have I thanked the people who helped me grow as a writer?
- Have I processed all the feelings I am experiencing as I finish this project successfully?

Celebrate progress by checking off "I can" statements:

- ✓ I can feel good about my accomplishments.
- ✓ I can imagine how to turn my poem into a story, my research paper into a book, my story into a movie (for example).
- ✓ I can explain my process as a writer to others and grow in my identity as a writer in multiple genres.

This final chapter about stages of thinking involved in the revision of writing ends our in-depth review of the thinking behind writing. In the next chapter, we explore how ThinkWrite does not have to be approached linearly (prewriting, writing, revision), and how changing stages of thinking can enhance writing through what we call *toggling*.

CHAPTER 6

Toggling to Assist Variability and Flexibility

Writing is the highest form of thinking. To be able to express yourself in written form is the most difficult mental task we ask of our brains not only due to the sheer number of neural networks involved, but also because we ask the brain to fire up these networks *simultaneously.* Writing is not only a question of pairing up the right combination of letters, but also selecting the appropriate word, placing it in just the right spot, matching it with the precise tone, ensuring it fits the right context of the assignment, and then doing this a hundred more times to complete a paragraph. The student must then manage to do this while existing in their social and emotional contexts, including how nervous they feel about whether the sandwich from lunch is still on their breath when they talk to someone they like, if they can make it to both sports practice and the after-school job on time, and if Grandpa's health will hold through the holidays. That is, our identities as writers live both in the idea generation world and in our daily contact with others.

In celebration of Holly Atkins and Lin Carver's declaration that *Writing Is Thinking* (2022), we'd also like to suggest it's not only a "snapshot of thinking" (p. 49), but that the writing process itself is thinking. This higher-order thinking involves the coordination of many distinct neural processes that force the writer to process the discovery and communication of ideas. Consequently, the better the thinking, the better the writing, and the better the writing, the better the thinking. Writing involves internal feelings, neural mechanisms, and influences from one's surrounding community and culture. It involves memory, attention, and choices. Writing is a catharsis for inner emotions as well as a functional tool for success in society. Writing is personal but serves the group as a permanent record, unlike a fleeting thought that can live in your mind momentarily but then be gone. Writing allows communication across time and space, and its ubiquity can disguise its complexity and magic. Because of the constant, dynamic exchange between internal and external worlds, the writing brain must manage very different neural networks at very distinct levels of consciousness simultaneously. To negotiate all these different levels of thinking, one must first be aware they exist. Once we can label these different ways of thinking, we can begin to leverage them to our advantage.

NAME IT TO TAME IT

"Name it to tame it!" is a mantra used in elementary school classrooms to help kids with social–emotional learning. Just as the youngest learners need to learn how to name their emotions to manage them, we believe that naming the different stages of thinking is also the first step in learning to use them correctly. The names used in this book (prewriting stages, writing stages, and revise stages) are meant to be intelligible to the youngest of children, so that they can begin to label their thinking stages in a shared vocabulary with their teachers starting in grade 1. Once labeled, these stages of thinking can then be used to identify challenges and strengths and to provide student writers with greater awareness and choice in their writing process. The 15 evidence-based stages of thinking in ThinkWrite are complementary to earlier process-based strategies for writing instruction in that a key element of ThinkWrite is student autonomy about where to begin the process. An important lesson from neuroscience research about the brain and consciousness is that it is natural for humans to jump from one stage of thinking to another. What is *un*natural is to believe that all students in a class can go through that process in the same order in the same amount of time. Different people need different things at different times to achieve the same results. One of the keys to great writing is giving each student what they need when they need it in terms of stages of thinking.

Prewriting, writing, and revision are great guidelines for writing, and breaking them down into even smaller stages of thinking seen in Chapters 3, 4, and 5 helps us appreciate the complex writing process in manageable chunks. Prewriting consists of understanding, knowing things, mind wandering, reflection, and mapping and connecting. Each of those stages of thinking is broken down into hundreds of neural networks. The same is true for writing (outlining, planning, researching, drafting) and revision (peer exchange, feedback and feedforward, editing, revision, proofreading, and completing and commencing). The focus of this chapter is to help readers understand that the brain doesn't just jump between prewriting and writing and revision, *it jumps between different stages and neural networks.* All stages of thinking are important, but they play different roles in completing any given writing assignment. Knowing when one stage is more beneficial than another is the key to knowing where to start in the ThinkWrite process and where to move next.

While each of the 15 stages is necessary and might even be intuitive to good writing teachers, one thing they often are not is ordered so neatly as described in this book. It may sound logical to first understand the assignment before making an outline, but some people do the opposite; some make an outline and then get feedback before they understand what they need to do. And while many people might draft their work and then get feedback, others like to get feedback on their unwritten ideas before putting anything into a draft. Similarly, while many people might reflect, then map out their ideas, and then edit, others may map, then edit, then reflect, and then edit some more. The bottom line is that there is no correct order in which to think about writing; different people will start at different stages because no two brains will approach the same writing assignments in an identical way due to each person's unique prior experiences.

As we experienced the many ways people approached writing assignments, we wondered what caused one person to first *plan*, then *draft*, and then *complete* a project in one sitting while it took a month for someone else to *research*, bounce ideas off others in *peer exchange*, and then *complete* the assignment? Why did someone else in the same class spend a day *understanding* the assignment and then another get formal *feedback* before zipping through a *draft* in an hour? The differences between individuals suggested that writing is impacted by a learner's familiarity with the genre as well as their motivation and time, but there were two more revelations that led us to the importance of toggling, the movement from one stage of thinking to another: how well the student knew the topic of the writing assignment and how frequently the teacher had used the same assignment structure before. These five differences are explained below.

Writers do not go through all 15 stages of thinking in every writing project due to:

- **Expertise in a genre:** Some people have a lot of experience in a particular genre, which means they have rehearsed it so often they can spend less time deciphering rules.
- **Personal motivation.**
- **Time availability.**
- **Familiarity with the topic:** The more familiar you are with a topic, the less time you need to review it.
- **Experience with the assignment:** Some students know the "drill" of a teacher's assignment structure. Repetition of the same assignment reduces the amount of time on the assignment.

FAMILIARITY, REPETITION, AND PRACTICE

All stages of thinking are not always employed in all writing projects. To become a quick and efficient writer, normally familiarity, repetition, and practice are required (Reedy & Riley, 1999). Sometimes the writer's familiarity with the topic and assignment means they can speed through stages of understanding or knowing things, appearing to skip them. This happens when a person knows their topic so well they can jump straight to drafting without outlining or researching beforehand—steps that a person less familiar with the topic would need to do. Expertise allows people to skip stages in thinking due to knowledge of topics, genres, or writing tasks. "Intuition" is hard to explain in neuroscience, but "hypercognition" explains how a person can "skip" thinking steps and reach fast results due to heuristics (Conway-Smith, 2020).

Second, different people need different amounts of time in different stages of thinking depending on the writing project. Not only can some students write a poem in a few minutes while others take days, but to write the poem, the first student may simply need to reflect and then write, while others may need to research, get feedback, draft, and then revise their poem. Another person might be able to write a newspaper article in no time by just copying from a worked model, while the same person might take ages to write out instructions about how to clean a fish tank after they have really understood the process, looked up the right vocabulary words, and then reviewed examples of instruction booklets before starting. Similarly, independent of the genre or assignment, some students may regularly spend a great deal of time understanding, drafting, or editing as their habituated practices have ingrained taking time in these stages more so than in others.

Many teachers know that when they teach a genre of writing to a class, it can take many students a lot longer to write a successful first draft. Students might be amazing at writing free-verse poetry but then take ages to write a haiku; even though both are genres of poetry, they differ significantly in expectations and success criteria. Some students might have heard their whole lives that they are great writers, only to be told by another teacher they have to work on their skills because the writing expectations of a new genre are different; research and a five-paragraph essay differ in their goals, their success criteria, and their thinking processes.

Additionally, different people go through the stages of writing in different orders depending on the writing project itself and their familiarity with teacher expectations. For teacher-experts in their topic or genre form, many have acquired routines enabling them to jump through the writing stages often without being conscious, and therefore their experience of flow may come almost immediately, leading them to think their students follow suit just as easily. Many students, however, might be inexperienced with the way the assignment should be completed and need much more time to get accustomed to the task. This means they may spend time in all of the 15 stages of thinking as they strive to write well. Teachers can help students become better at working at the right pace and through the appropriate thinking stages by first helping them understand what level of thinking occurs at each stage and then reflecting on how they normally go through the stages as they approach writing tasks. It's key to remember that the end product does not depend on the order of the stages but on the appropriate choice of stage ordering based on individual needs.

The quality of a writing project can be equally good coming from a person who understands, outlines, drafts, and then edits as from someone who outlines, drafts, edits, and then understands. The order of the steps and the amount of time spent in each step reflect the individual needs of learners, not the quality of their writing. The 15 stages of ThinkWrite are purposefully represented in a circle (see Figure 1.1) because any stage can be the starting point, any order of stages can lead to success, and this process is expected to change with the learner's context.

Documenting Stages of Thinking and Your Personal Writing Process: A quick exercise to figure out what you (or your students) could do differently the next time in the ThinkWrite process is to use a spider rubric (Figure 7.1) to make visible the starting point and pathway(s) towards the writing goal.

Steps in Toggling for Students and Teachers

Students	Teachers
As a writer, think about a recent writing project:	**As a teacher, think about a student writer:**
• In which of the 15 stages of thinking did you spend the most time (and the least time)?	• In which of the 15 stages of thinking do you think the student spent the most time (and the least time)?
• In which order did you move from one stage to another?	• In which order do you think the student moved from one stage to another?
• What stage do you enjoy (and which do you hate or avoid)?	• What stage does the student enjoy (and hate or avoid)?
• What could you try differently the next time you write?	• What could you try differently the next time you guide this student?

Skipping writing stages because of expertise is a good thing, but in some cases, students skip stages for the wrong reasons, missing important thinking along the way. In the worst-case scenario, sometimes students are asked to do activities related to writing for which they are not prepared because either the teacher or the student has not taken the time to establish the learner's true starting point. This creates the bad habit on the part of students to blindly follow our/teacher directions, even if it was to the detriment of their writing. Sometimes instructors assume what is obvious or easy for them is just as obvious or natural for their students, and there is no good guard against this as many students will faithfully follow directions without thinking about the information they really need to get the assignment done. For example, sometimes writers are instructed to outline a paper *before* they even understand what they need to do or have thought through what they already know about it. Other times they are asked to get feedback from peers before they even have a solid idea of what they will be writing about because they have not connected ideas or mapped out the concepts. Or they may be told they need to edit, proofread, or revise their paper for formatting mistakes but have no idea what the correct formatting looks like and need to first review worked models for clarity. In short, a teacher can have a great plan, but it might not be what every learner needs. In fact, the only one who knows what he really needs is the learner himself.

If teachers first confirm which stage of thinking their students are starting from before asking for an outline (or for peer feedback or revisions), more students will find success and fewer teachers would be frustrated by missing information in the student texts. A key shift in ThinkWrite is to motivate students' understanding of the thinking behind the writing to give them more autonomy to structure their own learning approaches to writing assignments.

STUDENT CHOICE

The ultimate goal of ThinkWrite is to develop writers by nurturing learner autonomy through self-understanding. We know ThinkWrite processes work when students themselves can effectively choose which stage of thinking will advance their writing. Allowing students the choice of thinking stage based on their own assessment of needs is a core objective of good writing and a key step toward lifelong, independent learners. ThinkWrite builds off the work that gives choice and agency to students to identify their inner motivations to write (Hamel, 2017) by reminding us that not everyone is doing the same thing at the same time; different people are working on different parts of their product using different tools at different times. Some students may need to sit down and reflect on the assignments, others will need to dig deep into memory to identify what they already know, while others might be ready to dive into "flash-drafting" (Calkins, 2020, p. 35), "revise in groups" (Tompkins, 2013, p. 116), or take time to understand and unearth "the big idea" (Burke, 2010). In ThinkWrite, the choice of thinking stage is best made by the learner, but each learns to make this choice through guidance.

There are some things that are natural for the brain, and some things a brain cannot do without the help of a teacher. For example, the brain cannot help but have language. Humans are born with an innate "language sense" (Dehaene-Lambertz et al., 2008; Pietroski & Crain, 2005), but they cannot learn to read without guidance (Dehaene, 2009), nor write without rehearsal. Humans begin to talk by imitating others around them; they cannot learn to write without explicit instruction. The brain cannot *not* learn—its sole purpose is to learn as that increases the chances of survival. But while basic learning comes naturally to the brain, higher-order thinking skills can't be learned without the guidance of teachers (Elder & Paul, 1994). Higher-order cognition, including metacognitive abilities, come from strong models, explicit guidance, and teachers who know how to craft feedback that becomes students' future personal "voice in their heads." Knowing which stage of thinking best serves writing depends on the individual. Teachers should help their students understand the different types of thinking so that the choice can then be made by the students themselves.

In July 2022, young children were invited to be a part of a Zoom conference for teachers in the Mideast to tell them what they liked most about school and what they found most challenging. There were commonalities in the children's testimonies. All the students grades 1–5 shared stories of loving the way they felt known by teachers who called them by name or said hello to them in the hallways. All the children also mentioned *time* as one of the biggest challenges in their education, as they are asked to switch tasks before they are ready or to complete tasks before they are completed (personal conversation, St. Andrew's CTTL conference, July 2022). Every single child mentioned feeling rushed through work and having to move on to something new before they were ready. One 5th-grader said his biggest frustration in school was that he was slower than the other kids, not because he thought or moved more slowly, but because he was new at school and didn't know the routines. Others echoed that the biggest detriment to their learning was needing more time to get through all the steps in an activity. Just as they felt they were beginning to get into the groove of a lesson, not only were they told it was time to "move on," but sometimes they were even told to "move off" that topic and go to another subject matter. A little 2nd-grader shared that she was probably "the only one" who got caught daydreaming but felt she couldn't help but do this sometime. She did not realize that everyone daydreams, and when the grown-up teachers in the room assured her that they, too, needed to daydream sometimes (mind wander), the child lit up with a sense of relief. She had never been told that being off topic was normal, that daydreaming was something everyone did, or that being caught doing it shouldn't be a point of shame. The typical school structure does not celebrate the invisible aspects of writing, such as the need to mind wander or the amount of time that different students need to work through the different thinking processes.

The thinking underpinning the writing—the invisible parts of writing—are the time-consuming elements in the writing process. Teaching students to toggle effectively could be one way to better use the time we have in schools to teach writing.

TOGGLING FOR BETTER LEARNING

The different stages of ThinkWrite require different amounts of energy in different neural networks; too much time in any one network is exhausting, which is why the brain naturally moves from one network to another. The learning science literature uses the term *toggle* to talk about jumping from one stage of thinking to another or to switch from one option to another (Merriam-Webster, 2023). It seems that toggling between different stages of thinking is beneficial and may even be necessary (Cai et al., 2020) to advance thinking processes and especially helpful to higher-order thinking, such as that involved in writing. The brain cannot stay focused on one single way of thinking forever, as seen in the natural tendency to "mind wander" after long bouts of focused attention (Poerio et al., 2017). This is analogous to a person carrying a heavy bag as they walk home. That person will generally hold the bag in one hand and then after a while switch to the other hand to balance out the weight over time, toggling between them. Just as it feels easier to switch the bag back and forth rather than burden just one arm with the whole load the whole time, managing mental energy is also important for good thinking.

It takes energy to think, which is known as "cognitive load" (Vergara et al., 2019). Cognitive load is measured by tracking blood flow to different areas of the brain. Your brain is the most energy-hungry organ in the body, consuming around 20% of the entire body's resources despite only being around 2% of its total weight. Efficiency means the brain has to conserve energy and reduce cognitive load, which it can do in different ways (Phan & Ngu, 2021). We posit that one way to be efficient is to avoid getting stuck by staying in any one stage of thinking for too long or as with the bag, carrying it for too long with one arm.

As writers, when we get stuck in one kind of thinking, we experience writer's block, and it seems as if no progress is to be made. Writer's block can be avoided by toggling between distinct stages of thinking, which permits a kind of "refresh" button on energy use in the brain by diverting blood flow and its accompanying oxygen to different areas. This phenomenon is evident in neuroscience literature that tracks blood flow during task switching (e.g., Baller et al., 2022; Loftus et al., 2017). While blood is flowing throughout the brain all the time (just like both arms are working all the time), subtle changes in oxygenation, especially in working memory networks (Zuo et al., 2019), indicate heavier or lighter cognitive load. We have known this for more than 30 years (Rosenthal & Sick, 1989), but it's never really been applied to school settings. Some overused or exhausted neural networks can "get a break" when blood flow is switched to a different pathway. Within the blood flow, along with oxygen, different chemicals are exchanged between different areas of the brain, depending on a learner's mental state.

Most teachers have heard about dopamine, related to positive emotional states, and cortisol, related to stress. These are just two neurotransmitters in the brain that circulate throughout the different networks through the blood. While this has been known in laboratories for the past few decades (e.g., Schneider & Logan, 2009), teachers can now leverage the balance of different neurotransmitters and the cognitive load to benefit learning when they toggle between neural networks.

Toggling avoids heavy cognitive load on any single neural network.

One of the newest ways to measure cognitive load in real classrooms is with wearable headbands that combine electrical signals (EEG) with blood flow measures of oxygen (fNIRS) (e.g., Bevilacqua et al., 2019). Some studies also consider neurochemical exchanges by taking saliva samples during classroom exchanges to gauge stress (e.g., Castillo-Navarrete et al., 2023). Some current studies use this special technique to show how different activities trigger the use of different neural networks in the brain, and it can even show how whole groups of students appear to "get in sync" in these measurements when there is a common reaction to the activity (e.g., Czeszumski et al., 2020). Jumping around (toggling) to different stages of thinking is not only beneficial in writing activities, but also inevitable, and if managed, can be helpful in executing all cognitive tasks.

Shifting Focus to Save Energy

One of the most interesting insights from studies in real classrooms is that it seems that by toggling between stages of thinking, the brain avoids overworking any single group of networks. This was hinted at by Dehaene's *Consciousness in the Brain* (2015) and suggested in Baars's *Global Workspace Theory of Consciousness* (2005). This could explain why some people have amazing insights as they go for a run after spending hours trying to write without success, or why people give each other advice to "just sleep on it." By taking a run or falling asleep, they relieve the pressure on one network's taxing the demand for blood flow (Loftus et al., 2017; Murata & Suzuki, 2015), switch energy to another, and in doing so, create the conditions for better thinking.

Back in 2008, Kounios and colleagues did some of the first studies that showed how there were at least two different paths to creative insight and problem solving: "(A) methodical, conscious, search of problem-state transformations, and (B) sudden insight" (p. 281). This line of thinking grew into what is now known as the link between the default mode network and creativity (Deshayes et al., 2021; Dietrich & Haider, 2017). Whereas path "A" meant focusing attention on the problem, path "B" suggests letting go of thought processes and allowing connections to naturally occur, often leading to big *aha!* moments in problem resolution (e.g., Sunavsky & Poppenk, 2020). This "letting go" is an implicit act of toggling, or shifting the demands of deliberate processing on the neural networks and thereby allowing other networks to contribute their capacities to problem solving. These important studies help teachers know that getting kids to think about writing is getting them to think at many different levels, or as we call this in ThinkWrite, stages of thinking. By toggling between different stages of thinking, students increase the opportunity to truly experience creative insight in their own work.

Toggling as Task Switching

Task switching itself costs the brain energy when it is not naturally chosen by the learner. That is, when you begin to mind wander after a long bout of concentration, your brain is protecting itself from overuse, which has positive effects. A note of caution here: When you are *forced* to shift between stages of thinking by someone else, it can place an even *heavier* cognitive load on the brain (Klepsch & Seufert, 2020). The key to leveraging the stages is to help students best manage their own toggling. Teachers have a big influence over the stage of thinking students find themselves in within the classroom, and some even have the illusion that they control how and when students pay attention by the types of activities they conduct. This may be partially true, but good pedagogy is more about knowing how to guide students toward the right choices at a buffet than about serving a set menu. The key to successful toggling depends more on the student *choosing* their own combination of thinking stages to toggle between, which we will explore in Chapter 9. The main idea of this chapter is to appreciate that people can consciously change the networks for themselves and that teachers can nudge their students into appropriate stages.

Task switching in classrooms happens continuously each time we move to a new activity. A student might be focused on playing a game during recess and then be asked to shift to focusing on a math problem as they return to class; or they might be working on the math problem in class and be asked to switch attention from facing the board at the front of the class to working on the paper in front of them. Any time we change the focus of attention, or where students invest their cognitive load in a shift of thinking, we are asking them to task switch. This is true for both cognitive and emotional tasks (Kraft et al., 2020). Expanding cognitive load should be done conscientiously and carefully; otherwise it is just wasting good energy. This is probably why so many kids feel exhausted at the end of a school day.

Understanding how someone else feels is the ability to feel empathy. Empathy and understanding others' feelings are different from understanding what someone else is thinking, which is called mentalizing (Arioli et al., 2021). Moving between thinking and feeling are distinct neural pathways in the brain (Frith, 2016) and require energy to move from one state to another, and we ask this of students all the time, often without realizing how much effort and energy it takes. For example, students might be feeling empathy for a friend who is sad, but the teacher might call on them in class to explain what van Gogh intended when he painted his *Sunflowers*, or which math formulas can be used to resolve a problem. The teacher might not realize it, but this asks the student to go from a reflective, emotional state to an analytic, mentalizing state, which are very distinct neural networks in the brain, a shift that requires a lot of energy to make (Weigand & Jacobsen, 2022). Furthermore, asking the student to talk about a visually emotional image also uses different neural networks of the brain (Feng et al., 2021) than a neutral image, as does choosing the best math formula from memory (Bates et al., 2021), further taxing cognitive load. This explains why it might be hard to get a student to focus on the task at hand despite the teacher's best-planned class activities; much of the student's ability to do the work has nothing to do with the teacher, the topic, or the activity under way and everything to do with where their mind is giving the priority use of energy to their friend's situation. Each shift in thinking requires changes in the neural pathways that are used, which redirects the blood flow to different areas of the brain and modifies the balance of neurochemical exchanges. Because thinking is complex and uses so many different neural networks, learning how to manage different stages of thinking is key to successful teaching and learning. Understanding how and when to toggle requires new learning from both teacher and learner.

Mindfulness can help. Transitional activities such as mindfulness meditation (a kind of reflection) between different class topics has been shown to prepare the brain for what's to come and focuses attention (Grecucci et al., 2015). School is full of intense instruction, rushes between classes, and little downtime for students to mentally digest between learning moments. Task switching is eased by permitting students to toggle at their own pace. Mindfulness exercises, or "brain breaks" as schools like to call the few minutes of downtime, give students time before rushing to the next activity, to reflect and consolidate ideas before moving on to the next idea. Simply having students sit or lie in place and center their focus and quiet their minds is an activity that not only helps transition, but also teaches an element of self-regulation (Tang et al., 2014). Mindfulness activities also honor the natural shift of networks from one type of thinking to another. To leverage toggling in the best way possible, teachers need to rehearse transitional activities to develop habituated practice.

THE BRAIN ADAPTS TO WHAT IT DOES MOST

Some people are very good at shifting between different types of thinking, not because they are born that way but rather because they have rehearsed that kind of task switching a lot, and it has therefore become automated. Automation is based on habituation. The brain adapts to what it does most, which means that even very complicated tasks can become routine if they are done enough times (Bhangal et al., 2016). Some people think that emergency medical technicians (EMTs) are naturally good at task switching or can "multitask," but multitasking is a myth. EMTs can manage multiple scenarios at once (the car turned over with the trapped child in the backseat, the fire starting under the left tire and the unconscious mother in the front seat) not because they are multitasking but rather because they have *rehearsed* that scenario so many times before that it has become second nature and is no longer a heavy cognitive load task to switch attention. Because they have rescued the child a hundred times before in simulations, they are able to do so in real life with little mental energy, whereas most of us would suffer from "analysis paralysis" in which we fumbled over all our options. Practice may not make perfect, but it does make permanent, which means that task rehearsal benefits quick toggling behavior.

One way that correct habituation of writing stages happens is through metacognitive awareness (Ramadhanti & Yanda, 2021). People with a good sense of self-understanding can learn through life experiences which types of thinking serve them best under which situations. There is a lot of research going on to determine how changing from one thinking stage to another occurs naturally and how it can be shaped in a classroom. For example, does mind wandering on-demand have the same results as mind wandering spontaneously (Murray & Krasich, 2022)? What we know so far is that in the least it habituates an understanding of different stages of thinking, and at best, it primes students to learn to do this on their own. Learning when you are best served by reflection time, research time, planning time, or even mind wandering time can improve writing outcomes. The key for classroom teachers is to first label these stages explicitly, scaffold choices about the best strategies, and then give students the choice of moving from stage to stage when it best suits them.

People can learn to toggle through:

- Use of mindfulness activities between different tasks
- Self-knowledge coupled with the labels of the 15 different stages of consciousness involved in writing
- Habituated practice
- The guidance of teachers who understand the many stages of thinking behind the writing.

While many expert writers have learned to leverage toggling on their own, most students need teachers who can help them learn to do this. One way to begin to help students "see" the invisible thinking behind writing is by labeling the 15 thinking stages and then helping them recognize when they need to be in one stage or another.

INTRODUCING THINKWRITE TO STUDENTS

To integrate ThinkWrite into any classroom, the first step is shared vocabulary. We recommend using the 5E model to explore ThinkWrite, though other models also work. In 5E, the teacher first gets students to **E**ngage in the idea and then lets them **E**xplore and discuss among themselves. The teacher then asks them to **E**xplain what they think is going on, after which the teacher **E**laborates on their observations, improves vocabulary, and improves on any misunderstandings. Once the students have clarified any doubts, **E**valuation can take place. This might look like the following.

Teacher: Today we're going to explore the thinking behind writing. [Hand out infographic with the ThinkWrite stages of thinking.] Learning scientists have identified 15 stages of thinking that contribute to writing.

Students: [Ask any spontaneous questions that may come up as the infographic is distributed.]

Teacher: At which stage do you actually submit written work in this model?

Students (hopefully): Outline? Draft? Complete and Commence?

Teacher: There seems to be just three places where we have a written product here, right? When we submit an outline, when we turn in a draft, and when we complete the paper.

Students: [Ask any spontaneous questions.]

Teacher: Twelve of the 15 stages focus on thinking processes rather than on writing product. It seems the key to good writing products is a good writing process. Writing products depend on thinking processes, right? Good writing requires good thinking. What do you notice about the 15 stages of thinking?

Students: [Observations about prewriting, writing, revision; questions about word meaning; observations about "play" on the fringes of the model; questions about the gray verbs on the edges]

Teacher: What do you think happens in your brain when you "understand" something? [Allow students to respond.]

Teacher: I hear some great answers here! To let everyone have the chance to think and talk about the stages, we are going to get into groups of three. In your small groups, try to define "understand" and give each other's examples of how you think your brain comes to understand. We'll take five minutes, then come back to the larger group. . . .

Once the students have had the chance to discuss the first thinking stage, the teacher should then elaborate on their findings to ensure a complete definition of "understanding." It would be helpful to reinforce student contributions through either an electronic whiteboard or a shared drive where all contributions can be documented. At the end of each session, a word cloud of all of the terms surrounding understanding should be shared.

Teacher: Now, what role does understanding play in writing? Why do we need to understand to write well?

While the students' examples are likely to be sufficient, the teacher can also chime in with additional ideas, such as what would happen if we did *not* understand before we wrote or if we skipped this stage in the writing process.

After understanding is clearly understood, the teacher can go through the same process with all of the other stages of thinking. This shared discovery of the different stages of thinking assures the group shares definitions and an understanding of the different types of thinking that go into writing. Once all 15 stages have been reviewed, the teacher can cold-call students to talk about any of the 15 stages to see if the class has begun to manage the vocabulary of ThinkWrite and shares definitions.

Once students understand the stages of thinking, they can become more autonomous in choosing which activities they want to engage in. If the students don't make this choice on their own, or if the teacher feels the choice is wrong, the teacher can nudge learners into different areas by using prompts.

Teacher: Today, everyone will choose an activity or two to help them advance their writing. Just sit for a minute and quietly think to yourself, *what do I*

> *need to do to advance my writing today?* Think about what you are able to do without many problems and what gives you trouble. Then think of all 15 stages of thinking and choose where you would like to work today. If anyone needs help deciding, let me know and we can talk about options.

To help students understand which stage of thinking would benefit them most, teachers can use the Table 6.1 handout.

Sometimes it is helpful for both the students and teacher if the entire class uses all 15 stages in the same order to improve clarity about how they work. Once familiar, they can begin jumping around (toggling). This is like everyone making the same fruit salad with the exact same proportions together and then letting everyone make their own salad with their own balance of fruits on their own. Once most of the class is comfortable with the stages of thinking and how to find related activities, the teacher should allow for choice, reminding students to document in which stage of thinking they spend their time on the spider rubrics. Toggling should be encouraged!

In practice, in real classrooms, this means knowing when a student needs to shift from the researching phase of a project and take time to reflect, or when talking through a draft idea would be more beneficial than making editorial corrections. Teachers can help students learn to toggle by helping them habituate a questioning structure that points to appropriate stages of thinking. A way to begin to learn to toggle is to discuss an example of how a student's mind might leverage toggling. Here we provide one typical scenario of what toggling might look like in a university research assignment (Table 6.2). There are additional elementary and middle school examples in Appendix B for elementary and middle school levels.

Labeling the thinking behind the writing gives teachers and students the vocabulary to talk about what each person needs to do to improve their process. One could parallel this with knowing that there are many different typefaces and colors that can be used in advertising, but some combinations are considered better than others depending on the product being sold or what audience it is being pitched to. Or, similarly, that you might have a range of clothes you can wear today, but some things are more appropriate given the weather, where you are going, and whom you are seeing. All thinking is good for writing, but some stages are better than others, depending on the needs. Explicitly learning what kinds of thinking work best can improve students' and teachers' choices about which activities best match each student's needs. Smart choices are the key to good advertising, appropriate dress, and to writing. One of the main reasons that learning to label the different kinds of thinking is valuable is because it can lead to flow, which is a sense of effortless (low cognitive load) attention (Huskey et al., 2018).

Table 6.1. Help Students Identify What Stage of Thinking Will Advance Their Writing

Ask yourself which of these statements seems closest to what you are thinking:	
If you feel this:	**Then work on this stage of thinking:**
• I can't understand the text better by interpreting the author's thinking. • I can't understand the instructions when I read them more than once. • I can't understand how to write a ____ (genre) even when I deconstruct its form. • I don't take the time to ensure I understand my assignment before I start. • I don't know what to do if I don't understand something. • I can't define and use all the key terms needed for my writing project. • I can't tell you how I will know if I have done a good job. • I can't explain what I have to do to another person. • I don't know the proper voice or verb tense to use in this writing task.	• Understand
• I don't realize I know things when I form networks between ideas. • I don't realize I know things when I can categorize them together. • I don't compare the new thing to things that look similar. • I don't know my own heuristics and bias. • I don't know how analogies help me know things. • I can't connect ideas. • I can't use my memory or imagination to connect ideas. • I can't find a way to make this assignment connect to my real life outside school.	• Know Things
• I don't know I have been mind wandering when I unconsciously link ideas together without knowing how I did it. • I don't know what role mind wandering serves in my experience as a writer. • I don't value mind wandering. • I don't have a way to capture the fruits of my mind wandering • I don't understand how to explain mind wandering and its value to writing to my fellow teachers, parents, and students. • I don't know how to build the underlying social and emotional and environmental conditions for mind wandering to flourish. • I don't work with students or other writers to help them assess, strengthen, and value their mind wandering and use it to enrich their written work.	• Mind Wander
• I can't reflect by taking time to contemplate the important ideas in the passage. • I can't reflect by dissecting each part of the dialogue I am going to write. • I can't reflect by being mindful of my choices. • I don't know what role has reflection served in your own experience as a thinker, writer, teacher, or person? • I don't value reflection time. • I don't think reflection is as important as study time. • I can't center my focus and attention. • I can't identify my own feelings. • I can't mindfully acknowledge spaces for improvement. • I don't think of myself as a writer.	• Reflect

Ask yourself which of these statements seems closest to what you are thinking:	
If you feel this:	**Then work on this stage of thinking:**
• When I map and connect, I can't join and link my thoughts. • To map and connect, I don't try to find bridges between concepts. • To map and connect I can't show how ideas crisscross and overlap. • I don't use any mapping tools. • I don't know how information can be connected logically. • I can't show the natural relationships between ideas. • I can't draw or write out categories of ideas. • I can't map and connect ideas to create a strong outline from written work.	• Map and Connect
• I don't know how to make a thumbnail sketch of all my ideas. • I don't know how to make an inventory of all the pieces that need to go into my paper. • I don't know how to enumerate all the main points in the "right order." • I don't always write an outline before starting a writing project. • I don't understand how a good outline guarantees a strong opening and closing to my paper. • I can't use a variety of tools to visually map ideas. • I can't write a clear outline that covers all major ideas. • I don't know how to order my ideas in different ways.	• Outline
• I don't know how to organize my time. • I don't lay out all the tasks before I start. • I didn't make a complete to-do list before I started. • I don't make a timeline for completion. • I don't always make reasonable plans. • I can't use a variety of planning tools. • I can't meet my deadlines by following a plan. • I can't set realistic goals with good planning. • I can't accurately estimate the time that a writing task will take.	• Plan
• I am not sure I have done complete research when I examine every source of information. • I don't know if I did good research when I interview lots of different people. • I don't know if my research is thorough. • I don't know how to discern good information sources from fake ones. • I don't know how to identify quality information. • I am not sure what my biases are about my topic. • I can't use a variety of sources (people and technology) to research. • I can't spot fake news. • I can't conduct unbiased research. • I don't understand the frameworks or vocabulary used in the domain or area that I am researching. • I don't know how to keep track of my research findings.	• Research

(*continued*)

Table 6.1. (*continued*)

Ask yourself which of these statements seems closest to what you are thinking:	
If you feel this:	**Then work on this stage of thinking:**
• In my first draft I don't always run through the big ideas before adding details. • I don't use my first draft to experiment with the order of my thoughts. • I don't know if I have a good draft. • I don't know how to compare my draft with a worked model. • I don't always plan for one or more drafts in my writing assignments. • I don't always treat each draft as if it were a final paper (spell-checked, review instructions). • I don't always flexibly modify my outline when the draft seems like it's missing something. • I can't get my ideas out into words in draft form. • I can't use the outline and template to write a strong first draft.	• Draft
• I don't know when I have a good peer exchange. • I don't know how to give reasons for my comments to my peer. • I don't know how to communicate my ideas clearly. • I don't know how to share views and listen to other people's ideas. • I find receiving peer feedback hard. • I find giving peer feedback hard. • I don't like listening to others' ideas about my writing. • I don't know how to learn to enjoy peer feedback more. • I can't be intellectually humble. • I can't be open to new ideas. • I can't learn from others' perspectives.	• Peer Exchange
• I don't know how to use feedback to feedforward. • I don't feel inspired to work harder after feedback. • I don't know how to react to feedback. • I don't feel motivated after feedback. • I don't feel supported in my writing. • I feel pushed to do things after feedback, not engaged. • I am not very open to feedback. • I do not embrace evaluation as a teaching tool. • I don't like [written][spoken][peer][teacher] feedback. • I can't be open to feedback. • I can't use feedback to improve. • I can't understand either rubrics or the written feedback. • I don't use feedback to find other things that need to be fixed in my writing beyond what is marked. • I don't understand the rules or principles that are behind what has been marked up. • I don't know how to learn from positive feedback.	• Feedback and Feedforward

Ask yourself which of these statements seems closest to what you are thinking:	
If you feel this:	**Then work on this stage of thinking:**
• I don't know how to make my paper coherent. • I don't know how to spell-check the paper before submitting it. • I don't know how to trim down unnecessary words. • I do not use all the tools available to me (spellchecker, grammar check, templates)? • I don't know which tools I can use and which I can't. • I can't pay attention to details. • I can't catch spelling errors. • I don't know how to identify grammar problems. • I am not good at identifying punctuation errors.	• Edit
• I don't know how to regroup all the similar ideas into one paragraph. • I don't know how to reorganize the sections for better logic. • I don't realize I have a lot of missing details. • I have not gone back to the instructions to ensure I am submitting the right assignment. • I don't know how to add visual representations to facilitate understanding. • I can't assure my work is complete by reading it from start to finish. • I can't confirm I have incorporated all feedback I found useful. • I have not asked anyone else to read my paper to see if it makes sense. • I can't hear my own voice in the paper. • I can't ensure each word is well placed. • I can't write a well-organized and error-free paper. • I don't always correct all of the errors that I find.	• Revise
• I don't know how to review misspelled words. • I don't know how to avoid word repetition. • I don't know how to bring out my own voice. • I don't know how to read my paper out loud. • I don't know how to listen to a clear narrative.	• Proofread
• I don't feel any sense of celebration when I finish my work. • I don't think my writing merits celebration. • When I finish, I have no desire to start anything new. • I have not thought about how this work potentially leads to new work. • I don't usually feel good about my accomplishments. • I can't imagine how to turn my poem into a story, my research paper into a book, my story into a movie. . . . • I don't know what I learned that I could use to begin the next writing project.	• Complete and Commence

Table 6.2. An Example of Toggling in a University Mind, Brain, Health, and Education (MBHE) Paper

<table>
<tr><th>University Research Paper</th><th>Assignment</th><th colspan="2">Stage of Thinking</th></tr>
<tr><td rowspan="8">INTRODUCTION
Submission One
HINTS:
• Familiarize yourself with the literature in order to find key studies on your subject of interest. Consider what these studies have already shown and what is not yet known.
• Be sure to consider perspectives across the MBHE disciplines and to cite the sources used to support your ideas.
• Remember that anything stated as a fact should be supported by evidence, which means you must include an in-text citation for the statement and the full reference in the References list.
• The Introduction asks you to ground the reader in an MBHE topic in broad terms. This is where you'll provide a "big picture" overview that explains the importance of your topic.
• The Background asks you to share what is already known about your topic and requires you to cite literature that establishes this.
• Write efficiently. If your topic is, for example, on youth in jails, this might be formulated in the following way: "Incarcerated youth, defined as ___ by authors X and Y, comprise an estimated ___% of the population in the United Kingdom. More than half of incarcerated youth are [characteristic] (author, year), and ___% have speech impediments (author, year)."</td>
<td rowspan="4">#1
What do you want to know? Why?

#2
After doing initial research, can you determine if what you want to know is truly a gap in the literature (or is it just something you don't know)? Research what is already known about what you want to know. What solutions have already been proposed? What gaps exist in the literature in terms of research? Remember to indicate your "problems, plans, and help" at the end of your assignment.</td>
<td>Understand</td><td></td></tr>
<tr><td>Know Things</td><td></td></tr>
<tr><td>Mind Wander</td><td></td></tr>
<tr><td>Reflect</td><td></td></tr>
<tr><td rowspan="4">#3
Based on the gaps in the literature from a transdisciplinary perspective, what is not yet known and justifies your area of research? What is the draft of your research question in the format "How and to what extent does X [influence][impact] Y?" Remember to indicate your "problems, plans, and help" at the end of your assignment.</td>
<td>Map and Connect</td><td>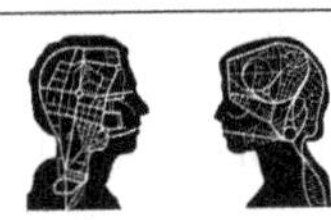</td></tr>
<tr><td>Outline</td><td>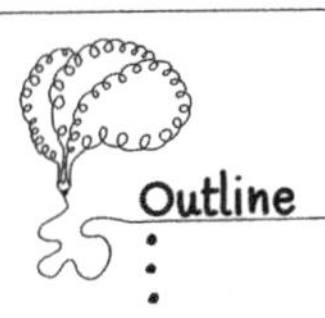</td></tr>
<tr><td>Plan</td><td></td></tr>
<tr><td>Research</td><td></td></tr>
</table>

Table 6.2. (*continued*)

University Research Paper	Assignment	Stage of Thinking	
These kinds of sentences integrate findings from your initial review of the literature, define terms, and offer background information to your topic. • The Problem Statement identifies what is not yet known about your topic. It is often harder to see what is "not known" than what is "known" about a topic. This can be formulated in the following structure: "While X and Y are well established in the literature, Z is less understood." • The Problem Statement should naturally lead to your Research Question. Please write your Research Question in this format: "How and to what extent does X [influence] [change][modify] Y?" For example, "How and to what extent would early intervention for speech impediments reduce incarceration for minority youth?"	#4 *Use the template and submit the Introduction, Background, Problem Statement, and Research Question.* *Be sure to address any unresolved feedback regarding previous submissions.*	Draft	
LITERATURE REVIEW *Submission Two* HINTS: • As a transdisciplinary paper, one should consider organizing the literature at the intersections of two or more elements. For example, a topic might be entitled "expressive language disorders from an MBHE perspective" and include subsections on speech challenges from a neuro- or biological perspective, from a psychological perspective, from a health and well-being perspective, and from an education perspective.	#5 *Identify each piece of feedback (global comments and themes) and explain how you plan to resolve the query, concern, or recommendation made by the teaching team. Remember to indicate your "problems, plans and help" at the end of your assignment.*	Feedback and Feedforward	
		Reflect	
		Plan	

(*continued*)

Table 6.2. (*continued*)

<table>
<tr><th>University Research Paper</th><th>Assignment</th><th colspan="2">Stage of Thinking</th></tr>
<tr><td rowspan="7">• Remember that your outline must create a logical structure for the information you present (consider heading levels as you organize your information). Provide in-text citations as needed (anything that is not common knowledge must be cited).</td><td rowspan="4">#6
What are the Literature Review topics and subtopics you will research in order to answer your research question or to explore your topic? Write your list of topics and subtopics (not the full content) and indicate 2–6 good research articles you have found so far. Remember to indicate your "problems, plans and help" at the end of your assignment. Remember, your Semester Project must be transdisciplinary, covering perspectives of Mind, Brain, Health, and Education science.</td><td>Understand</td><td>

</td></tr>
<tr><td>Research</td><td>

</td></tr>
<tr><td>Map and Connect</td><td>
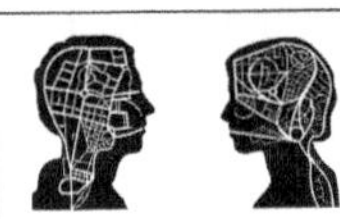
</td></tr>
<tr><td>Outline</td><td>

</td></tr>
<tr><td rowspan="3">#7
Create an annotated bibliography by adding specific comments, ideas and narrative to each of your topics and subtopics using the feedback you received in week 6. Remember to indicate your "problems, plans, and help" at the end of your assignment. Remember, you will eventually have to write this in a narrative form, but for the time being just worry about the content.</td><td>Feedback and Feedforward</td><td>

</td></tr>
<tr><td>Edit</td><td>

</td></tr>
<tr><td>Research</td><td>

</td></tr>
</table>

Table 6.2. (*continued*)

University Research Paper	Assignment	Stage of Thinking	
	#8 *Use the template and submit your Literature Review (attached to your Introduction).* *Be sure to address any unresolved feedback regarding previous submissions.*	Draft	
METHODOLOGY *Submission Three* HINTS: • The Methodology should describe how you found the evidence. In an academic paper this means that a person could follow your steps and would come up with the same results.	#9 *Write a concise and thoughtful self-assessment of your work thus far on your Semester Project. You should critique both yourself and the assignments. Also include any comments you want to share on the risk and protective factors that have impacted your work. Explain how your process so far has worked or has not worked. Remember to indicate your "problems, plans, and help" at the end of your assignment.*	Feedback and Feedforward	
		Reflect	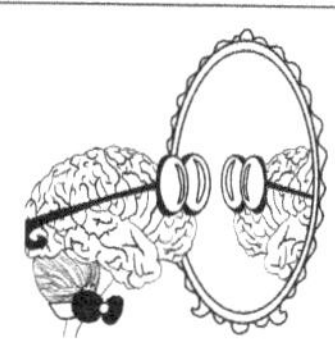
		Understand	
		Mind Wander	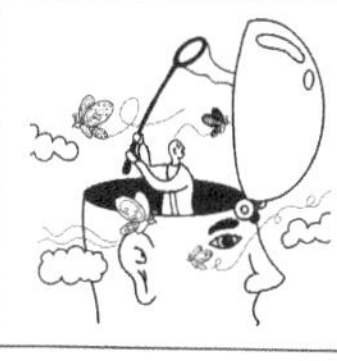
	#10 *Use the template and submit your Methodology (attached to your Introduction and Literature Review).* *Be sure to address any unresolved feedback regarding previous submissions.*	Revise	
		Draft	

(*continued*)

Table 6.2. (*continued*)

University Research Paper	Assignment	Stage of Thinking	
ANALYSIS *Submission Four* Hints: • The Analysis, along with the Conclusions, are the most creative parts of an Academic Paper. The author has the opportunity to reach a higher level of thinking in order to convey new ideas that are based on personal experiences and their cumulative MBHE research. The goal is to establish their existing understanding of the problem or question and synthesize findings from the different MBHE fields into a cohesive analysis section. • Remember that Analysis involves much more than just reporting information. Whereas you can report what others said in the Literature Review, Analysis requires that you join together the pieces of the puzzle in a unique way. Remember: "The whole is greater than the sum of its parts." This means you need to make sense of all the individual elements you found in the literature review and string them together in a way that tells a new story. • Think about the many ideas that other researchers have come up with related to your topic. Now think of the problems that still exist. How has previous research helped respond to the problem? How is it still inadequate? Take the time to think of paradoxes and unusual or contradictory thinking that may have occurred as you read different authors' perspectives.	#11 *Analyze the research evidence you have identified so far. What does the synthesis of the body of the literature tell you that each individual article or field of study could not? What did you find that you expected to find? What did you find that you did not expect to find? What new questions do you have now? Did you notice any deficiencies, gaps, or conflicts in the literature? Does your peer see what you see? What is your new understanding of your research question? Remember to indicate your "problems, plans, and help" at the end of your assignment.*	Know Things	
		Research	
		Revise	
		Mind Wander	
		Map and Connect	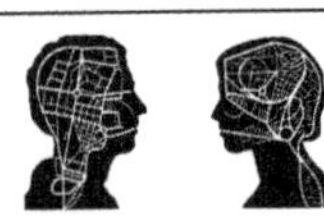
		Peer Exchange	
	#12 *Use the template and submit your Analysis (attached to your Methodology, Literature Review and Introduction).* *Be sure to address any unresolved feedback regarding previous submissions.*	Draft	

Table 6.2. (*continued*)

University Research Paper	Assignment	Stage of Thinking	
• The Analysis section is where you are critical with the Literature and identify gaps in knowledge. This is also where you point out the importance of a transdisciplinary view of the Literature. Explicitly call out connections you have made to this transdisciplinary way of approaching your problem.			
CONCLUSION *Submission Five* HINTS: • Remember that the first thing the reader wants to know in the Conclusions are the answers to the research questions or problems that were being tackled. • At the start of the semester, you were asked to think about what you wanted to know and why. In the Conclusions, you should respond to that initial prompt. Some conclusions are anticipated, and others are surprises. Take the time to identify what it was you expected to find and what you did not expect to find. You should write this section in the present tense (e.g., "There are four conclusions, two of which were expected and two of which were unexpected . . ."; "It is surprising and also intriguing to realize that . . ."). • The Conclusions are where you can be critical of yourself; where you critique your own process and challenge your assumptions. Think about answering one or more of the following questions: • Were you able to answer your question? Why or why not?	#13 *The Answer(s). What is the answer to your Research Question or what is the solution to your problem? In the Academic Paper, please answer your question in two parts: "How" and "To what extent." If you were unable to answer your research question, explain why. Remember to indicate your "problems, plans, and help" at the end of your assignment.*	Feedback and Feedforward	
		Mind Wander	
	#14 *Choose one or more of the following questions to complete your prompt: What were the limitations of your research process? Based on the limitations, what are your recommendations for future research? Related to the limitations: Were you able to answer your question? Why or why not? Where do you wish you had spent more or less time? How did your initial research question change after you reviewed the literature? Related to the recommendations: Did you identify how your findings lead to usable knowledge in the field? What suggestions for future study might you make based on your research? Remember to indicate your "problems, plans, and help" at the end of your assignment.*	Understand	
		Revise	
		Proofread	

(*continued*)

Table 6.2. (*continued*)

University Research Paper	Assignment	Stage of Thinking	
• Did you notice any deficiencies, gaps, or conflicts in the literature? • What is your new understanding of your research question? • Did you identify how your findings lead to usable knowledge in the field? • What suggestions for future study might you make based on your research thus far? • How did your initial research question change after you reviewed the literature?		Edit	
		Peer Exchange	
• Where do you wish you had spent more time (less time?) • If you were to self-assess at this stage, how would you grade yourself in terms of your final product, your research process, and your personal progress? • Finally, the best researchers take time to note all of the new, unanswered questions this process generated. Making space in a paper for this tends to support intentional and intellectually humble final papers. This shows how each Conclusion is really a new beginning to another new set of questions or problems.	#15 *Use the template and submit your Conclusions (attached to your Analysis, Methodology, Literature Review and Introduction).* *Be sure to address any unresolved feedback regarding previous submissions.*	Draft	
		Complete & Commence	

Variety Keeps Thinking Fresh and Focused

Being in the right stage of thinking at the right time is the feeling of flow. In entering the flow state, the feeling of pleasurable focus sustains the attention to the task at hand (Huskey et al., 2018). Expert writers know when to attend to negative affect and switch stages, and when to press on, recruiting the memory of past work to engage their executive control systems (Kellogg, 2018). Experienced writers have learned, often through trial and error, what works for them to catalyze flow. One way to think of flow and writing is that it is the opposite of writer's block. In *Writer's Block: The Cognitive Dimension* (1980), author Mike Rose explains that writer's block is psychological, but we suggest it can be explained with neurophysiological processes involving networks and chemicals. That is, when a person feels a lack of motivation for a project, the confidence to complete a writing challenge, or an inability to access creative thoughts—all partial definitions of writer's block—this is due to neurophysiological changes in the brain. We suggest that writer's block can be avoided if one understands the 15 stages of writing in ThinkWrite and toggles *between* them purposefully.

Efficient toggling depends on knowing yourself and your own needs. Self-understanding is the key to effective toggling. Developing writers can benefit from direct guidance and practice in building these same capacities of strategic engagement of diverse neural networks, strengthening executive control (Diaz, 2013). While some writers have extensive experience in toggling through the writing process, student writers can benefit from being explicitly taught the stages of thinking underlying the writing process and from being coached by a knowledgeable teacher, one who knows them as individual thinkers as well as having some expertise on the thinking processes involved in writing. In some cases, for instance, teachers might be advised to coach persistence in one type of thinking rather than the toggling out of a writing stage too soon, depending on the learner and the circumstances. For example, in moments involving creative ideation, research has shown underlying beliefs about creativity can cause some people to shorten the ideation process and consequently never arrive at their best insights, believing falsely that the best ideas come in an initial flash of insight and that creative ideation declines over time, a concept known as the "creative cliff" illusion (Lucas & Nordgren 2020). To avoid writer's block, achieve flow, and enhance creative insight, learners should be taught to toggle effectively.

Time for Toggling?

An impediment to using toggling in real classrooms is time. Teacher knowledge of the stages of thinking is just the beginning. Being able to label the different stages of thinking is a must, and once named, the key to enhancing writing through toggling is to help students understand how to choose the right stage. This is metaphorically like driving a car. The teacher needs to know how the car functions best and all that it can do, but they also need to show good decision-making about when to use which feature of the car. Sometimes it is beneficial to speed up, like on a long stretch of unhindered road. Other times it is good to use the windshield wipers, like in a rainstorm. At another moment it is good to use the rear-view mirror or camera to back into a parking place. All the different features of the car serve a different purpose. They are not necessarily all meant to be used at the same time, however, nor are some features to be ignored because they are not well understood or seem too difficult to understand. For a smooth ride, the driver should know all the possibilities and features of the car, which permits them a wider range of choices of what to use depending on the situation. To be a great teacher of driving or of writing, teachers need to first understand the machine (the brain), when to use which features (stages of thinking), and then the steps in forming independent drivers (learners) using good guidance (pedagogy).

We will show how ThinkWrite can be adapted to any curriculum using UDL (Universal Design For Learning) in Chapter 8. First, however, we turn to the practical tools in ThinkWrite that help to coach the toggling of thinking stages for better writing.

CHAPTER 7

Tools for Coaching the Thinking Behind Writing

The skill of leveraging the most appropriate stage of thinking at just the right moment through toggling requires development and practice (see Chapter 6). A writing coach, like any coach, is not expecting perfection from their students all at once. Instead, they begin by assessing where the student is starting from and how the student can get to the goal. We think there's no replacement for a writing sample in figuring out where a learner is in their thinking and what they need to capitalize on the potential of their work. The sample can be a past assignment or a worked example, or as we propose in ThinkWrite, a response to a single writing activity. Great teachers know they will never have a homogeneous group of writers; everyone comes into class at different levels, and despite the range of learners, the teacher is responsible for helping each learner advance.

COACHING STUDENTS TO TOGGLE

Below we share steps to coach toggling, including a list of questioning prompts. This is followed by a brief overview of five new tools from ThinkWrite to improve the evaluation of student writing. We end with a commentary about generative AI, specifically ChatGPT's call to action for educators, and a word about the challenges posed to current evaluation practices.

Teacher Diagnoses: What Stage of Thinking Would Benefit a Student's Writing?

To guide the choice of thinking stages and to toggle more purposefully, teachers can use the checklist in Table 7.1.

Once teachers know which stage would most benefit a student, feedback is needed to move students in that direction. Generally, a great way to prompt students to toggle is to ask questions such as: *What would happen if you tried X activity? How do your ideas change after trying X activity? What stage of thinking do you think you need next?* All three questions encourage experimentation with the ThinkWrite process while nudging students to recognize how different stages of thinking help their ideas to grow. After Table 7.1 below, teachers can find examples of prompts that can deepen student engagement in each stage of thinking during the writing process (Table 7.2).

Table 7.1. Teacher Checklist to Support Student Toggling

If you notice . . .	Then recommend activities for this stage of thinking:
• Inaccurate facts or descriptions of source materials • A disconnect between the assignment goal and the student's work • Failure to comply with a specified format • Misuse of key terminology or core ideas	Understand
• Overuse or overreliance on the ideas or words of other people's works • Inability to make analogies or relate one idea to that of others • A disconnect between the student's written submission and their personal goals • Missing data or information or ideas that one would expect based on previous learning or recent experience	Know Things
• Regurgitated solutions or overly typical responses to a problem • A lack of originality in the written assignment, despite accurate or thoughtful ideas • Weak associations between ideas	Mind Wander
• Inability to identify and/or use important ideas from source materials • Difficulty in making a personal connection to the writing • Tendency to skip over feedback or avoid making changes based on feedback • Jumps between one idea to another with no explicit connections	Reflect
• Illogical leaps between ideas or concepts • Disjointed writing or failure to see similarities and differences between parts of the written product • Difficulty in describing the relationship between multiple ideas	Map and Connect
• Trailing away from main point or main objective • Unorganized approach to sharing what are otherwise sound and related ideas • A struggle to convey the order and hierarchy of the written work • A weak opening and/or closing of ideas	Outline
• Written work that appears rushed or completed in one sitting • Missed deadlines and/or stressing about deadlines • A missing connection between the assignment and what the student hopes to achieve with it	Plan
• Missed opportunities to include key voices/authors on the topic • A mixture of good and questionable sources of information • Leaning on sources expressing only similar viewpoints to that of the author • Missing or mistaken factual material or inaccuracies in the use of domain-specific vocabulary or schema	Research

Table 7.1. (*continued*)

If you notice . . .	Then recommend activities for this stage of thinking:
• Difficulty in conveying thoughts or ideas in written form despite clear communication in other modalities • An avoidance of writing, or preference to share out in other ways	Draft
• Trouble with tone or messaging of the written ideas • An overreliance on self-confirming evidence • Difficulty in separating main ideas from supporting details • Desire to please the teacher; writing for the teacher's goals	Peer Exchange
• Revisions to the written work are minimal to none • Disengagement from the project after receiving feedback • A difference in reactions to feedback based on modality or who gives the feedback • Limiting response to feedback to correcting only marked errors and not finding the same or similar errors elsewhere • Limiting responses in feedback to only positive, "face-saving" feedback	Feedback and Feedforward
• A lot of unnecessary repetition or wordiness • Organizational issues • Evidence problems • Inappropriate transitions or gaps in transitions • Logical fallacies • Poor word choice or word choice inappropriate to audience or task • Inappropriate tone • Gaps in connecting the pieces (details) to the larger ideas (the whole)	Edit
• Haphazard revisions after feedback, or missed opportunities to step back and see how all the pieces go back together • Missing details or gaps in the connections across the main ideas • Writing that trails away from the point of the assignment or the student's goals	Revise
• Poor word choice, misspellings, and many grammatical errors • A lack of unique voice in the student's writing	Proofread
• The final grade is the student's main reason for celebration (or feelings of failure) • Unmet potential for the written work to be shared beyond the assignment submission	Complete and Commence

Table 7.2. Asking Questions to Prompt Toggling

When this stage is needed . . .	Ask . . .
Understand	What do you want to know and why? How would you explain this assignment to a friend?
Know Things	What else do you already know about this? What does this information mean to you?
Mind Wander	Have you tried taking a break or daydreaming? What connections do you see between different ideas?
Reflect	How did you come up with that idea? What will you do better/differently next time?
Map and Connect	What are the topics and subtopics you need to respond to the assignment or to explore your topic? What are different ways to group the ideas?
Outline	What would happen if you tried talking about X, then Y, and then Z? In what order would you share these ideas with a friend (or other audience)?
Plan	Where do you wish you had spent more or less time? What do you want to do? What do you need to do?
Research	Are there other perspectives you might use? What would happen if you also included Y?
Draft	Who do you want reading your work? How could you convince those people that your topic is important to them too?
Peer Exchange	Who can give the best feedback related to the genre or topic? Emotional support? Writing skills? A member of the target audience? Someone with technical knowledge of your topic?
Feedback and Feedforward	What next steps will you take based on the feedback? What categories of feedback do you see? How could you benefit from the feedback?
Edit	What is the intention of each paragraph? What is the relationship between two paragraphs? What about the next two?
Revise	Are there typical errors or verbal tics you often include that you want to edit out? What is your "center of gravity" or the central ideas you are conveying based on the passion in your voice? Have you given those areas appropriate attention in your writing?
Proofread	What are the kinds of tiny errors previous readers have marked up for you? How could you leverage tools to help you better understand when or how to apply rules for punctuation or grammar?
Complete and Commence	How did it feel to share your finished product with others? What else could come out of your writing project? In what other forms could your ideas be shared?

Evaluating End Products vs. Coaching Thinkers

No form of evaluation is objective, and this holds especially true for writing. In 1912, Starch and Elliot took two English essays by high school students and had teachers assign a grade. One-hundred-forty-two teachers graded these same two essays, and the result was a vast range of overall scores. An essay rated highly by one teacher received a failing grade from another. Even teachers in the same school district looking at the same essay and trained in scoring using a specific rubric gave grades differing by as much as 40 points or more on a scale of 100 (Brimi, 2011). While table grading, in which a group of teachers evaluate sample essays and reconcile their scoring, can help internalize standards, the practice seems to work best with frequent repetition, and the "norming" may drift with a new assignment. Teachers and students alike probably can name many occasions where it was obvious to them that subjectivity is inherent in evaluating writing.

It turns out that attempts to refine scoring criteria, develop training for scorers, and achieve consistency in grading across teachers are rooted in assumptions that we've known for a while to be untrue (e.g., see Huot, 1996). Writing has no fixed quality, there is no single set of features that defines all "good" writing, and any student's ability to write is never fully represented through a few numerical scales. This is not to say that having some shared criteria is fruitless. The movement in the 1990s toward rubrics was a response to the understanding that grades are indeed subjective. Portfolios have pushed us to see and assess multiple points of progress from a student rather than a single final paper. Yet, while we've progressed in our desire to reach a more holistic view of assessing writing, the tools we're using still pass subjective judgment of not just a written work but of a person (often unintentionally) and do so based on writing tending to be brief in length, completed over short spans of time, and in limited genres. Though perhaps we cannot achieve complete objectivity in evaluating writing, we can inch closer to measuring and coaching for what really matters: the development of *thinkers* as much as the tech-correct aspects of writing.

Thinking to write and writing to think ultimately aim at "good writing" as an end product. But how do we know when writing is of high quality? This is one of the oldest dilemmas in education as writing is judged both on technical merit and creative merit. To share criteria about good writing, this chapter considers the use of modified versions of familiar tools, such as rubrics, for both students and teachers. We also suggest a shift from evaluating the end products to coaching the thinking behind the writing throughout the process, which necessitates not only modified tools but also adjustments to where we spend our valuable time as teachers.

As Peter Elbow (2000) says, "writing wasn't meant to be read in stacks of twenty-five, fifty, or seventy-five," (p.452). Yet we often find ourselves in such circumstances, where we are challenged to find ways to like and judge the piles of student writing before us. We posit that any disappointment felt about the quality of writing is because the scaffolding to get to a more impressive product wasn't quite there in the first place. Instead of spending hours wondering what went wrong, how to correct, what to grade, and what to justify, if we spread our efforts and interactions over time, we not only give better spacing to our teaching efforts but also intervene earlier and become familiar sooner with what a student is thinking, where they are headed and what they need from us. Part of the dread of final grading is not knowing precisely what the issue was and being too far along in the class timeline to backtrack and figure it out. By chunking the process (into ThinkWrite stages) and sprinkling in formative feedback at each part of the process (with ThinkWrite activities and tools), we can better support student growth and avoid being surprised or taxed for time when we get whatever we deem to be the "final" product from our student.

This is precisely why the best teachers refocus their efforts on *developing* or coaching students as great thinkers and great writers. As Huot (2002) described,

> When we grade or test writing, the student receives some score, grade or label. Although the articulated judgment is based upon writing, the person is the object of that articulation. If, instead, we respond to the writing without a grade, score or label, then the writing remains the object. . . . Grading or testing involves little or no learning or teaching. (p. 62)

If we aim to grow a learner's ability to think critically and be effective communicators, we must first extend our view of writing beyond its final product. Hairston referred back in 1982 to a focus on the writing process as part of a paradigm shift in the teaching of writing, which also included using writing as a tool for learning. Across different subjects from science to math to philosophy to social studies, writing is leveraged for learning content (e.g., Graham et al., 2020) as well as for thinking (e.g., Holdinga et al., 2021; Kayaalp et al., 2020; Woldt & Nenad, 2021). The value of the process writers engage in while writing has been known for some time by rhetoric studies, reaching even disciplines such as history (e.g., Carter & Korostyshevsky, 2021). Because teachers recognize that there is an underlying process that leads to a great product—whether an academic paper or a poem—making that process just as visible as the written artifact allows for formative feedback to coach the thinking as well as the writing.

Though we often generate a visible written product (an *artifact*), the thinking itself occurs in many invisible ways. We don't, for example, see the way in which a writer may grapple with feedback or how a writer connects many ideas while out on a walk. From a friendly conversation that spurs a new draft to the reflection that occurs while staring at a wall, what we now might describe as the thinking moments, or perhaps what our students apologize for as "wasted time," can be underappreciated in preference for what is written on the page. Yet thinking and writing are inextricably linked (Langer & Applebee, 1987), and writing makes thinking visible (Kaag & van Belle, 2024). The ThinkWrite model calls on us to celebrate the invisible thinking behind visible writing, inspired by and adapting activities from visible thinking (Ritchhart et al., 2011) and visible learning (Hattie, 2012). By removing the veil of "great" writing and breaking down the thinking–writing process into its smaller parts, teachers can intervene and coach their learners in a way consistent with how our brain learns: through a dynamic process of interaction with the environment and experience (e.g., Zelazo, 2015), and adapting based on error detection (Dehaene, 2014).

ThinkWrite provides tools and activities that enable this kind of formative commentary to correct misunderstandings, respond to questions, or to enhance thinking processes sooner rather than later. ThinkWrite asks teachers to make different kinds of observations of their students at each stage of the process and to leverage new kinds of data or information they might not have had access to before. ThinkWrite also embraces *Understanding by Design* by Wiggins and McTighe (2005), to keep clear objectives in focus. If our goal in education is for students to develop a writing identity, make meaning, and be critical thinkers, we must change the tools we use to measure writing and the evidence we accept so that we can be better writing coaches. The changes and debates brought on through the COVID pandemic and from technology such as generative AI (e.g., ChatGPT) have made it more important than ever to step back and reconsider our goals as educators and the paths toward them. That is, if being a great writer means just the final product, then perhaps tools like ChatGPT win. But if being a great writer means becoming a great thinker, then society wins.

VALUING THE THINKING AS MUCH AS THE WRITING

There are many ways that teachers already cultivate writing skills in classrooms. Some of these methods prize the written artifact above all else, and many place value on meeting a particular objective in a certain amount of time. When taking on the role of a coach, as a guide in the cognitive development of the student, existing writing and assessment tools can be complemented by ThinkWrite (Table 7.3). While the scope of this book does not allow for an in-depth explanation of each additional tool we propose, their introduction and purpose are described below.

Tracking Starting Points and Progress: Spider Rubrics

When assessing the invisible thinking behind the writing, one method to reduce subjectivity is by creating shared criteria that will be used to grade a student. The best tool for that to date is a rubric (Stanley, 2021). But rubrics themselves are faulty in that the weight given and criteria chosen are normally made by the

Table 7.3. Using ThinkWrite to Expand Current Tools Commonly Used in Teaching Writing

Instead of relying solely on . . .	Also consider this from ThinkWrite . . .
"On-time" grade percentages	Use a spider rubric (Figure 7.1) to help writers understand where they start and where they spend their time.
Writing rubrics	Use a product-process-progress-potential (PPPP) rubric (Table 7.4) to increase a writer's grade based on their development over time.
Draft and final written products	Use ThinkWrite activities to get "mini" products (see Chapters 3, 4, and 5) that show a student's thinking and allow for frequent, formative feedback.
Common Core writing categories	Use the Genres of Writing list (Figure 1.5) to normalize students' struggles in different genres, represent a truer range of writing that exists outside of school, and invite students to extend their ideas.
Transition Word charts	Use the Relationships (Transitions) in Writing guide (Table 7.5) to direct students to the thinking behind the word choice.

teacher, and these weights can vary widely from one teacher to the next. For some, clarity is weighted more than formatting, for others spelling or evidence takes on more weight. We propose a rubric that emphasizes the thinking behind the writing. The spider rubric (Figure 7.1), named after its spiderweb form, gives a teacher a view into the approaches that got a student to the end product they submitted. Not only does this spider rubric expose different people's approaches and starting points, it also helps an educator work with a student to figure out precisely where that student may benefit from more time or practice.

The spider rubric can be used to mark the order and number of activities a student completes for that stage of thinking, or even more simply, the estimated number of hours (or days, or weeks) they spend in one particular stage. The rubric doesn't require any specialized knowledge and can be applied as a first step in implementing the ThinkWrite model across disciplines, as all disciplines leverage and aim to improve their students' thinking and reasoning even with very different end products. Let's explain further.

To give a clearer idea of how ThinkWrite works in a nonlinear way, we share three scenarios mapped onto the ThinkWrite spider rubric. Spider rubrics show how much time and at which stage of thinking learners focused their attention. This allows both teachers and learners to visually assess how students spend their time in order to make the thinking behind the writing more visible. These are just a few possibilities out of many but we hope it serves the purpose of showing the flexibility of the model.

In the first scenario, there may be some students who work through each of the stages in a step-by-step fashion and cover all of the bases evenly (Figure 7.2). This can be due to the teacher's decision about how to structure writing lessons or to the student's choice about where to begin, depending on course design. A step-by-step writing process would cover all 15 stages in order, beginning with *Understand* and circling all around through *Complete and Commence*.

In a second scenario (Figure 7.3), a student who is very familiar with the assigned topic might begin with *Drafting* and then get *Feedback* before they realize they did not *Understand* part of the instructions and then backtrack to do more *Research* before finally submitting.

In a third scenario (Figure 7.4), a student might know very little about the assigned topic and start by doing *Research*, then *Outlining*, and then get some *Peer Exchange* comments before *Editing* and submitting their work.

Figure 7.1. Spider Rubric

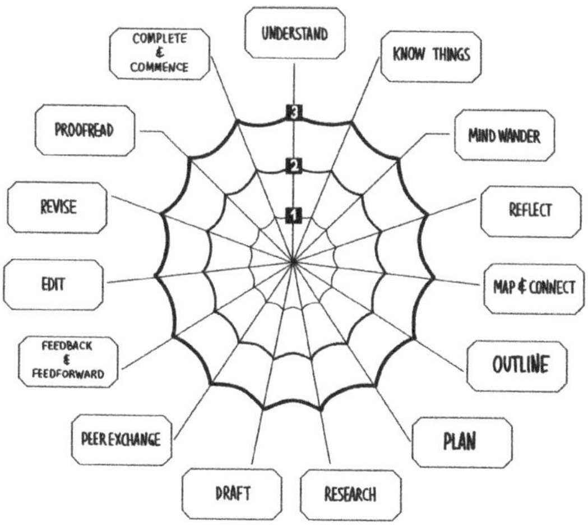

Figure 7.2. Spider Rubric Example of a Linear Writing Process

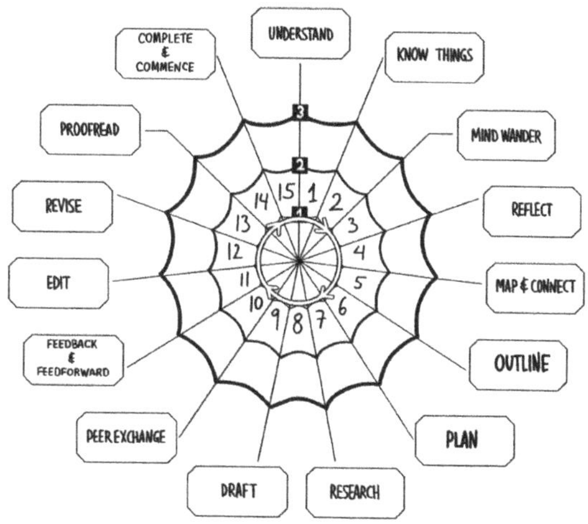

Figure 7.3. Spider Rubric Example of a Writing Process That Prioritizes Drafting but Not Planning or Outlining

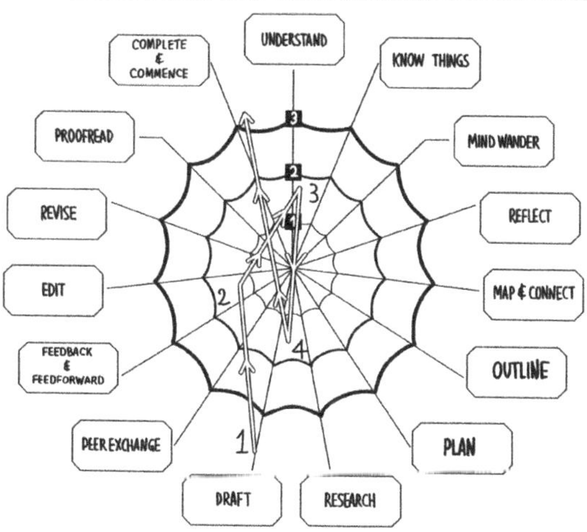

Figure 7.4. Spider Rubric Example That Prioritizes Peer Feedback but Not Understanding

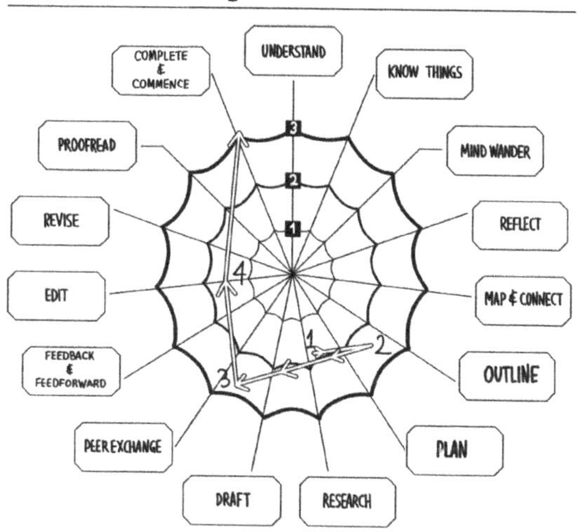

This means that while a typical path toward a successful writing project might start with prewriting, we know that this all depends on multiple variables related to the student and to the teacher. The spider rubric can be used along with the students' writing submissions to discuss their process. Teachers can indicate how more time in one stage or another might yield a superior result and point the student to possible activities from the ThinkWrite list in those areas. The teacher and student can discuss what the student would do differently the next time, based on the path they took and the results they achieved (feed*forward*). The big-picture view enabled by the spider rubric gives credit to all the effort put into different stages of thinking, celebrates individual variability, and could even be used as a point of comparison not just for one single assignment but for how a student adapts their approach across time and disciplinary contexts.

Expanding Dimensions of Evaluation: PPPP Rubrics

A single rubric can take into consideration the outcome or *product*, the writer's thinking *process*, the revisions made over time and lessons learned or *progress*, and that person's *potential* to be a great writer (Table 7.4). This product-process-progress-potential (PPPP) rubric enables us to evaluate writing more holistically, in a way that accounts for not just a single product but one's learning over time. The rubric further breaks down the ratings into ThinkWrite's stages, giving precise feedback on where a writer may excel or benefit from exploring more in the future. Whereas traditional rubrics tend to be fault finding (we minus points from a total), the PPPP rubric can replace final grades, when possible, or can be used to raise a writer's grade based on their development over time. That is, if a writer made substantial progress in the assignment product, adapted their process, and tried different activities, whatever initial grade they received can be increased to recognize their growth. No single product at one point in time is enough to judge potential, but several products (or revisions) over time move us away from assessing writing as though it is fixed. The PPPP rubric at a minimum can be highly useful in formative feedback and developing metacognitive awareness of the writer's own processes and progress. The PPPP rubric can be used alone or in combination with existing rubrics; the point is to use it as a coaching tool to recognize a student's strengths and development.

Observing Thinking: Activities by Stages

Frequent, formative feedback is only possible when the invisible thinking behind writing becomes visible (observable) to teachers. Each ThinkWrite stage includes a range of activities a writer can complete to benefit from that form of thinking, examples of which were shared in Chapters 3, 4, and 5. Each activity results in a "mini" product or form that is evidence of their thinking process, which teachers then use to inform what that writer might need next. Figure 7.5 shows an example

Table 7.4. Product-Process-Progress-Potential Rubric

Criteria	Area of achievement	Scale 1	2	3	4	Total
UNDERSTAND	Product (writing project)					
	Process (number and quality of activities)					
	Progress (advancement from previous work)					
	Potential (promising direction for future work)					
KNOW THINGS	Product (writing project)					
	Process (number and quality of activities)					
	Progress (advancement from previous work)					
	Potential (promising direction for future work)					
MIND WANDER	Product (writing project)					
	Process (number and quality of activities)					
	Progress (advancement from previous work)					
	Potential (promising direction for future work)					
REFLECT	Product (writing project)					
	Process (number and quality of activities)					
	Progress (advancement from previous work)					
	Potential (promising direction for future work)					
MAP AND CONNECT	Product (writing project)					
	Process (number and quality of activities)					
	Progress (advancement from previous work)					
	Potential (promising direction for future work)					
OUTLINE	Product (writing project)					
	Process (number and quality of activities)					
	Progress (advancement from previous work)					
	Potential (promising direction for future work)					
PLAN	Product (writing project)					
	Process (number and quality of activities)					
	Progress (advancement from previous work)					
	Potential (promising direction for future work)					
RESEARCH	Product (writing project)					
	Process (number and quality of activities)					
	Progress (advancement from previous work)					
	Potential (promising direction for future work)					
DRAFT	Product (writing project)					
	Process (number and quality of activities)					
	Progress (advancement from previous work)					
	Potential (promising direction for future work)					

Table 7.4. (*continued*)

Criteria	Area of achievement	Scale 1	2	3	4	Total
PEER EXCHANGE	Product (writing project)					
	Process (number and quality of activities)					
	Progress (advancement from previous work)					
	Potential (promising direction for future work)					
FEEDBACK AND FEEDFORWARD	Product (writing project)					
	Process (number and quality of activities)					
	Progress (advancement from previous work)					
	Potential (promising direction for future work)					
EDIT	Product (writing project)					
	Process (number and quality of activities)					
	Progress (advancement from previous work)					
	Potential (promising direction for future work)					
REVISE	Product (writing project)					
	Process (number and quality of activities)					
	Progress (advancement from previous work)					
	Potential (promising direction for future work)					
PROOFREAD	Product (writing project)					
	Process (number and quality of activities)					
	Progress (advancement from previous work)					
	Potential (promising direction for future work)					
COMPLETE AND COMMENCE	Product (writing project)					
	Process (number and quality of activities)					
	Progress (advancement from previous work)					
	Potential (promising direction for future work)					
TOTAL:						

Source: Authors

workflow of a writer who leverages a single activity (from Map and Connect) to generate a miniproduct (the photo of grouped ideas) and then can explain and get feedback from others. In this example, a peer or teacher may offer additional ways to connect ideas or expose gaps in the writer's rationale, and all this input informs the writer's thinking early in the process.

The activities are sometimes completed individually, sometimes in small groups, and other times prompt the writer to seek out a partner's opinion. The activities also span modalities, from simply talking out loud, to drawing or writing,

Figure 7.5. Example Process: From "Map and Connect" Activity to Miniproduct to Explanation

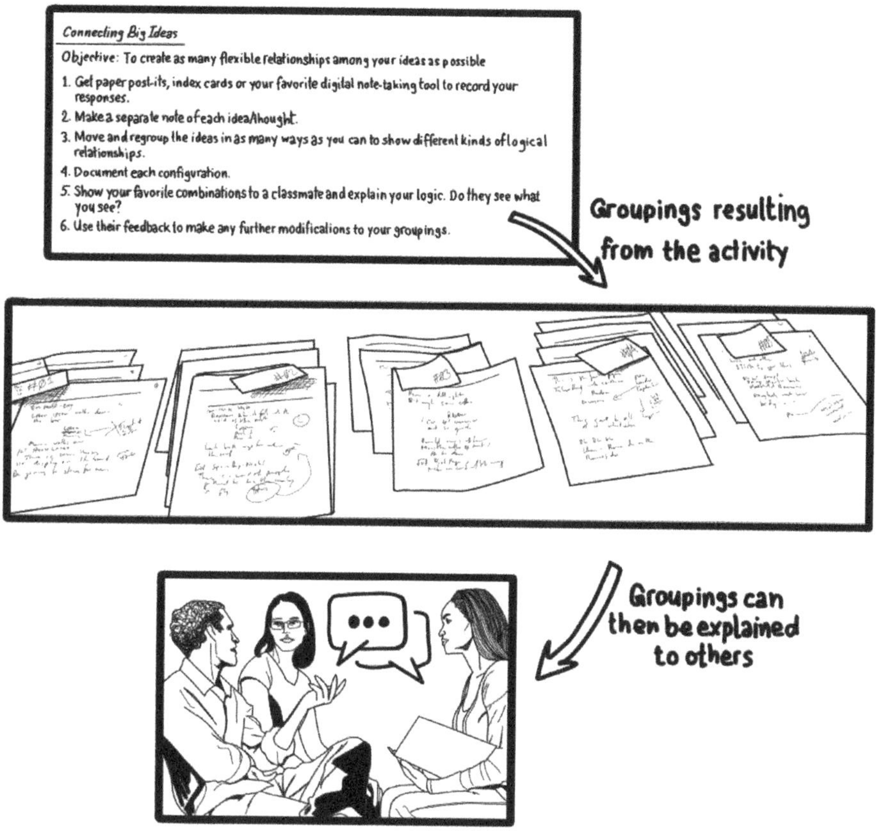

to listening, or even using audio, video, or other potentially helpful digital tools (in Figure 7.5, for example, a student could have instead used Post-its or digital whiteboards to achieve the same goal). Allowing student choice about the activity and modality is important, as each activity specifies an objective that meets a different writing objective, unique to the learner. Teachers and students alike can select the activity that best serves their needs based on what outcome they could benefit from the most. A sampling of activities is provided in Chapters 3, 4, and 5, though the full range of options are available at ThinkWriteMBE.com.

Expanding Ways of Expression: List of Writing Artifacts

Expertise in writing varies greatly because of the vast range of ways that exist to write. Some of us may have developed expertise in particular genres or forms of writing, such as when a student becomes proficient in literary analysis, while others have habituated writing a science report. In Chapter 6, we described how expertise in a specific form of writing affects when/how a writer moves through the thinking processes and how/when that writer encounters an unfamiliar genre, they may need additional time because of the shift in writing expectations between genres. What student writers may not realize is that the struggle they may feel when stretching into an unknown form of writing is totally normal. As Figure 1.5 shows, there are over 200 kinds of writing. Each artifact of writing comes with its own set of expectations from the audience, allows for various kinds of voices, and serves quite different purposes and goals. Genres promote a set of expectations that guides a reader to activate certain frameworks and schema in their meaning-making process; the delineation of subgenres shows how these expectations can grow increasingly specific, requiring the novice in the field to engage in research to begin to grasp and possibly apply them. ThinkWrite motivates reading and writing cross-genre exercises and the benefits they bring and encourages a broader range of writing artifact development (see Chapter 1), more closely resembling the range of writing that exists outside of school.

Additionally, in the real world, it is easy to find ideas that are extended, such as with sequels, the way songs are used in ads, a lab report that morphs into a science fiction novel, or a series of memoirs that become a saga. By extending the options available to students, we emphasize that it is not just about what the students finish or submit but where they are headed with their ideas. A narrow band of thinking (single genre evaluation, for example) may make students think they are not good at writing because our assessments fail to value the range of thinking a student is doing. It is not only beneficial to invite exploration across genres but also natural for the brain to want to extend what it is doing. A student may start with a research paper and then decide to turn that into an infographic (see Figure 7.6 for an example Complete and Commence activity to do just this!).

Figure 7.6. Example Activity to Extend Work to Another Genre

Infographic or Poster

Objective: *To extend your audience by synthesizing your work*

1. Search for infographics or posters on your topic for inspiration.
2. Note the main ideas or message from your completed written project that you want to convey.
3. Make an infographic or poster out of your written work.
4. Upload or display your infographic or poster to a public space.
5. Reflect and take notes on the following questions: How did it feel to share your finished product with others? How did the possibilities of an infographic or poster expand your understanding of your own work? Would you do anything differently the next time?

Another may turn in a lab report and then realize the importance of sharing results through other mediums like a blog post or scripting a vlog. The invitation to explore is a core benefit of offering a wider range of writing artifacts, as it is no longer only the writing that matters but the thinking that each student carries forward.

Turning Stylistic Choices Into Thinking Exercises: Relationships (Transitions) in Writing

Many teachers are already familiar with transition charts that give writers a template of connecting words to move between ideas. Guides like transition charts become valuable go-to resources for students as they communicate their ideas. To take this idea one step further, ThinkWrite focuses not only on the words or phrases themselves but also the *relationships* they denote. Words as well as punctuation marks indicate relationships between one sentence, paragraph, or idea and the next one. Errors in selecting the best transition are not just syntactical but also expose errors in logic or thinking. Some students make these transition errors because they have been taught a limited number of relationships, and because they have been taught to use select transitions in a single order. One of the authors recalls a university student who spoke English as a second language repeatedly used "hence," followed by "therefore," and ended with "in conclusion," in every single paragraph! Teachers can support student thinking by asking them to explicitly identify the relationships they are after. Understanding that "furthermore" builds off of the previous idea, while "on the contrary" opposes it, and "as a consequence" summarizes its effects, are all valuable lessons not only in rhetoric, but also logic.

Relationships between ideas in writing are shown via transitions, from conjunctions such as "but" to denote a conditional statement or "because" for cause/effect, to phrases such as "even though" to signal comparing/contrasting ideas, to "to demonstrate," which connects a stated idea with an example. The relationships are also shown through punctuation marks such as connecting lists with a comma or a semicolon to contrast ideas, and through formatting such as italic or bold font for emphasis. Sometimes no transition is needed at all, meaning that writers must learn when transitions are needed or not and how to leverage them. Learning how relationships are defined by the placement of these words in sentences, and even the use of punctation or formatting, helps writers think through their conceptual understanding of the ideas in their paper. By providing the Relationships in Writing Guide (Table 7.5), teachers help developing writers think about how they see the relationships between their ideas.

Table 7.5. Relationships (Transitions) in Writing Guide

EMPHASIS		ADDITION	
Above all	Indeed	A further	In addition (to this)
Absolutely	It should be noted	Additionally	In fact
Actually	More importantly	Again	In other words
Again	Moreover	Along with	In support (of)
Also	Never	Also	Like
And	Notably	An additional	Likewise
Another point is	Obviously	And (then)	Moreover
As it happens	Of course	Another	Neither . . . nor . . .
As well as	On top of that	Apart from this	Next
Certainly	Only	As (well) (as that)	Not only . . . but also . . .
Clearly	Particularly	Besides	Not to mention
Definitely	Significantly	Both . . . and . . .	Or
Especially	Specifically	By the same token	Similarly
Furthermore	To be sure	Equally (important)	Then
Importantly	Too	Finally	To say nothing of
In addition	Truly	Further	Too
In fact	Undoubtedly	Furthermore	Uniquely
In particular	Unquestionable	Identically	
In reality	Without a doubt		
COMPARE		**CONTRAST**	
Also	In contrast	Albeit	Instead (of)
Alternatively	In like manner	Alternatively	Nevertheless
As if	In the same way	Although	Nonetheless
As with	Instead (of)	Apart from	Notwithstanding
As . . . as . . .	Just as (. . . so too)	As much as	Of contrast
Both . . . and . . .	Like	At the same time	On the contrary
By the same token	Likewise	But	On the other hand
Comparable	Of contrast	Contrary to	Or
Despite this	Same as	Conversely	Others may say
Either . . . or . . .	Similar to	Despite	Others think
Equally	Similarly	Different(from)	Otherwise
Even though	Unless	Either . . . or . . .	Rather
In comparison	Whether or		

Table 7.5. (*continued*)

OPINION		CONTRAST	
As far as I know	In my opinion	Even if	Some believe
As for me	In my view	Even so	Still
I believe	It seems likely	Even though	Though
I feel	It seems to be	Even when	Uniquely
I think	It seems to me	Except	Unless
I'd say that	Personally (I think)	Having said that	Unlike
If I am not mistaken	To me	However	Whereas
In my experience	What I mean to say is	If	While
		In contrast (to)	Yet
		In spite of	
SIMILARITY		**SUMMARY**	
Additionally	In like manner	Accordingly	In conclusion
As well as	Just as	After all	In general
Both . . . and . . .	Likewise	All in all	In most cases
Comparatively	Moreover	Altogether	In other words
Correspondingly	Of course	As a result	In short
Equally important	Similarly	As a rule	In sum
Furthermore	The same as	As has been noted	In summary
Identically	Together with	As shown above	In the end
In either case		As you can see	On balance
		Briefly	On the whole
		By and large	Overall
		Finally	Thus
		For all of those reasons	To be sure
		For the most part	To sum up
		Generally	To summarize
		In a word	With this in mind
		In brief	

Table 7.5. (*continued*)

RESULT/CONCLUDE		ILLUSTRATION/EXAMPLE	
Above all	In conclusion	According to	In other words
Accordingly	In consequence	An instance (of this)	In particular
All in all	In essence	As an example	In the case of
All things considered	In fact	As can be seen	In this case
As a consequence (of)	In light of	As proof	Including
As a result	In response to	As revealed by	Like
As explained	In short	As shown by	Namely
Based on	In summary	Based on	One example is
Because of	It seems	By	Proof of this
Consequently	On the whole	Finally	So
Due to	Overall	For example	Specifically
Evidently	So	For instance	Such as
Finally	Then	For one thing	Take . . .
For this reason	Therefore	If	That is
Generally (speaking)	Thereupon	Illustrated by	This can be seen in
Given these points	Thus	In fact	To begin with
Hence	To be sure	In one case	To clarify
In a word	To conclude	In one example	To demonstrate
In brief	To sum up	In one instance	To illustrate
	Without a doubt	In one respect	To show that

CAUSE & EFFECT		CONDITION	
As a consequence of	In fact	As/so long as	Lest
As a result (of)	In the consequence of	Because (of)	On (the condition) (that)
Because (of)	Is caused by	But	Provided that
Being that	Is due to	Depending on	Since
Brings about	Is the result of	Even if	Unless
Causes	Leads to	For that reason	When
Consequently	Owing to	If	Whether
Contributes to	Results from	In order to	With this in mind
Due to	Since	In that case	
For	So	In the event that	
For that reason	Therefore		
Hence	Thus		

Table 7.5. (*continued*)

DIRECTION & PLACE		SPACE	
Above	In the distance	Above	Inside
At	Into	Across	Into
At that point	Nearby	Against	Near
Behind	Next to	Along	Next to
Beside	On	Among	Off
Beyond	On the other side	Around	On
Close to	Opposite to	Behind	On top (of)
Down	Over there	Below	Opposite
From	There	Beneath	Outside
Here	To	Between	Over
In	To the left/right	By	Through
In front of	Toward	In back (of)	Throughout
In the back	Under	In front (of)	Under
PERSUASION/ARGUMENT		**CONCESSION**	
Admittedly	Indeed	Admittedly	Even so
Again	It is clear that	All the same	Even though
Besides	Most importantly	Although	However
Best of all	Obviously	As much as	In spite of
Certainly	Of course	Even if	Up to this point
Cleary	Really		
Decidedly	Surely		
Especially	Understandably		
Evidently	Undoubtedly		
For this reason	Worst of all		
In fact			

(*continued*)

Table 7.5. (*continued*)

TIME/SEQUENCE		ORDER	
About	Later	Above all	Last but not least
After	Long ago	After	Next
Afterward	Meanwhile	At this time	Previously
As soon as	Next	Before	Second/secondly
As time passes	No sooner then	Finally	Subsequently
At last	Not for a long time	First and foremost	Then
At the same time	Now	First/firstly	Third/thirdly
At the start	One (two, multiple) time(s)	Following	
Before (long)	Presently		
Beginning with	Scarcely when		
Currently	Since		
During	Someday		
Earlier	Soon		
Eventually	Subsequently		
Finally	That day		
First (of all)	The next day		
Following	Then		
Formerly	Thereafter		
Immediately	These days		
In a little while	To begin with		
In modern times	Today/tomorrow		
In the future	Until		
In the meantime	When		
In the past	Whenever		
Initially			
Last(ly)			

Source: Authors

WRITING IS NO LONGER JUST ABOUT PENCIL AND PAPER: EMBRACING EDTECH

Good writing used to be measured by what a person could do with pencil and paper. Nowadays, multiple edtech tools can support the writing processes. Indeed, generative AI has caused some of the hottest debates in literacy in the past 50 years. Rather than take sides in this debate, we wanted to add an additional angle. Before generative AI (e.g., ChatGPT), writing products were mainly the result of complex mental processes and good thinking skills. ChatGPT has shown you can skip the thinking and still come up with a decent writing product (much like when someone is hired to write an assignment for someone else.) What is at stake is not just the quality of writing, it is the quality of *thinking*. If school evaluation only rewards the product, there is no need to nurture the thinking behind the writing, but also remember that if ChatGPT replaces the actual writing process, then those neural networks go unused and good thinking goes undeveloped. In neuroscience there is a saying, "use it or lose it." When we use technology like generative AI to shortcut rather than force thinking, we don't push ourselves to use or reinforce the neural underpinnings of great thinking. This means good writing can exist without great thinking, as a result of tools like ChatGPT, but unfortunately, great thinking does not develop without pushing the brain to write.

Pairing Tools With Writing Objectives

Finally, we want to call attention to the evaluation of writing. A key roadblock to innovation in literacy practice is the circular logic with which success is defined. The articulation of competencies has been a major (and politically charged) focus of educational reform since the turn of the millennium. The impressive list of competencies that have been articulated continues to be deeply focused both on the written product and on ensuring standardization and increased efficiencies in the measurement process. As many of the testing companies are also textbook producers, a limited range of writing skills is evaluated on standardized tests. The textbooks geared to these measurements are likewise limited in scope. Writing instruction is complex and can be approached in a number of ways. While not universal, one practical "fallback" in formal education has been the one-size-fits all approach—one task, a set sequencing of activities, one deadline, one set of formal standards to attain. This can be an approach in service of the mastery of universally desirable skills (e.g., the five-paragraph essay) and is, in part, a practical adaptation in terms of the individual teacher's workflow.

The industrial model of education would have us smooth over individual differences in the interest of practical processing and production. Rather than respecting these uniquely successful brains who have learned to adapt to their environment through experience, we come to view those who don't fit the mold as deficient. Some "do school" well and thrive; many do not and find their strengths are seldom recognized or celebrated. They may come to think of themselves as not being good writers or as lacking the potential to be. Conversely, those who thrive within a traditional classroom may not reach their full potential as writers and thinkers because certain thinking stages have not been addressed or well developed through direct instruction and feedback. Current school structures push all kids to make writing standards on a timetable that may not be their own. One way to create more time is to have students self-assess where they need to work more by identifying the stage(s) of ThinkWrite that would advance the writing and to toggle accordingly.

We hope this chapter gives teachers an introduction to a range of tools that add to the discussion about not just judging written artifacts but also the quality of thinking behind them. We hope they find inspiration in the checklist and guiding questions (Tables 7.1 and 7.2) to help students toggle between stages of thinking. We nudge teachers to use the spider rubric (Figure 7.1) to help students visualize their current approaches to writing, and then think about how to modify their toggling for even better results in the future. We encourage the incorporation of PPPP rubrics (Table 7.4) to call attention to thinking-stage successes and where there is room for improvement. We highly recommend the use of new genres (Figure 1.5) to inspire instruction in multiple artifact forms, with a focus on thinking rather than just the product. We hope teachers will use the relationships (transition word) guide (Table 7.5) to launch conversations about many ways ideas can be linked. And finally, we hope teachers see the overall societal benefits of developing great thinkers through the process of writing rather than relinquishing this great task to generative AI. Writing can be augmented by using generative AI as a mental sparring partner, but it should never replace the invisible thinking that is a prerequisite to good writing.

The key to great literacy instruction is to first identify what missing knowledge a student has and then to pair it with the right level of thinking. While current educational structures are generally good about identifying deficits in student knowledge (what content they missed), we are less successful in giving learners the time they need to fill in those gaps in their process. By shifting the way we spend our time, and by modifying the tools we employ, we can become more precise in filling those gaps and in coaching the thinking needed to enhance writing. Next, we discuss how this all can be done through Universal Design for Learning.

CHAPTER 8

Implementing ThinkWrite With Universal Design for Learning

The ThinkWrite model has a strong theoretical framework grounded in the learning sciences. To be practical, however, it needs to convert into usable knowledge. One way to do this is through Universal Design for Learning, which is closely linked to mastery learning.

Almost 70 years ago, Benjamin Bloom and 33 of the brightest minds of the day set out to establish a taxonomy of educational objectives (1956). He continued to innovate and celebrate the human mind, and in his observation of children, came to realize something that many great teachers know intuitively: Pretty much anyone in any class can learn anything under the right conditions. Bloom suggested that although students vary widely in their learning rates and modalities, if teachers could provide the necessary time and appropriate learning conditions, nearly all students could reach a high level of achievement. Roughly 10% of students have learning difficulties that prevent them from mastering the content such as severe intellectual disabilities, blindness, deafness, or mobility issues. The vast majority (90%+) of students can achieve grade-level expectations so long as they have enough *time* to fill in any missing prerequisite pieces of content information. This means that the real work of teachers is in designing the conditions for learning in which *a whole class moves forward when each student has their own starting point for writing.*

WHAT IS UNIVERSAL DESIGN FOR LEARNING IN EDUCATION?

Universal Design for Learning (UDL) is a teaching and learning structure that has its origins in architecture's attempts to design environments that can meet multiple needs. For example, modern crosswalks now have slight ramps that include raised bumps rather than old-fashioned curbs, to help the blind, people with baby carriages, and old people who have trouble with steps. UDL started with a "barrier-free" movement in 1961 and solidified as a design movement in the 1980s led by Ronald Mace to be as inclusive as possible (EIDD Stockholm Declaration).

The core mantra in UDL is that some people can do stairs and everyone can do ramps, therefore, we should build ramps to cast the widest net possible. In 1984, the Center for Applied Special Technology (CAST) was created at the Harvard University Education School to show how education could be redesigned from a one-size-fits-all model to a more inclusive structure if just a handful of design concepts were used as guides. Led by Todd Rose and Ann Meyer, the center began an important movement to approach the teaching and learning dynamic as a design problem that could respond to the needs of all learners, independent of disability, age, gender, culture, or linguistic background (Rose et al., 2013). The framework of UDL embraces the idea that *all students can reach high levels of expectation*, that the *barriers to success are in our systems of education and not in the children*, that *human variability is the norm* not the exception, and that *a continual reflection on one's processes would lead to lifelong learners and eventual expertise*. These noble goals led to the first practical applications of UDL, which were to change teacher mindsets about what is meant to reach all learners through differentiation and inclusion. To plan for this broad variety of learners, CAST recommends that classes be designed with three ideas in mind.

First, to offer options for different ways of perceiving information, information should have ***multiple forms of representation***. In writing, students should learn that words can be written in different fonts: *WORDS*, **WORDS**, WORDS, as well as in CAPITAL and small letters, and that nonletter symbols like "" ! ? .,: make a big difference in what we communicate. This gets really interesting when you learn that different punctuation changes the meaning of the exact same words. For example, "Let's eat Grandma" and "Let's eat, Grandma" carry completely different ideas. In ThinkWrite, we respond to this first UDL idea by offering dozens of different choices for each of the 15 stages of thinking. These include activities a student does alone, in pairs, in small groups, and with the entire class. The ThinkWrite model includes activities to reinforce each thinking stage using all senses and pays attention to all cognitive levels of understanding as well as the social and emotional aspects of the writing process.

A second element of UDL is that there are always ***multiple means of engagement***, including the use of multimedia tools, readings, videos, podcasts, gamification, worksheets, and all other digital and analog ways of making the information of interest to the learner. ThinkWrite's activities take advantage of all these modalities and leverage both edtech and traditional tools. Each ThinkWrite thinking stage gives students the choice to use AI tools such as voice-to-text apps, closed captioning for reading assistance, ChatGPT as a mental sparring partner, among others, as well as drawing, talking, and writing activity options. This variety is flexible, self-selected by the learner, and offers multiple forms of reinforcement of each thinking stage.

ThinkWrite's teaching methods rests on students' autonomy to choose, which in turn increases their motivation and individual meaning-making, leading to better overall thinking skills. And this is a two-way street! Not only do students choose to take in the new information in different forms, but they are also given the opportunity to use ***multiple means of expression*** to show what they have learned. This leads to the spin-off of the co-construction of the curriculum by teacher and learner in which the learner plays a more active role, both in the choices around how they learn and in the many ways they can show what they have learned.

In their original model, Rose and Meyer point to three "UDL Guidelines" that align with certain brain regions: (a) ***engagement*** through the *affective networks* to explain the **why** of learning; (b) ***representation*** through the *recognition networks* to explain the **what** of learning; and (c) ***action and expression*** through the *strategic networks* to explain the **how** of learning. While real teaching and learning dynamics involve many elements and more complex networks, this general framework remains an easy-to-follow guide and engagement, representation, action and expression are now seen to be a small part of the dozens of pathways documented in typical neural networks for learning. ThinkWrite uses the basic scaffolding of UDL as a foundation. On top of this, we add the reminder that learning should be aimed at mastery goals, and that writing needs to be approached via a clear trajectory of skills.

DIFFERENTIATION THROUGH UDL

Bloom said pretty much anyone could learn, so it had to be asked, *why, then, do so many fail?* The success of UDL was initially measured as the way in which the burden of adaptation went from the learner to the school. For a hundred years, students who did not fit into the school mold were marginalized because "success" criteria were chosen for schools and translated into standardized test scores from a multiple-choice exam, not on quality writing. The UDL model thought of education as a design problem, not a learning problem, which changed everything.

When the backlash against teaching-to-the-test reached its peak in 2020 just before COVID hit, the pandemic catalyzed a rejection of the single-standard model (Bennett, 2022). This opened the floodgate to a myriad of options that had been waiting in the wings and used by some great teachers but not applied widely. Accepting that the barriers to success were those we ourselves have created by using standardized tests instead of investing in the time it takes to assess good writing well was a realization that helped tip some schools into the UDL camp. UDL helped spotlight the myth of the average in school and to celebrate that human variability is the norm, not the exception (Hartman, 2015). One way to think of differentiation is to accept that while the means of evaluation can change, the objectives are shared by all, no matter how far ahead or behind they seem to be. Differentiation takes into consideration learner variance (Tomlinson, 2017). Most great teachers know that differentiation in teaching is beneficial to students and personalizes their learning process (Tomlinson, 2021). The idea of lifting each learner to their own potential has gained a lot of traction thanks to evidence from the learning sciences that shows that *all* students have "special needs" (Eikeland & Ohna, 2022) that can be met through UDL.

WHY DO STUDENTS VARY IN THEIR STARTING POINTS AS WRITERS?

Wisdom from the experts (see Appendix A) tells us that there are at least six reasons students don't all start at the same point as writers.

Genre of Writing

People begin their writing journey at different stages depending on the writing genre. Some students are strong at five-paragraph argumentative essays and poorer at lab reports, while others are excellent at stories but lacking in poetic grace.

Subject Matter

People also begin their writing at different points due to their familiarity with the subject matter. If the assignment is about pets and the student has a dog, a cat, or a rabbit, they will likely be able to write more speedily than a student who has never owned an animal before.

Prior Knowledge

Students also have different starting points based on their understanding of the assignment. Depending on a person's prior knowledge and familiarity with the vocabulary being used to explain the task, they will also have different starting points. A child in Lima, Peru, who is asked to write something in non-native English about rain, which does not occur often in his neighborhood, will have a harder time beginning the assignment than a British child who is familiar with changes in weather.

Personal Relevance

Children also vary greatly in the importance they give the work. Sometimes it's a matter of pride to do well, independent of the task, and for others it might gain them social status to downplay the assignment as a sign of defiance toward the teacher, which gains them clout with their clique.

Organization

People also begin at different starting points depending on how much time they have; whether it is due to good or bad planning on the students' part or the teacher's part, to procrastination, or other issues, time crunches change the quality and quantity of work.

Motivation

Finally, different students approach the same assignment with different degrees of enthusiasm and motivation based on personal interest. What motivates one person does not necessarily motivate another. Some students might be motivated by the topic, grade, process, or the teacher, and yet others by none of these. Depending on all these issues and more, people start writing from different points, and progress is based on all these combined factors.

Why must we differentiate? People start their writing journeys from different spaces depending on:

- Their familiarity with the writing genre (Understand)
- Familiarity with the subject matter (Know Things, Research, Map and Connect)
- Their understanding of what is expected of them (Understand, Feedback)
- Prior knowledge (Research)
- Attitude and level of motivation (Reflect, Feedback and Feedforward, Peer Exchange)
- Time available for the task (Plan, Mind Wander)

Think of a student in your class and go through this list once more. Where is their strongest point? Where is their weakest point? What stage of thinking is needed to help them advance?

DIFFERENTIATING WITH THINKWRITE

To successfully differentiate with ThinkWrite, we need to appreciate the many reasons a student might not do well on a particular writing task. Once we target their area of need, we can identify what stage of ThinkWrite corresponds to their gaps in order to suggest activities to shore up that area. For example, if the student is struggling to write poetry (or a narrative essay, or blog, or research paper), they may just not *understand* the genre. Some activities that would help this student include seeing worked models or example pieces. On the other hand, if the student is struggling because they do not have a lot of experience with the subject matter, then the teacher can recommend activities that either help the student *know things* (what they already know but are unaware of), for example, through analogy development, or by showing the student how to gather information or *research* ideas on the subject. Another way to stimulate a greater familiarity with the topic is by helping the learner *map and connect* what they already know onto what is not yet known, and so on.

This movement from one thinking stage to another might sound complex compared to the typical scripted prewriting–write–edit activities of curriculum guides, but it is the natural way the brain learns and more in tune with the variability of individual brains. While some people might work best under a straightforward, orderly step-by-step process, many writers have invisible thinking needs that are not met by the normal writing instruction in typical classrooms. Differentiating means attending to different stages of thinking. Thinking is not linear and consequently neither is writing. Jumping around, or toggling, can help, as indicated in Chapter 6.

Finally, to leverage the benefits of toggling and apply ThinkWrite in a UDL classroom, teachers should answer two important questions: *What is the range of learners?* And *which resources do you have?* To gauge this, there are a variety of tools to establish a baseline.

DETERMINING THE RANGE OF LEARNERS

To apply UDL well, one has to know the students. What does the highest flier need? What is the neediest student bound to require? Some experienced teachers use their knowledge to presume a range of learners, but nothing works better than asking for a sample of written work on the first day of class. Getting a writing sample from the start can help establish the outer boundaries of understanding as well as those kids who need remediation. Teachers are often tempted to use the prior year's test scores to judge a student's abilities. While this is a useful piece of information, it never replaces an actual writing sample in the current moment.

Another way to understand the range of learners is to create spider rubrics for the classroom level. These are called radar charts (Figure 8.1). The quantity of activities completed by individual students can be compiled into a single spreadsheet, giving a dashboard-like view into where the group tends to be strong or weak in the

Figure 8.1 Radar Charts: Making the Range of Learners Visible in ThinkWrite

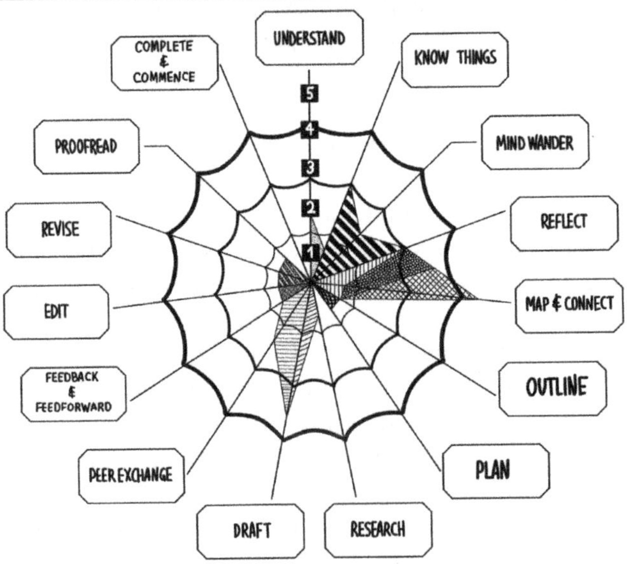

Source: Authors

ThinkWrite process. At a quick glance, it becomes clear that this 10-student group consists of writers who tend to skip over many stages of the ThinkWrite process (such as planning, revising, editing, to name a few), and seem to spend quite a bit of time mapping and connecting and drafting. This suggests that the teacher needs to nudge students into areas of weakness to strengthen the writing as a whole.

DETERMINING THE SCOPE OF ACTIVITIES

Determining the scope or range of activities in UDL depends on the group of students in your class. With this UDL requirement in mind, the ThinkWrite model offers a broad range of novice-to-expert activities for the 15 stages of thinking.

One basic resource that benefits all levels of writers is the use of worked examples. Seeing what a finished product looks like is often the fastest path to successful transfer of writing skills (Yancey et al., 2014). A space in children's literature that is very slim and needs improvement is that of child authors. The vast number of examples students see are written by adults (some might be surprised to learn that books like *The Diary of a Wimpy Kid* and *Harriet the Spy* are not written by kids). Worked examples like *The Diary of Anne Frank* (Franks & Jameson, 1958) help children see how kids Anne's age write. Test prep books (i.e., SAT, PSAT, or SSAT) often include example essays from the target age group, which serve as worked models but do so only for a very specific testing purpose. Websites such as the *Frontiers for Young Minds* (https://kids.frontiersin.org/) encourage younger audiences to contribute to science writing, albeit alongside the expert adult. Worked models offer realistic goals. Unlike mentor texts, which are inspirational but often not attainable and normally written by master writers, worked models give writers the basic idea of a form upon which the learner can add their own creative ideas.

We also highly recommend using "bundles" or curated collections of resources on the topic. Bundles use podcasts, interactions with ChatGPT, gamification, and other apps to personalize homework and meet students at their own starting points with the subject matter. The use of ThinkWrite Activities, worked models, and bundles offers a solid foundation to build a UDL classroom.

HOW THINKWRITE RESPONDS TO ALL ASPECTS OF UDL COURSE DESIGN

In UDL and in ThinkWrite:

- All learners know the objective of the class and several paths toward it
- The teacher ensures there are always intentional, flexible options for all students to use.
- Students always have access to a range of resources from the start of a lesson.
- Students are always building and internalizing their own learning.

To confirm that ThinkWrite can work in a UDL structure, we compare the CAST UDL guidelines with ThinkWrite's structure below (Table 8.1).

Table 8.1. UDL Guidelines and ThinkWrite's Design

Provide multiple means of engagement	ThinkWrite's responses:
1. How can I engage all students in my class? *2. In what ways do I give students choice and autonomy?* *3. How do I make learning relevant to students' needs and wants?* *4. In what ways is my classroom accepting and supportive of all students?*	1. By listening to their individual interests and needs and becoming knowledgeable of their strengths and challenges. 2. Allow students to choose between any of the 15 stages of thinking (use choice menus for working toward goals). Allow for students to choose any of the numerous exercises in each of the thinking stages. 3. Permit students' choice within assignments (state learning goals clearly and in a way that feels relevant to students). 4. The classroom accepts that all students have "special needs"; that is, human variability is great enough that everyone needs "extra support" at some time, so resources are varied and flexible.

Provide multiple means of representation	ThinkWrite's responses:
1. How can I present information in ways that reach all learners? *2. Have I considered options for how printed texts, pictures, and charts are displayed?* *3. What options do I provide for students who need support engaging with texts and/or with auditory learning?*	1. Presents all instructions and requirements in multiple formats (alt text, digital, audio, print). 2. Present all instructions, requirements, and support materials in modifiable formats (text sizes, text-to-speech, audiobooks, partner reading). 3a.Use "alt-texts" with all figures and charts; use subtitles on all videos. 3b.Provide mentor and worked models for writing tasks.

Provide multiple means of action and expression	ThinkWrite's responses:
1. How can I offer purposeful options for students to show what they know? *2. When can I provide flexibility with timing and pacing?* *3. Have I considered methods aside from paper-and-pencil tasks for students to show what they know?* *4. Am I providing students access to assistive technology (AT)?*	1. Allow students options in the ways they demonstrate their competencies (allow them to show what they know through a variety of formats). 2. Rather than being given hard deadlines, students submit work in a neuroconstructivist design based on their starting point and advances toward mastery. 3. As the goal of writing depends on the written word, students are given the opportunity to show advances through activity completion, and their content knowledge can be shown through multimedia formats, but the ultimate display of written language must be in written form. 4. Students are encouraged to appropriately use generative AI (as a sparring partner or to catalyze idea generation) but may not use it to write.

ThinkWrite is a Universal Design for Learning program that respects the individual variability in learners. Other benefits include its goal to make thinking visible. Designing a class is important for success, but the single most important element in teaching of writing is the teacher themselves. We now turn to a final chapter to consider student–teacher relationship and how ThinkWrite lays the foundation for better writing.

CHAPTER 9

From Theory to Practice

In this chapter, we seek to link theory and practice, and we remind you that while ThinkWrite can be used as a programmatic approach to writing and planning, its elements can be adapted to complement an existing writing curriculum. We begin with the "why" of ThinkWrite followed by brief overview of "how" for those excited to implement ThinkWrite programmatically. This is followed by a look at some of the most important learning science concepts related to ThinkWrite and their application in the classroom. Some teachers may find themselves limited by constraints when aligning writing instruction with the findings of the learning sciences, so we then discuss possible adaptations of the ThinkWrite model in classrooms for those interested but seeking a more complementary approach to their existing program.

WHY THINKWRITE?

The ThinkWrite model:

- Opens the focus of instruction and feedback to the process as well as the product of writing;
- Makes visible the invisible thinking of writing, allowing it to be accessible for coaching by the teacher;
- Gives writers an awareness of the neuroplasticity that results from learning experiences, which allows students and teachers to make informed decisions about leaning into challenges and about how and when to use technology, including AI;
- Taps into motivational circuits of the brain by allowing for choice and reflection;
- Provides activities for differentiation that are responsive to individual learner needs;
- Is rooted in the transdisciplinary research of the learning sciences, most notably Mind (psychology), Brain (neuroscience), and Education) (MBE);

- Can be used as a complete writing program or integrated into an existing program;
- Provides hundreds of activities and allows us to increase the frequency of the rehearsal of neural networks for all 15 stages of thinking involved in writing.

While major writing projects may be spaced out over greater periods of time than is ideal for consolidating these thinking skills, you do not have to limit activities to those linked to a specific writing assignment; many activities can be used independently to rehearse and strengthen specific thinking stages as a "bell ringer" at the start of class, as playful interludes or moments of transition during class or as an exit ticket.

HOW TO THINKWRITE (THE QUICK GUIDE)

Use the ThinkWrite model itself as a design process to incorporate ThinkWrite into your writing instruction; note that, just as with your students, the iterative nature of ThinkWrite means you can revisit stages and progress through these steps in a "non-linear" fashion. Track your process using the spider rubric!

Understand the reasoning and structure of ThinkWrite by reading this book, taking notes, and asking questions. What is your goal in applying this? It helps to begin with the end in mind. Make a checklist of the 15 thinking stages to keep your implementation process focused and complete.

Know Things: Connect what you are learning in this book to your previous understanding about the brain and your experience as a writing instructor. How does this connect and extend what you know and have been doing?

Mind Wander: Take a walk, take a shower, spend some time in the garden letting your mind wander freely, allowing your brain to combine and connect freely; imagine how and where ThinkWrite activities and approaches might make a difference. Allow yourself to fantasize a bit about using ThinkWrite. Keep a notebook close to capture any insights and inspirations.

Reflect: Journal purposefully about your values and ideals as a teacher, about what makes writing important, about your students, about how ThinkWrite can help you bring those values to life. Make your values explicit and access the motivational power of transcendent thinking and meaning-making.

By yourself or with a partner, spend some time with some sticky notes or whiteboard and **map and connect** the elements of ThinkWrite and what you have learned here to what you are currently doing and would like to do in your writing instruction.

Outline: Choose an existing assignment to revise or design a new one using the ThinkWrite model and tools to map out activities and sequence an instructional unit. Use the outline process to deepen your understanding of the relationships between these activities. Use the 15 thinking stages to create a template for your lesson planning, and include a selection of ThinkWrite activities for each thinking stage in your lesson plan. Are there opportunities for choice of genre? If the lesson is meant to teach a specific genre, might its conclusion lead on to presenting the learning in another genre?

Plan by using a calendar, first, to map out the time frame within which you have to complete the process, and second, to map out how the activities might be integrated in your curriculum calendar. If your students are new to ThinkWrite, decide how you can best scaffold by incorporating lessons or reminders about neuroplasticity and how you will take students through each stage of thinking. Consider where student choice might be incorporated and where taking them through the stages as a group works best for you.

Research: If you need to, revisit parts of this text for clarification; research the citations independently; explore the complete literature review and other materials including the activities and information on ThinkWriteMBE.com. Consider what individual activities might be the most useful for your students. **Draft** a lesson plan and sequence. Familiarize yourself with the rubrics and other tools in Chapters 7 and 8.

Exchange your plan with a fellow teacher for **peer feedback**. Respond to their questions and use the feedback to **edit** and **revise** your lesson plan. **Proofread** and polish your plan to present to students and share with other teachers. Once you have completed the process, implement the plan. Adapt the "Introducing ThinkWrite to Students" dialog in Chapter 6 to your class. Share the spider rubric (Figure 7.1) with students to help them track their thinking. In conferences, use the "Asking Questions to Prompt Toggling" (Table 7.2) and the "Help Students Identify What Stages of Thinking Will Advance Their Writing" (Table 6.1) tools. During the writing process, apply the "Teacher Checklist to Support Student Toggling" (Table 7.1) tool and the product-process-progress-potential rubric (Table 7.4) to give feedback on their work.

Celebrate! as you **complete** your work and **commence** anew.

Ask yourself and your students, what were the sticking points? What worked well? Recognize that building the underlying neural circuitry will take time and repeated practice.

Feedforward: Try again based on what you have learned, and follow the same process with a new writing assignment. You will find your ability to use the process with your students has grown due to having immersed yourself in it.

CORE PRINCIPLES FROM THE LEARNING SCIENCES AND THEIR IMPLICATIONS FOR INSTRUCTION

If you have read this far, we hope you have been disabused of archaic beliefs such as we only use 10% of our brain, that right-brained learners are more creative than left-brained learners, and that girls are better than boys at language.

Understanding the neuroscience underpinning the thinking stages during writing can help us move beyond the simplistic, unhelpful neuromyths such as grouping our students by "learning styles." As we have tried to make clear, good writing involves the activation and coordination of many complex neural networks across the whole brain, more so than any cognitive activity, from its most basic physiological functions to its most abstract cognitive capacities. So, we have come to see writing as the highest form of thinking. Our brains' neuroplastic responses to our experiences mean each of our students is an individual thinker with unique strengths and challenges, and the learning sciences direct us toward individual differentiation of instruction as an ideal.

On the other hand, the social neuroscience of learning has helped us see that writing involves not just the activation of numerous networks within the individual brain but activation across the divide of individuals, from one brain to another. Writing is an expressive form that activates neural networks in other people, by engaging, informing, entertaining, and persuading them. Writing well, therefore, involves learning to engage in cognitive empathy or perspective taking, getting out of our individualistic perspective to better connect with the reader. Additionally, the findings in the learning sciences point to the important role of social connection (Kulahci & Quinn, 2019), emotions in learning (Hachem, 2022), and the role the teacher plays as a neuromodulator in the writing classroom (Roberts, 2021). While writing instruction may indeed involve learning about thesis statements and comma rules, the learning sciences point to a whole new realm of instruction related to awareness of the role of emotions, social contagion, and emotional attunement in writing and teaching. Finally, ThinkWrite melds all these social–emotional and cognitive elements and points us back to the mutual dependency and mutually instructive role that thinking and writing have with one another.

There are just a handful of agreed-on principles and tenets in Mind, Brain, and Education, and those most related to classroom practices when using ThinkWrite are summarized below.

Neuroplasticity

Perhaps the foremost concept for teachers and students to understand is the role of neuroplasticity in learning. Brain networks change due to repeated practice and effort, whether that is practicing recall of vocabulary, a song on the piano, reading, or writing. Learning involves physical changes in the brain that result from our experience, the interaction of our innate potential for development and our environment, including the classroom. These neuroplastic responses to challenges—the strengthening and quickening of some neural connections and the weakening or pruning of others—continue throughout a lifetime and result in the unique intelligences of our individual students.

Each of the 15 stages of the ThinkWrite model is a complex cognitive task in itself, involving the coordinated firing of distinct sets of neural networks and drawing on diverse memory systems as outlined in Chapters 3, 4, and 5. The repeated rehearsal of these distinct thinking tasks strengthens the connections between neurons within and between these networks, leading to greater efficiency in the firing of these signals over time. Telling students that the tasks selected for writing are actually designed to target and develop new physical changes in their brains can be a powerful motivator. Each thinking stage we rehearse in turn improves both writing ability and thinking ability. And while the brain is not a muscle, for those who know of the concept, the analogy of those who "skip their leg days" in the weight room can be a useful reminder of why good writers would want to develop all the neural networks underlying good writing through frequent practice of each of the ThinkWrite stages. The brain's neuroplastic responses to the stimulation of the activities, while invisible, eventually manifest in behavioral changes, like better writing and thinking.

While ThinkWrite can be used without detailed knowledge of the brain, we think it's empowering for students to see how their actions can result in physical changes in the brain. We hope that this knowledge leads to more informed choices on their part as they eventually autonomously toggle through the different stages of thinking. This metacognitive awareness can be a powerful motivator and help move students beyond merely "doing school" to becoming more strategically engaged in their own learning. While brain science and neural development may feel unfamiliar to some teachers, the resulting motivation that this knowledge of plasticity and the connection of specific behaviors and thinking to one's ability to learn and grow sets the MBE-literate classroom apart. We recommend teaching students about neuroplasticity and the link between practice and the physical strengthening of distinct neural networks which can take the form of direct, age-appropriate instruction about neuroplasticity and visual reminders in the classroom. ThinkWrite tools such as the spider rubric (Figure 7.1) and the product-process-progress-potential rubric (Table 7.4) can help students and teachers monitor which thinking stages are being actively and regularly engaged, reinforced, and strengthened and which may need more attention.

Neurodiversity and Human Variability

Neurodiversity is another concept from the learning sciences that both teachers and students should be aware of. While there are general patterns of neural network development for skills, each of us has individual experiences that have wired our brains uniquely; as a result, each of us has our own strengths, challenges, and inclinations. Consequently, everyone will follow a different path through the writing process and thinking stages, and these paths will continue to change as one grows, depending on the writing task and context. Our brain structure is more unique than our DNA; while identical twins share DNA, their unique experiences mean that their brains are distinct and individualized. Experience, both incidental and deliberate, changes us. Consequently, in approaching the writing task we know that people will have greater facility with some of the over 200 genres than others. Similarly, some will find different thinking stages easier to apply than others and even discover new ways of thinking they had never used before. Some will be good at mind wandering; others will be skilled outliners; others, peer-editors. As each writer both learns to value their strengths and leans into the process and challenge of growing all their capacities, they will continue to develop their brains and thinking across a lifetime.

The ThinkWrite model respects individual differences, another core concept of MBE literacy. MBE tenets support the idea that individual differences due to human variability need to be respected and accounted for through differentiation in instruction. ThinkWrite gives us the tools to differentiate writing instruction for all learners. In addition to providing such differentiation, we recommend teaching students to recognize and value their own individual strengths and to confidently lean into areas of challenge.

Also, the acquisition of strengths in some areas versus others will vary by individual students. Not seeing universal growth across all thinking and executive capacities simultaneously does not mean that the growth that will eventually allow these to eventually "click" into place is not already taking place. The neural networks underpinning writing and thinking take time to develop. We have often heard writing teachers lament that even though they have taught particular skills or concepts repeatedly, students are still making the same mistakes. While this may in some cases be due to how the lessons or concepts were taught or student inattention, it is worth remembering how many neural networks are being called on to grow during writing instruction.

ThinkWrite tools such as the Teacher Checklist to Support Student Toggling (Table 7.1) and the Asking Questions to Prompt Toggling list (Table 7.2), the Help Students Identify What Stage of Thinking Will Advance Their Writing questions (Table 6.1), along with the appropriate tasks from the ThinkWrite Activities list and the spider (Figures 7.1–7.4) rubric and PPPP rubric (Table 7.4), can all help students and teachers recognize areas of strength and target and address areas of challenge in developing and complexifying students' thinking and writing abilities. Radar charts such as those in Figure 8.1 can be a means for teachers to assess their writing instruction with an eye toward offering a program that addresses and strengthens the full range of thinking stages involved.

Executive Functions and Self-Regulation

Yet another core concept in MBE science is the important role of executive functions in learning. While there is no universally shared, singular definition or model of the executive functions, they are broadly understood to be those neural networks underpinning the management of behaviors such as planning, initiating, monitoring, and modulating tasks, and depend on strong working memory, inhibitory control, and cognitive flexibility. Good executive skills are universally recognized as central to the self-regulation necessary for sustained academic and social success. Writing, because of the necessary toggling between the numerous neural networks discussed above, makes some of the greatest demands imaginable on our brain's executive capacities. Executive functions are also subject to strengthening via the brain's neuroplastic response to repeated learning experiences. Teachers initially serve as a source of "auxiliary executive functioning" by guiding metacognitive, reflective practices in their students, but a key goal in education is the eventual autonomy of these learners. Shepherding students' EF rehearsal by getting them to respond to the questions posed in Table 7.2 or even those as basic as "What should we do next and why?" or "Why should we set aside a separate time for proofreading?" help students pause and reflect and help habituate them to self-reflective learning.

By disaggregating the thinking stages that underlie the phases of the writing process, ThinkWrite activities and tools allow both teachers and student writers to target thinking stages more precisely and to strategically toggle between them. Initially, the teacher will likely need to either take a more directive approach in purposefully structuring lessons or offer specific options for "next steps" before students are able to make good choices independently beginning with the dialogue "Introducing ThinkWrite to Students" in Chapter 6. In working with individual students, teachers may need to take an inquiry-based, experimental, or "trial-error-assess" approach to these suggested activities to discover just which thinking stage an individual needs to work on next to best realize the potential in his writing and thinking. As teachers come to know their students better as individual thinkers and as students come to understand the thinking stages and their own strengths and challenges as writers in the ThinkWrite approach, the collaborative process between teacher and student can lead to student autonomy. Both teacher and student learn and evolve their understanding, leading to greater independence and student ownership of the learning. As all brains are unique, this process may take longer for some students than others. Additionally, while shifting to an unfamiliar genre may liberate some writers to discover unacknowledged strengths as writers, it may simultaneously tax students who excelled previously in genres they were more familiar with, in part due to being habituated by previous training and in part due to new executive function demands that such a shift entails.

As an example of neurodiversity and executive support in action, we recall introducing mind mapping as a tool for capturing the fruits of mind wandering to a class of high school freshmen for whom this was a new practice. Suddenly, writers who had struggled when told to begin with generating a thesis or outlining discovered their previously hidden talents for associative thinking. Conversely, some students who had performed well in those more linear approaches struggled when they discovered the paucity of their findings in this same exercise. On the one hand, the teacher could serve as one who affirmed the value of these students' newfound strengths and then help coach them how best to select and move from their associations and findings to incorporate these materials in an outline or draft. On the other hand, for those who struggled, the teacher could note and affirm the challenging nature of the work, recall their strengths elsewhere, and affirm the effort involved in this novel task. The teacher's role turned into one of a coach who explained the different types of thinking behind these different writing tasks and then encouraged perseverance to help them find the quality in their efforts. In both cases, the teacher acted as an "executive function assistant," a strategic partner and reflective friend to the students, the aim of which was to eventually build more independence on the part of the writers.

Over time, great teachers shift the executive demands of writing and learning onto the students through appropriate scaffolding that encourages the development of these very skills. As a bridging strategy, the Institute of Education Sciences' "What Works Clearinghouse" *Teaching Elementary Students to be Effective Writers* (Graham et al., 2012) and *Teaching Secondary Students to Write Effectively* (Graham et al., 2016) suggest that teachers modeling writing and cycles of instructor modeling of the stages of the writing process, followed by student practice and reflection, are particularly effective strategies at both the elementary and secondary levels (Gilbert & Graham, 2010; Olson et al., 2018). Worked models can provide an important instructional strategy as well, and we would suggest the use of *student* or peer examples as particularly effective in instruction. In their own modeling, teachers might want to be alert, however, to the fact that the fluidity of their own seeming mastery of these writing strategies can be intimidating to developing writers. But seeing the teacher write, hesitate, "make mistakes," and reconsider can be very helpful in normalizing the toggling and probing nature of the writing process. This can be especially effective if the teacher talks through or narrates the "hidden" decision-making process, including sharing their emotional "flow," as they toggle through the thinking stages. The writing instructor can also explain their thinking as they consider how to transfer the knowledge, insights, and discoveries from one thinking stage (e.g., mind wandering) to another (e.g., outlining or drafting). Making the inner and embodied, emotional experience of writing visible for students is one of the most significant ways human-to-human teaching can help shape developing writers.

These competencies are rarely covered in most writing rubrics but are essential for developing confident writers. Such modelling can help developing writers learn to value their own thinking. The process, progress, and potential columns in the PPPP rubric can help students increase the metacognitive awareness of their past of growth and future promise, and be more aware of the link between their active engagement and better writing, giving the executive networks vital information for directing effort and engaging motivation for further growth.

Affect, Emotion, and Cognition

The learning sciences also tell us that great teachers help support their students' development by attending to the role of emotions, relationships, and culture in the learning process. This means we must prioritize building supportive relationships and environments for developing writers to better access their own executive skills and model (openly reflect on) good executive processing and consequent emotions during that process. Teachers can lead social contagion by co-regulating the emotional temperature of the classroom to establish the best climate for autonomous, creative learning.

While much popular or folk psychology sets emotion in opposition to good reasoning, the learning sciences reveal it is impossible to reason effectively without attending to emotional information. The role of emotions in cognition and learning is an important principle in the learning sciences. Emotion plays a significant role in directing attention, and its valences—positive and negative—have a strong influence on behaviors such as approaching, repeating, or avoidance. Where the student's emotion is centered, this is where the attention is centered and where learning takes place. This has a number of implications for the classroom teacher both involving the specific neurobiological bases of the thinking stages of writing and in developing classrooms in which emotions are managed to best free up students' cognitive load and to focus their learning on the tasks at hand: good writing and thinking. Thoughtful instructors can prioritize the role of emotion and emotional intelligence in writing instruction no matter the circumstances or institutional constraints. They can also help students recognize the role of emotional intelligence in the writing process.

Related to affect is intellectual empathy and perspective taking. To be successful, a writer must learn to be aware of what potential readers know, how they might react emotionally and intellectually as they read, and what questions or objections they might raise as they do so. This toggling from one's own expressive needs and into the perspective of another is both a benefit of good writing instruction (and one that contributes to writing's ability to build better-equipped citizens) and one of its most complex demands on the developing writer. Good writing teachers can help support and model this process, in part by talking through their own challenges and thinking as they model this aspect of the writing process for students.

Attending to and managing one's own emotions while editing one's work is also a significant area for instruction attuned to the learning sciences. The flow of emotion can give us important information about what is working or not in our writing. Being able to manage the emotions around giving and receiving feedback from peers and instructors furthermore involves significant skills important to good thinking, writing, and social interactions generally. These skills are often assumed or only addressed in passing, but a prominent idea in ThinkWrite activities is that *you can't teach them if you don't know them.* This means that the social context of learning makes it important for teachers to invest in building strong relationships with students, getting to know them genuinely as individuals. There is no better way to do that than to "get into their heads" to better understand the thinking behind their writing. In addition to the formative feedback on the writing process and thinking stages, student–teacher relationships are a significant leverage point for advancing learning (Hattie, 2012). Louis Cozolino's *The Social Neuroscience of Education* (2013) delves into the role of emotions and social contagion in teaching and learning more thoroughly, advising teachers of the importance of building social and emotional connections within the classroom. Positive and authentic relationships help free up students' cognitive load and shift their attention toward the learning task and better access their other thinking skills and internal resources, intellectual and emotional, to apply to the writing task at hand. Moreover, knowing a student's interests and motivations and sensitivities can inform better writing coaching. MBE-aligned teaching prioritizes attention to these factors.

While positive emotions are generally desirable for allowing the playful intelligence necessary for good writing to do its work, dealing with negative emotions can also be important factors in writing and writing instruction. While confidence and swagger may help with inspiration and the initiation of a new writing project, it may be that mild irritation or doubt put us in a good frame of mind for editing or proofreading. Strong positive or negative emotions may give us the energy for other moments in the writing task such as drafting activities or in reflection, while they may inhibit other detailed-oriented thinking like understanding the task or identifying errors. Teaching students to attend to and manage their feelings can help them make better decisions as they write.

Playing, gaming, and learning are related. The focus of emotion is also an issue in a writing teacher's choices of activities. While one might adopt a playful gamified lesson or fun project to engage students' attention around a topic in grammar, if those emotions are directed on the excitement of the game's mechanics and one's team "winning" and not on the content of the lesson, students are less likely to recall the content conveyed (Willingham, 2009). Are they thinking about the fun they just had with their peers as they leave the classroom or the cool things they can do with their newly acquired knowledge of some aspect of syntax? Similarly, mechanical learning programs can help target skills for instruction and gamify the learning process; however, transfer of these targeted skills can be a problem in part because of the programs' inability to redirect the emotions of the learning process from "winning the game" to the thrill of mastery and further application of content and skills. Here, good writing instruction should be attentive to where the emotions of the lesson are really centered. Helping students shift their emotions away from the social play toward the fun or pleasure of building new and challenging sentences, for instance, should be an important goal in considering how to sequence lessons. If the emotions are centered on the excitement of writing an effective sentence, applying an effective rhetorical strategy or thoughtful transition, then that can be highly motivating in the future and is more likely to support future memory of and ability to apply the grammar skills independently and strategically in the future.

Positive emotional support is a gateway to the ultimate goal of learning, intrinsic motivation. The pleasure of mastery, or the pleasure one takes in a well-wrought sentence, the confidence that memories of difficult tasks met and overcome imparts, the alignment of one's developing identity or self-concept as a writer with the challenge of a new writing task—these should be the ultimate goals in helping our students manage their emotions for stronger writing in the future. ThinkWrite, through allowing microteaching and coaching of these thinking stages along with opportunities for metacognitive reflection on one's writing and evolving sense of purpose, helps leverage these emotions for better recall and better writing. Regardless of the other constraints a teacher feels, critical attention to the focus of emotion can help optimize learning.

Purpose and Identity

Evolving research in MBE sciences indicates that a student's sense of purpose and identity can be a powerful driver for the acquisition of the more basic skills one hopes to address in instruction. The research of Mary Helen Immordino-Yang's lab makes it increasingly clear that students' capacities to reflect on purpose and meaning beyond the concrete present instance, to abstract and engage in meaning-making, to engage in reflection that transcends the particular and that links the moment, story, or assignment to a bigger picture or larger purpose over time all predict greater brain growth and even increased well-being in students (Immordino-Yang & Knecht, 2020). This research suggests that habituating a student's reflection on the big picture and developing a sense of purpose and identity as a writer can be powerful drivers for mastery of more basic competencies and of sustaining students' social and emotional well-being over time. Such practices tap into the emerging values and motivational circuits within the student and drive their achievement from within. George McCloskey's work also suggests that the ability of students to consider questions of meaning and purpose, what he terms "self-generation" capacities, can help students overcome some degrees of weakness in other "lower" self-regulating executive capacities that otherwise inhibit their success (McCloskey et al., 2009). Writing and the ThinkWrite stages, particularly mind wandering and reflection, can be powerful tools in helping develop these capacities in all students.

Additionally, research reminds us of the important role of culture in MBE-aligned writing instruction (Hammond, 2014). The instructor's cultural competencies should be developed and employed to reduce stereotype threat and unproductive stressors, and to free up cognitive load, which would allow students a safe space to flourish. In this context as well, it is worth considering how broadening the range of genres in writing instruction can help students find their voice and identity as good writers in addition to the role played by offering a broad range of culturally responsive and representative models of accomplished writers in the curriculum.

"I Am a Writer": The Role of Mindsets

One important and popular concept to arise in education has been mindset and its impact on learning. Students' mindsets about talent and intelligence can also have an important impact on plasticity. Carol Dweck's work on growth versus fixed mindsets also provides effective tools for working with students, encouraging their perseverance in the face of challenges in writing. Core to a growth mindset is how the type of feedback we give students encourages or discourages perseverance in the face of challenge, the subsequent plasticity that occurs from grappling with such challenges, and the learning that results. Simply put, feedback that reinforces the notion that talent or intelligence is innate and part of one's enduring identity—even when it is "positive" (e.g., "You are a good writer!")—*dis*courages perseverance in the face of challenges and undermines subsequent long-term development and achievement (Mangels et al., 2006; Mueller & Dweck, 1998). To a student who is encouraged to believe their intelligence or talent is part of their identity, any perceived challenge to that intelligence is a threat to the student's identity. These students can feel exposed when asked to do a more difficult writing task, work in an unfamiliar genre, or develop unfamiliar thinking skills, which reveal "weaknesses." Consequently, such students avoid increased or novel challenges, which impacts the plastic responses of the brain and consequently learning. On the other hand, those students who are praised accurately for their perseverance and effort in the face of challenge, encouraging an incremental or growth mindset about learning, tend to respond to such increased challenges with perseverance, even choosing more challenging tasks in the future, consequently catalyzing greater plasticity and deeper, stronger learning. Classrooms that directly address mindset and teachers whose feedback is guided by Dweck's work can encourage greater growth in their developing writers over time.

Additionally, as teachers we should model the mindsets around intelligence that we hope to cultivate in our students. ThinkWrite presumes everyone can become a great writer. Sometimes this is a matter of discovering strengths or developing them more fully. Other times it may require working in a new genre of writing. Or it could possibly mean toggling from a different stage of thinking about the topic at hand to a new one. Teachers who approach their students with a growth mindset, knowledgeable about the role of appropriate challenge, feedback, and plasticity, are more likely to persevere in their own efforts to help all students reach their potential. As teachers, how do we face obstacles, challenging students, or those who struggle? We hope ThinkWrite offers new tools to persevere, nudges us to learn more, and helps us see the challenges as interesting opportunities to grow.

THE BRIDGE BETWEEN OUR CURRENT PRACTICE AND THINKWRITE

With this reminder of the role of MBE in ThinkWrite, we now turn to bridging our current practice with ThinkWrite.

We begin by asking teachers to consider to what extent their current practices are already aligned with the learning sciences and to build on that. We believe most teachers will agree that they *already* rely on students' understanding, knowing things, thoughtfully reflecting, knowing how to outline and draft, edit, engage in peer review, revise, and format their work. This suggests that aspects of ThinkWrite model are not entirely new to teachers, but perhaps the recommended structure poses challenges to implementation at the level of change management. The main roadblocks to implementation can be grouped into four categories: a perceived lack of expertise, a lack of instructor autonomy, a perceived lack of time, and a perceived lack of alignment with institutional educational philosophy (e.g., essentialism vs. progressivism).

ThinkWrite is predicated on the learning sciences, and not all teachers have been trained in these areas. Only starting in 2017 has teacher knowledge about the brain and learning been recommended widely (Guerriero, 2017), meaning many teachers trained before this time have not been privy to insights from the learning sciences.

For those open and excited to dive into the learning sciences, there are many resources available to teachers, including this suggestion for MBE school teachers: "101 Books and Articles for MBE Teachers" available here:

Challenging Circumstances: Time and School Policies

We realize that even well-informed, engaged, and motivated teachers may feel constrained by pressures of time, perceptions of a lack of autonomy to act on such knowledge, and questions about whether such practices align with institutional philosophy. Furthermore, some may have concerns about their expertise in the learning sciences (*do I know enough?*). Others might not be completely sure how to differentiate for the range of student needs which may feel like an additional challenge.

The ultimate goal of writing instruction is mastery and student autonomy. The nonlinear, "choose your own path" approach to the writing process that we have discussed throughout this book comes from the realization that individual brains solve problems differently (Graham et al., 2016, p. 8). By allowing some degree of choice in the prompt and in the process, students can better access their existing executive skills as choice frees up the cognitive load of the task. We know, however, that this is not always easy to cultivate in all learning contexts. In addition to the potential roadblocks of individualizing the writing process, teachers may feel constrained by their situation and unable to offer such individualized choices, even if they feel it would be ideal to do so. Restraints on time, student-to-teacher ratios, limited energy, and having to stay "in sync" with other classes in the building can all make us feel as if we are being restricted from more individualized approaches to writing and learning. Initial unfamiliarity with the ThinkWrite process and/or a perceived lack of expertise and lack of confidence may also cause some teachers to shy away from offering such individualized approaches to the writing process. Even so, students' thinking and writing skills will benefit from engaging with the ThinkWrite activities and tools whether they do so en masse, as a whole class at the same time or in parts. This is to say that ThinkWrite can also be introduced gradually, following the current structure you may be using today, with no other changes needed except to call attention to the different stages of thinking. While the ultimate goal of ThinkWrite is full student autonomy about choosing learning activities and toggling between the most appropriate stages of thinking, some teachers may choose to start with the lower-hanging fruit of awareness of the stages of thinking.

In the face of such concerns, we would like to turn to some practical steps that have minimal impact on instructional time, work even in the context of limited autonomy, and support or deepen writing instruction no matter the larger instructional philosophy.

PRACTICAL STEPS TO GROUND WRITING INSTRUCTION IN THE LEARNING SCIENCES

We humbly suggest 12 steps to help start your use of ThinkWrite in your classroom. Each of these steps elevates the presence of visible thinking in the writing classroom.

1. **Acquaint yourself with ThinkWrite and MBE generally and then practice the ThinkWrite model in your own writing.** Try the activities; discover how toggling between them can serve your own needs. Discover what comes easily and where you find your own challenges. Such an acquaintance can help you adapt ThinkWrite to your own evolving understanding and instructional needs. Engaging with it for yourself can allow you to teach with greater authenticity and better bridge between your students' experiences and the ThinkWrite tools that would serve them best. Once you are comfortable, introduce ThinkWrite to your students (as shared in Chapter 6).
2. **Use the 15 thinking stages to audit your school's writing program's curriculum.** Where are there assumptions of understanding versus direct instruction and feedback on these thinking stages within the writing process? What assignments address them directly? What types of thinking are currently excluded or neglected? Such an interrogation can help identify where ThinkWrite activities might be plugged into an existing program to best support writing instruction.
3. **Use the 15 stages of thinking to guide teacher classroom observations.** Where are we assuming students' understanding of the thinking stages in the absence of explicit tools or feedback? If we are asking students to brainstorm, for instance, have we given them explicit tools for doing so? Do they engage with them independently? Using ThinkWrite in this way can, likewise, identify the low-hanging fruit and allow us to find opportunities to plug ThinkWrite tools and activities into one's existing instructional practices.

4. **Use the questions in Chapter 6 under "Help Students Identify What Stage of Thinking Will Advance Their Writing" (Table 6.1) to survey students during the writing process to identify areas of need,** whether individually or for all students. Once identified, make select activities in those areas available to those students with identified needs or consider adding these to existing classroom instruction. While this will have some impact on instructional time, explicitly addressing these areas may free up time needed for remediation later.
5. **Use the Scaling Up Learning Interventions guide** (Figure 2.10) along with professional support from learning specialists to diagnose the appropriate level of intervention with individual students.
6. If more basic roots of possible writing issues have been addressed (see step 5), use the **Teacher Checklist to Support Student Toggling** (Table 7.1) to diagnose what thinking stages might be addressed in individual students' work and address observed issues in student writing and thinking in formative feedback. Suggest activities in written feedback or a selection of activities to choose from in partnership with students during individual conferences if you are able to meet one-on-one.
7. **Use the "Asking Questions to Prompt Toggling" tool in Chapter 7** (Table 7.2) in your formative feedback on drafts. Again, students can then be provided with appropriate choices of ThinkWrite activities to prompt effective revision, which can be individualized helping to aid in differentiation.
8. **Identify those thinking stages that seem most familiar given your own current teaching of the writing process and begin implementing the activities within those stages** in the context of your current instruction. As you grow in comfort and expertise over time, consider adopting the teaching of thinking stages that may feel like more of a stretch but that you suspect are necessary next steps for your students' growth.
9. **Survey your own existing writing activities, and map them onto the 15 stages of thinking** in ThinkWrite to see how aligned your instruction already is to this research. In addition to the tools, lessons, and activities you already use, consider how the ThinkWrite activities can give you even more choices to support what you are already doing well. Add those that seem like a best fit to your own classroom instruction.
10. Alternatively, **identify the ThinkWrite activities** that make the most sense with what you are already doing and that align with your present understanding of good writing and your individual students' needs.
11. Consider adding **select Understanding activities or Reflection activities as possible "exit tickets"** to existing lesson plans to help consolidate learning and identify areas of concern, as well as to develop a student's reflective capacities and their sense of themselves as writers.

12. **Identify which ThinkWrite tools you can use immediately** without altering instructional time or routine at all, and share these with students without changing a thing that you do, such as giving them the spider rubric to use in self-tracking their thinking stages or the Relationships in Writing Guide (Table 7.5). Note how the latter encourages students to think about the relationships of one moment to another when making decisions about the vocabulary of transitions, and how it might aid in better outlining, mapping and connecting as well as drafting.

These 12 steps can help in four ways: They can ease the adaptation of the ThinkWrite approach, they can make a difference in prompting us to reflect on our own current writing instruction, they provide practical tools for our students' learning, and they celebrate the invisible thinking behind the writing already existing in our classrooms. Additionally, they can also be completed within the context of the instructional time demands and in most cases irrespective of the relative autonomy we feel as instructors. In our limited experience, we also feel it works within a wide range of existing educational philosophies, though more evidence is needed. Across one such continuum, for example, essentialist educational frameworks that emphasize the acquisition of specific skills and competencies to prepare for the next level or outside world will find the cause well served by activities, for instance in the understanding, outlining, and proofreading stages, and perhaps be appropriately challenged by mind wandering and reflection. Progressive educational programs will find that perhaps the opposite is the case, that some activities confirm and work well within the existing paradigm, and others address growth in areas that might otherwise go underdeveloped.

A Word About Deadlines

In plotting out their calendar for an upcoming lesson, some teachers optimistically anticipate students moving in unison through the writing process. An outline is due Tuesday; a first draft, Friday. Even as some accommodation may be made for absent students, such uniformity can feel necessary to keep the classroom manageable and may be supported by a superficial but practical notion of "fairness." There may even be institutional pressure to keep in step with other teachers' sections in the school. ThinkWrite activities that already align well with the uniform or shared schedule of lessons can be used to provide some degree of choice and autonomy in such situations. Other institutions may offer more individualized programs in which student choice, student–teacher conferencing, and individualization, including differentiating deadlines, are the norm. Some programs may adopt a workshop model in which students keep a number of writing tasks going at the same time, choosing what to work on when, depending on their individual preference for a particular classroom writing session. Such sessions may be interspersed with key lessons for common issues that arise in a particular class or that cover elements to be mastered for the year. These programs try to balance student autonomy with the need for common knowledge, skills, and vocabulary. The ThinkWrite stages can be addressed in the period of common instruction in such programs, and the activities can be provided for individual choice and differentiation. Other programs take a mastery approach to writing that emphasizes multiple opportunities for revisions and regradings, eliminating the familiar conception of a common due date on which everyone must demonstrate complete mastery of a set of skills on a summative assessment that itself signals the "end" of the unit and the last opportunity to demonstrate growth through that writing task. This approach puts heavy emphasis on the teacher in terms of feedback and record-keeping and leads to periods of particularly heavy workloads as students scramble to revise and get feedback before a grading period ends. In such a program, ThinkWrite activities and tools can help direct student efforts in revising toward specific learning targets and building thinking skills and away from merely manipulating their grade upward incrementally through responding mechanically to feedback. ThinkWrite has important contributions to make across even such varied, existing approaches to writing, and we hope the tools shared in Chapter 6 and 7 can support whatever system you find yourself in as a teacher. The approaches and emphases discussed above and the ThinkWrite activities can be applied within the context of varied scheduling philosophies.

One universal consideration in scheduling of lessons concerns providing for spaced (rather than massed) practice. While the superior learning impact of spaced or distributed practice has been widely supported by research, students and teachers alike have been slow to adopt such practices in part because massed practice feels more effective in the short term and in part due to the tendency of teachers to construct discrete units of study ending with noncumulative summative assessments (Son & Simon, 2012). The diverse neural networks that underpin the executive functions and those involved in the thinking stages are best strengthened through spaced rehearsal. Meaning that a single unit or lesson on "understanding" or any thinking stage is unlikely to provide sufficient rehearsal of the underlying neural networks to result in long-term retention and mastery. It will take repetition of the tasks under varied circumstances over the school year and beyond to get good at recalling and applying the thinking stages independently. Explicitly teaching each stage to students is good; repeatedly *practicing* each stage over time is better. Table 6.2 provides "An Example of Toggling in a University Research Paper" to show how the thinking stages are interleaved across a long-term academic project. Of course, to develop the neural circuitry underlying such skills fully is the work of years. See Appendix A for examples at other levels of schooling.

The acquisition of strengths in some areas versus others will also vary by individual students. Experienced writers take time to get things right, much more so than developing writers. ThinkWrite can increase our awareness of the demands on developing neural networks that learning to write demands, encourage our patience and our confidence that with repeated spaced practice, with actionable formative feedback, and strong relationships, this growth is taking place. Due to its grounding in the learning sciences, ThinkWrite can help us understand why what works well in current writing instruction works and how it can be optimized. Additionally, it can also help us understand why some perennial practices do not "move the needle" for many student writers and how this may be corrected. Why, for instance, after grammar lessons and apparent mastery of a skill in drills do we find so little transfer of this knowledge to the students' own writing and proofreading? The learning sciences suggest that the relative simplicity of recognizing a single targeted error in a practice sentence when cued to do so by the lesson and surrounding sentences has little to do with finding the same error "in the wild" in the more complex syntactical snarl of "actual" sentences and is, at best, a first step toward identifying a rule. That does not mean such learning is useless, only that it is just a part of what needs to happen in the classroom; careful attention should be given to scaffolding the students' ability to transfer such error recognition in simple drill situations to actual written work. This is but one small way that ThinkWrite and the learning sciences can help us think critically and constructively about our instruction and instructional habits. In ThinkWrite, such drills can complement specific activities in the Proofreading stage, for instance, and may be a helpful precursor to implementing them. Thus, the activities can help bridge specific isolated grammar lessons to application in the student's own writing. How can you use ThinkWrite and the learning sciences to interrogate your current writing instruction?

LEVERAGE POINTS TO CHANGE THE SYSTEM

When we speak of the holons of writing, we are mentally drawing a boundary around a complex system of literacy instruction. This system involves the interactions of holons—from those internal to the student writers from their different neural networks engaged in different types of thinking and stages of writing, to their interaction with the instructor who is busy trying to accurately read students' emotional states and be alert to the different knowledge arenas they will need to be successful, to the classroom as a whole, situated within the school and the larger community and even the natural environment. Each of these holons and all of their parts and wholes contribute to an ongoing dynamic relationship and exchange that makes up the messiness of the classroom. Systems thinking draws our attention in the opposite direction from reductionism; rather than breaking things down into parts alone, we can use holonic and systems thinking to consider the connections between holons and the resulting "wholes" and the dynamics that emerge from their interaction. While ThinkWrite can help us think about the complex dynamics of writing instruction, it also provides a means of asking ourselves how we might shift the system of writing instruction in powerful and positive ways.

Donella Meadows, a pathfinder in systems thinking, once articulated a hierarchical description of leverage points where a shift can most effect change in the system. Fourth from the top on her list of effective leverage points is "the power to add, change, evolve or self-organize system structure" (Meadows, 1999, p. 14). Her model in this is the diversity of mature natural systems and the rich resources that brings to the capacity of the system as a whole to prove resilient in the face of future challenges. Working in the opposite direction are institutional forces that try to reduce diversity to simplify and control outcomes. ThinkWrite's approach celebrates the diverse strengths of unique individual brains and the routes they might take to reach their potential as writers. It celebrates the diversity of genres in which writers might find their excellence, and it challenges us to make the classroom a place in which diverse cultures can be a resource for greater learning and building of community and empathetic engagement as well as a place to learn to communicate our perspectives and understandings and make ourselves understood to others. The learning sciences in which ThinkWrite is rooted encourage us to be suspicious of a single, simple, unified approach that supposedly works for everyone in lockstep. Furthermore, ThinkWrite does not just celebrate such diversity and student autonomy, it brings us the tools necessary to change the structure of writing instruction.

Third from the top of Meadows's leverage points for systemic change are "The Goals of the System." ThinkWrite encourages us to look beyond the dominant paradigm of writing instruction that focuses on the written *product* almost exclusively in its feedback and evaluation, and which therefore limits the learner's growth in developing a strong writing *process*. Rather than learning a narrow set of competencies alone as the goal of the system, ThinkWrite encourages teachers to consider students' personal growth and self-actualization as writers and thinkers as the true goal of writing instruction. Such ambitious targets are often mentioned in school mission statements, but integrating them into lesson planning has proven difficult and rare, and such expansive goals often remain a hopeful "by-product" of schooling, which seldom links such lofty outcomes to distinct lesson plans. ThinkWrite bridges that gap. By approaching writing from the holons of the different types of thinking involved in writing, ThinkWrite shifts the focus to the development of the writers' underlying neural capacity to think in different modes, strategically apply that thinking, self-regulate and attune, and become the great writers they can become and the great thinkers we need. When students are driven by that pursuit of mastery, they are all more likely to achieve the competencies that are the end of so much educational planning currently in place.

The second most powerful point of intervention in systems change according to Meadows is "the mindset or paradigm out of which the system—its goals, structure, rules, delays, parameters—arises" (Meadows, 1999, p. 17). ThinkWrite encourages us to think critically about the current paradigm in writing instruction as practiced in schools. This includes the confined thinking skills it reinforces, the limited genres it tends to emphasize, and the narrow range of coaching or feedback that the system trains us for, and then asks us to think critically about the quality of outcomes created by these structures, rules, and parameters. ThinkWrite suggests an alternative approach that celebrates and strengthens the thinking behind good writing and makes that thinking accessible to coaching and feedback in addition to the written product that emerges from that thinking.

The most important leverage point in Meadows's account is "the power to transcend paradigms" (Meadows, 1999, p. 19). Our hope is that this description of ThinkWrite has allowed you to step out of your current paradigm for a moment, to celebrate what you feel works well now, and perhaps entertain a new way of looking at writing instruction and finding ways to reach students who may have kept themselves at the periphery during writing instruction previously. ThinkWrite does not suggest that current writing instruction is wrong but rather that the learning sciences add a new dimension to our craft. ThinkWrite is in full accord with the best practices already in place in writing instruction. Having said that, thanks to its grounding in the learning sciences, ThinkWrite provides us a way to step outside of the current paradigm and consider additional approaches to writing instruction, a critical ground outside of traditional paradigms. We hope the grounding of ThinkWrite in the learning sciences provides you a means of advocating for sound critical thinking about writing instruction. The desired outcome is not just a change in the institution of writing instruction and practice; the real systemic outcome we hope for is the realization of every student writer's fullest potential as an expressive human being.

THE HOLONS OF THE LEARNER AND WHY AI WILL NOT REPLACE GOOD WRITING TEACHERS

Making Learning Whole is a wonderful book by David Perkins (2010) that celebrates the complexity of what goes into learning, starting from the person themselves who is in the context of their family, school, neighborhood, and within the space of their own self, including their emotions, memories, and worldviews. Perkins, a cofounder of Harvard Project Zero with Howard Gardner, has a beautiful way of reminding us that learning isn't a transaction between student and teacher but more like the relationships in a complex ecosystem. Perkins helps us understand that how people learn to write can be examined at the micro level of the brain—neurons, synapses, and networks—but they can also be examined at the social level—how culture and social values influence standard English, for example. Each student in our class learns through a combination of things they already know; the teacher's ability to instruct, select good activities, and adjust to individual needs; the student's potential for the subject; and more. Each of those things can be broken down into memories, teacher training, and DNA, among other things. On one extreme (macro), the learner can be analyzed in the context of their culture, and on the other extreme (micro), we can measure changes in neural networks in the brain. Thinking about the whole child helps assess how well they will do with a given assignment.

This means as teachers we need to learn to appreciate the many forces acting on students' abilities to learn, including those they have no influence over. Sometimes students have a hard time learning due to the genes they got from their parents or the quality of last year's teachers. Other times students *do* have control over things that impact their learning, but they don't know how things like sleep, diet, and exercise change their ability to perform their best. Humans are complex. Understanding the many influences on learning can help teachers select better interventions. Holonic thinking helps us understand what is going on when problems with writing occur. Thinking about learning through holons gives us the opportunity to diagnose writing challenges with more precision. Rather than blame ourselves and think our teaching methodology is wrong, we might explore other, more student-focused aspects of the teaching–learning dynamic using holons. For example, what else is going on in the student's life that is competing with the writing assignment? Or if it is the writing assignment that is troubling the student, which aspect or subskill of writing seems to be the problem? Thinking *holonically* about students and their needs can lead to better interventions, as we saw in Chapters 7 and 8.

When students arrive in the classroom, they each bring an entire universe of a separate lived experience with their particular genetic gifts; their individual, embodied brains; their individual executive networks with their own capacities for self-direction and social engagement; their individual salience networks with their own developing sense of meaning and what is important; their individual default mode networks with their own capacities for reflection and imagination. These have been sculpted, even optimized for their particular life; by their past experience to bring each of the unique students in your classes to the present moment. Much educational evaluation involves identifying and remediating weaknesses and faults. It can help shift the emotional tone of learning to pivot from this at times and consider how we might leverage the strengths that students have each developed to deal with their unique experiences. One of ThinkWrite's premises is that great teaching starts by understanding and leveraging the strengths within our students.

These brains, with their own predilections, insights, perceptions, and emotional life, have been shaped by their distinct past experiences, past learning, and the internalization of various cultures, including family culture, school culture, popular culture, and social media. Our students bring their past learning, their immediate history, and the resulting (and shifting) internal emotional states to us each day, along with their memories of past classrooms, their schema for meaning-making, their variable attention capacities, their strengths, and their challenges. They have been shaped by their individual experience and the larger history of the world around them. Each student is a holon, at once a part of many dynamic and meaningful systems outside the classroom; a part of the dynamic social, emotional, and educational systems within the classroom; and a unique and individual whole unto themselves. The social space of the classroom in turn is a dynamic system in which students shape one another's future development and in which the relationship between student and teacher also mutually shapes the future development of both the student and the teacher (Tokuhama-Espinosa & Borja, 2023).

Superhero comics and movies, science fiction, and theoretical physics have sparked the imaginations of many with the concept of the multiverse, a larger "whole" in which many unique and parallel universes simultaneously exist, and creative minds have entertained us with their ability to spin stories based on what might happen if these separate universes crossed over into one another. These stories have imagined the comic and cosmic possibilities that might ensue and led to thoughtful philosophical reflections about the power of context, circumstance, and choice in our lives. It is possible to see the classroom as a kind of multiverse containing the many universes that our students bring with them, combined with the complex holon of the teacher. Within this multiverse, the role of the teacher changes depending on the needs of the day. The teacher or coach is actually more of a designer, creator, observer, sage, monitor and modulator, responder, hypothesizing scientist, or probing sleuth at times. On other days, teachers are part superhero, part improvisational actor, part reflective philosopher. We are especially interested here, of course, in the writing teacher, by which we mean all teachers. The work of teaching writing makes protean demands on our intelligences and emotional capacities daily, which in turn, changes the multiverse. And as great teachers never stop learning, they also embody the holons of students as well.

Just as for students, teachers are subject to neuroplasticity and the ever-changing reshaping of perception, thinking, emotions, and actions due to influences from all of the systems relationships outlined above. The unique past experience and wiring of each teacher necessarily affects their dispositions, inclinations, and ability to "read the room" and guide individual and groups of students. Teachers are subject to continued inputs of various systems relationships, including the combinations of personalities of our current students, the habituated responses across the lifetime that become our heuristics and reactions to challenges, the new ideas we wanted to try out this semester that we picked up over the summer, expectations from parents and the administration, and dealing with challenges and experiencing life in and outside the classroom. Just as at the end of the year, our students are capable of thinking thoughts they could not think on first entering our classroom, we teachers have acquired new competencies—social, emotional, and academic—thanks to the brain's plastic responses to the curriculum, classroom experiences, interactions with colleagues. Teachers' as well as students' skills are dynamic and developing. Our brains physically change throughout the years as we teach, and we have capacities and perceptions due to our teaching experience we could not have had before we began. Each new piece helps us construct the holon of ourselves, professionally and personally.

GENERATIVE AI (CHATGPT)

We could not end this book without addressing a concern on many teachers' minds: generative AI, large language models, and the role of apps, like ChatGPT. We think two words point to why ChatGPT will not replace good writing teachers: *thinking* and *emotions*.

Generative AI can have a role in producing writing, but we are not convinced it aids thinking. It is clear that generative AI can quickly roll out pieces of writing, but it does not (yet) engage in intersubjective, human, embodied cognition, and its capacities for attending to its own bias and correcting its algorithms are limited and not steered by human emotion or the goal of deeper thinking but by alternative motives (including profit). Generative AI does not hesitate, as thinking people do, and seldom seems concerned if its information is accurate or ethically sourced. This is why human modeling of the writing process is so important for students to observe (Graham et al., 2016). Mechanical language programs are efficient at generating written products but do not nurture the invisible thinking process of their users as they quickly pick and pull from existing work to craft syntactically correct but unoriginal outcomes. Presently, generative AI programs display their written product via an animation of composition, showing the sentences rolling out dramatically and assuredly, suggesting an aura of competence that has little if anything to do with the actual writing process, which involves a wide range of thinking tasks, emotions, and errors. This illusory AI model of the writing process may be one of the most damaging impacts of the chatbot revolution as it further demeans the thinking behind the writing. The cultural transmission of writing skills from one generation to another is very much a human-to-human process, and it is built in a neuroconstructivist design that depends on understanding how life experiences shape learning outcomes, something AI will never have (at least for now). ThinkWrite, and the learning sciences generally, can provide a critical framework for how to best apply AI tools. We should ask ourselves, recalling the role of neural plasticity in learning, *What thinking skills (and what neural networks) are being activated by this use? Which are being ignored? Where does this interaction center our emotions (and therefore our learning)? How might we use these programs to better attend to the acquisition of skills and the training of the cognition involved in writing if we employ such programs ideally?* For instance, it might be useful to have AI give feedback on a draft; but, it is worth remembering that giving and receiving feedback through a peer review process builds important neural circuitry in cognition *and* affect.

If there is a task that makes more demands on our brain than writing, it may well be the teaching of writing. The development and marshaling of social and emotional competencies required of great teaching—the embodied self-awareness, self-regulation, social awareness, social skillfulness, critical minute-by-minute decision-making, and creative problem solving—are crucial to human learning and unlikely to be replicated by disembodied mechanical learning anytime soon. Some of the more promising AI programs do not answer questions but rather are being trained to engage student thinking by responding to student inquiries in the form of Socratic questions to engender and extend student thinking. Some teachers have employed AI products as a critical resource, putting generated documents in front of students for consideration of where the thinking is falling short versus its virtues that might be emulated. Other digital platforms employ algorithms that can personalize (adjust to one's learning level) the information with which one interacts. However, this can tend to send learners into a digital feedback loop, reinforcing existing bias rather than engaging students in different or critical thinking. The skills necessary in preparing students to interact in a world of other individual thinkers, each with their own particular histories and distinct neural development, require a much greater cognitive flexibility, cross-domain thinking, critical awareness, and emotional intelligence than such programs are presently trained for. Students need human teachers to embody and model the skills and values of good thinking and writing and to help them develop into better critical thinkers.

NURTURING WRITERS

ThinkWrite allows us to look beyond the narrow band of external competencies that we already have rubrics for and to become writing coaches who attend to students' development cognitively, socially, physically, and emotionally to nurture their thinking and guide their writing. The ThinkWrite activities target ***understanding***, not just of the writing assignment but also of the individual. By prompting memories about how we ***know things***, we trigger personal experiences as well as connect the dots between elements in the world. ThinkWrite celebrates the invisible and varied levels of consciousness that play into learning, and perhaps uniquely in education, promote the redeeming qualities of ***mind wandering***. While many writing programs remind learners of the ways ***reflection*** supports insight, ThinkWrite goes beyond mirrored reproductions of thinking toward careful steps that lead to deeper thought. ThinkWrite's stage of ***mapping & connecting*** is meant to identify relationships that can go unseen, reinforce those that are obvious, and prompt us to imagine ways things—people, literary styles, words—are linked to give order to what may seem chaotic at first. ***Outlining*** in ThinkWrite helps writers rein in thinking and offers parameters within which to work, while ***planning*** forces a reality check on those ambitions. In ThinkWrite, ***researching*** is a catalyst for stretching what we know, challenging what we thought we knew, and introducing the new. When students approach the ***drafting*** stage of writing, great ThinkWrite teachers realize we have asked them to voluntarily be vulnerable as they place their thinking, visible now in writing, out to the public for the first time. We push this vulnerability even further when we conduct ***peer exchange*** in which the writer and the peer-teacher both gain from the perspective taking added by having another set of eyes on the work. ThinkWrite's ***feedback*** approach insists on feed*forward* outcomes by asking the learner what they will do differently the next time to further improve, placing both autonomy and responsibility on the student. ***Editing*** in ThinkWrite becomes one of the most exciting stages of writing as learners chisel away at a form to give it definition and refinement, just as our memories get whittled down to a few choice representations of life. ***Revising*** is like a rebirth, where the writer is asked to reread and rethink the entire written work using fresh eyes to make final refinements to the content. And just before finishing, the writer, exhausted, is asked to be sure that the ***proofreading*** is complete, the instructions all followed, and the outward presentation is as beautiful as the inward thinking that went into getting the words on paper. To end and begin again, the ***complete and commence*** stage nudges writers and their audiences to celebrate what is done and how it can become something new. Each of the 15 stages of ThinkWrite keeps both the writing process and the writer center stage, directing our attention to how every holonic aspect of language and of the student can be nurtured in the best way possible.

Among the ThinkWrite activities are those that attend to social intelligence, emotional awareness, meaning-making, and reflection on one's own concept of oneself as a writer, because these capacities are what we bring to every writing endeavor. Activities that ask students to explicitly engage in explaining their understanding to others, categorize their ideas and evidence, consider alternative organizational possibilities, and think about the purpose of the assignment all help develop the metacognitive awareness and capacity to move through the writing process more strategically, and these aptitudes and abilities are useful across the content areas and life itself. We hope that you share our belief that ThinkWrite is a means to induce powerful, visible thinking, which makes it available for coaching. Specifically developing these capacities across the full spectrum in each and every student sets the ThinkWrite paradigm apart. That writing teachers should become thinking coaches may require us all to step out of our comfort zone and our naive hope for a simple and single sequence of instruction that works for all to become the teachers we could be, and, what's more, for all of our students to become the great writers they can be.

Index

About the Authors

Tracey Tokuhama-Espinosa is an instructor at the Harvard University Extension School and Summer School where she teaches a course called "The Neuroscience of Learning: An Introduction to Mind, Brain, Health and Education." She is an associate editor of *Nature* Partner Journal *Science of Learning* and is a former member of the OECD expert panel to redefine teachers' new pedagogical knowledge due to contributions from technology and neuroscience. She is co-founder of *Conexiones: The Learning Sciences Platform* (www.thelearningsciences.com), which provides evidence-based resources for teachers in Spanish and English. She has taught kindergarten through university, and now works closely with the Global Science of Learning Network; the International Mind, Brain, and Education Society; the American Educational Research Association's Special Interest Group on Brain, Neurosciences, and Education; and the UNESCO Chair for Education and Neuroscience. Her research focuses on the integration of Mind, Brain, and Education science into teachers' daily practice and professional development; transdisciplinary thinking; curriculum changes to enhance math and literacy skills; bilingualism and multilingualism; and the leveraging of technology to enhance learning outcomes. Her most recent books are *Bringing the Neuroscience of Learning to Online Teaching* and *Questions Kids Ask About Their Brains: Answers That Help Students Learn and Teachers Teach*. Originally from Berkeley, California, she has lived and worked professionally in Tokyo, Lima, Boston, New York, Geneva, and currently lives in Washington, DC, where she works with teachers, schools, governments, and NGOs in 40 different countries.

Jovi R. S. Nazareno graduated from the Mind, Brain, and Education master's program at Harvard Graduate School of Education. Her fascination with the brain grew from the course "The Neuroscience of Learning" at Harvard Extension School, which she took as a student and for which she later served as a teaching assistant for multiple years. Her curiosity about the brain and writing has its roots, though, in her undergraduate work and professional experience. She earned her B.A. in English and psychology at Hawaii Pacific University and then worked a decade as a writer and lead editor at an engineering firm. In her professional work, she developed writing toolkits and templates, conducted research of historical documents, and produced reports on environmental investigations.

Additionally, she worked with K–12 students in tutoring centers for writing and math, taught computer skills to adults, and tutored college students in writing. It is because of all these experiences that she focuses on a transdisciplinary approach to studying what best supports learning to write, a skill that helps people to learn, to think, and to progress in formal academia and employment. Her other research interests include how to teach about the brain and how to share evidence from the learning sciences—bridging research with practice. She currently works at MIT Open Learning as a learning science and education outreach specialist.

Christopher Rappleye is the Ethan A. H. Shepley '41 Chair of Distinguished Teaching in English and Composition at the Mary Institute and Saint Louis Country Day School in St. Louis, Missouri, where he has taught for over 3 decades. His teaching has been shaped by research in Mind, Brain, and Education science, which has also informed his work as a leader in developing social–emotional learning programming in the Upper School. He received his MFA in writing (poetry) from Washington University and has attended the Kenyon Writer's Workshop in Fiction. He has taught grades 7 through 12 and coaches varsity boys cross country and middle school track. He has been a reader and workshop consultant for Educational Testing Services for the Advanced Placement Examination in English Literature and Composition and served as a workshop consultant for ACT. His other research interests are driven by teaching senior electives in creativity, the Faust myth, and a life-long interest in the process of meaning making.

Printed and bound by CPI Group (UK) Ltd, Croydon, CR0 4YY

16/09/2026

14963486-0001